DATE DUE

DEMCO 38-296

VICTORIAN POETRY

THE MAGILL BIBLIOGRAPHIES

The American Presidents, by Norman S. Cohen, 1989
Black American Women Novelists, by Craig Werner, 1989
Classical Greek and Roman Drama, by Robert J. Forman, 1989
Contemporary Latin American Fiction, by Keith H. Brower, 1989
Masters of Mystery and Detective Fiction, by J. Randolph Cox, 1989
Nineteenth Century American Poetry, by Philip K. Jason, 1989
Restoration Drama, by Thomas J. Taylor, 1989
Twentieth Century European Short Story, by Charles E. May, 1989
The Victorian Novel, by Laurence W. Mazzeno, 1989
Women's Issues, by Laura Stempel Mumford, 1989
America in Space, by Russell R. Tobias, 1991
The American Constitution, by Robert J. Janosik, 1991
The Classic Epic, by Thomas J. Sienkewicz, 1991
English Romantic Poetry, by Brian Aubrey, 1991
Ethics, by John K. Roth, 1991
The Immigrant Experience, by Paul D. Mageli, 1991
The Modern American Novel, by Steven G. Kellman, 1991
Native Americans, by Frederick E. Hoxie and Harvey Markowitz, 1991
American Drama: 1918–1960, by R. Baird Shuman, 1992
American Ethnic Literatures, by David R. Peck, 1992
American Theater History, by Thomas J. Taylor, 1992
The Atomic Bomb, by Hans G. Graetzer and Larry M. Browning, 1992
Biography, by Carl Rollyson, 1992
The History of Science, by Gordon L. Miller, 1992
The Origin and Evolution of Life on Earth, by David W. Hollar, Jr., 1992
Pan-Africanism, by Michael W. Williams, 1992
Resources for Writers, by R. Baird Shuman, 1992
Shakespeare, by Joseph Rosenblum, 1992
The Vietnam War in Literature, by Philip K. Jason, 1992
Contemporary Southern Women Fiction Writers, by Rosemary M. Canfield Reisman and Christopher J. Canfield, 1994
Cycles in Humans and Nature, by John T. Burns, 1994
Environmental Studies, by Diane M. Fortner, 1994
Poverty in America, by Steven Pressman, 1994
The Short Story in English: Britain and North America, by Dean Baldwin and Gregory L. Morris, 1994

VICTORIAN POETRY
An Annotated Bibliography

by
LAURENCE W. MAZZENO

Magill Bibliographies

The Scarecrow Press, Inc.
Metuchen, N.J., & London
and
Salem Press
Pasadena, CA & Englewood Cliffs, N.J.
1995

British Library Cataloguing-in-Publication data available

Library of Congress Cataloging-in-Publication Data

Mazzeno, Laurence W.
   Victorian poetry : an annotated bibliography / by Laurence W.
Mazzeno.
      p.   cm.—(Magill bibliographies)
   Includes indexes.
   ISBN 0-8108-3008-6 (acid-free paper)
   1. English poetry—19th century—Bibliography.   I. Title.
II. Series.
Z2014.P7M35   1995
[PR591]
016.821'8—dc20   95-5328

This book is dedicated to Nancy Gore

CONTENTS

CONTENTS

ACKNOWLEDGMENTS

Though this volume has a single author, a number of individuals contributed to its production. The library staffs at Mesa State College and Ursuline College were both helpful and patient; among them, Judith Berzinsky deserves special mention for her cheerful assistance in processing the hundreds of inter-library loan requests submitted almost relentlessly over almost a year. The most significant acknowledgment, however, must be to Nancy Gore, a budding young scholar whose career has been sidetracked (one hopes only temporarily) by a serious illness.

INTRODUCTION

In the preface to his 1968 anthology of Pre-Raphaelite poets, the distinguished twentieth century scholar Cecil Y. Lang observes that the collection he has brought together is "meant to fill an obvious and urgent need," providing students and scholars easy access to "several poets nearly always short-changed in favor of the Victorian Trinity, Tennyson, [Robert] Browning, and Arnold." Professor Lang's assessment reveals much about Victorian poetry and criticism of Victorian poets. If one surveys the shelves in a typical college library, there is ample evidence that these writers have commanded the attention of critics in much greater measure than other poets of the age. Actually, Arnold's poetry was not as well received by his contemporaries as it has been by modern audiences, but he made up for his deficiencies as a poet by becoming the age's greatest critic of poetry. What is certain is that, during the decades of Victoria's rule in Britain, these three men achieved distinction among their contemporaries as literary luminaries, inheritors of the vatic mantle from their Romantic predecessors and innovators whose insight into the human condition was captured in verse that spoke to both the hearts and intellects of their readers. As a result, they were revered by contemporaries not only for their craftsmanship but also for their ideas; the reading public found in poets the certitude no longer afforded them in traditional religion, which had been undermined by the findings of science.

The dominance of Tennyson, Arnold, and Browning sometimes obscures the fact that hundreds of men and women published volumes of poetry during the nineteenth century. Of course, not all of them were distinguished—and there is little disagreement that much of the work which graced the drawing-room tables and library shelves of Victorian ladies and gentlemen is better forgotten. That is true of popular writing in any age, however. It is important to realize that the age of Tennyson and Browning was also the age of the Pre-Raphaelites, whose work was largely written in reaction to that of their more widely read contemporaries. It was the age, too, when England's first truly great woman poet, Elizabeth Barrett, achieved a reputation in her own right years before she ran off to elope with a much less well respected poet named Robert Browning.

It is exceptionally difficult to make sweeping generalizations about Victorian poetry, since variety and individuality characterize the age. Poets of the period showed special interest in experimentation, both with traditional forms and with hitherto untried techniques. Like their Romantic predecessors, they rebelled against the strictures so highly prized by neoclassic poets in favor of new meters, rhyme schemes, and rhythms. Examples of conventional lyrics and sonnets abound. Narratives both short and long were equally commonplace. While much popular poetry was overtly (and uncontrollably) sentimental, the age witnessed the production of several significant love poems and the publication of one of the language's greatest elegies, Tennyson's *In Memoriam*. Though they did not excel at poetic drama, they created an entirely new poetic genre, the dramatic monologue, a form that afforded them ample opportunity to display their remarkable insight into the human psyche.

Despite the variety of forms in which they excelled, Victorian poets shared several common interests. Most saw themselves as inheritors and perpetuators of a strong literary tradition; they may have felt compelled to modify it, but they were not interested in abandoning it, as their modern successors were wont to do. Like the novelists of the period, poets were deeply concerned about the social conditions that confronted them: a growing reverence for material wealth and comfort, a concurrent devaluation of religious values (especially as science began to challenge the very efficacy of religious belief), horrid working and living conditions for the poor and the working classes, an increasing tendency to regard the non-white peoples of the British Empire—and the Irish—as chattel to be exploited for the benefit of the citizens of England. Many of them confronted these problems directly. Others turned to the ideas and works of earlier ages, especially the Middle Ages, to escape the tumult of modern life, or to find in these forgotten times some example that could help encourage reform. Though the term is most often applied to Tennyson, more than one poet exhibited a consuming interest in what has come to be called "the passion of the past."

Common among men and women serious about their vocation as poets was a concern for what their mission and role should be. Was it their duty to expose the injustices, the evil, the squalor they saw around them? Was it better instead to provide some ideal that would appeal to people's better selves? In poem after countless poem, authors struggled to define for themselves and their readers the function of the poet as they saw it.

Perhaps better than any other genre and any other period, Victorian poetry exhibits the fate of work subjected to the vicissitudes and prejudices of the criticism of subsequent generations. In the waning years of the nineteenth century, the people who had turned to the work of Tennyson and Browning for spiritual comfort and philosophical wisdom were dying off, and their children and grandchildren were decidedly less prone to worship these writers and their contemporaries. By the start of World

War I, many Victorian poets had fallen into disfavor, and those who had not were soon to do so in the decades following the war. The 1920's and 1930's saw the publication of damning commentary on the once-revered giants; worse still, the majority of Victorian poets were simply dismissed out of hand by modern writers who found their work irrelevant. The sad case of Tennyson may serve as an example of the general demise. Once celebrated as one of the great thinkers of his age, and unquestionably its finest technician, he became in the hands of post-World War I critics such as Harold Nicolson a morbid, melancholy loner, hovering on the brink of psychological breakdown, whose few good works were lyrics that emulated the great Romantics. He was dismissed by W. H. Auden as undoubtedly "the stupidest" of English poets.

It is not surprising that little significant criticism was produced for nearly half a century. The tide began to shift ever so slightly in the years following World War II, but critics such as Lionel Trilling (whose 1939 study of Matthew Arnold has become recognized as a landmark in intellectual biography) and F. E. L. Priestly remained a vocal minority. Not until the 1960's did it become acceptable once more to study Victorian poets without preconceptions about their unwarranted optimism or their overzealous sentimentality.

Fortunately, much good work was done in the three decades from 1960. A gradual sifting has taken place in evaluating the merits of individual authors and works. While the fate of the Victorian Trinity mentioned by Lang remains secure, the reputations of others have undergone serious alteration. No one has seen his stock rise greater than Gerard Manley Hopkins. Unknown during his lifetime (he published virtually nothing while alive), by the 1970's Hopkins was commanding as much attention as those poets whose reputations were firmly established before their deaths. The Pre-Raphaelites, long dismissed as either morally suspect or ideologically inconsequential, have come to be recognized as important artists whose work deserves serious attention. Largely as a result of the feminist movement, the reputation of Elizabeth Barrett Browning has been enhanced; though she has not yet returned to the stature she held in her lifetime, when her works were more revered than those of her husband, she is now recognized as a serious champion of the cause of women and an exceptional master of technique.

Preparing a selected bibliography such as this one involves some hard choices about both authors and critical works. A brief review of the table of contents suggests that the selections for this volume follow conventional wisdom in the assessment of the continuing value of the works of Victorian poets. Tennyson, Browning, Arnold, and Hopkins are of course included, as are Elizabeth Barrett Browning, Algernon Charles Swinburne, Dante Gabriel Rossetti, his sister Christina Rossetti, and William Morris; few will quibble with these choices. The decision to include George Meredith (more noted as a novelist), and Coventry Patmore and James Thomson (each of whom produced only one work of lasting interest) may seem unusual. Perhaps equally noteworthy is the absence of figures such as Thomas Hardy and William Butler Yeats; both wrote much poetry before the end of the nineteenth century, and both are among the major figures of English literature. The tendency to include these writers in anthologies of modern poetry, and to treat their works as examples of the modernist movement, suggests that they would be more appropriately excluded from this volume.

The body of criticism on Victorian poets is substantial, though as one might expect, the bulk of scholarship is devoted to writers whose work is considered worthy of extended study. In the case of a few poets, such as Coventry Patmore or James Thomson, the limited number of book-length works or chapters in books makes a comprehensive survey appropriate. While there is no promise that the bibliographical entries are exhaustive, readers can be assured that the selections represent the majority of critical work produced during the twentieth century in book form. For poets considered more popular or critically important, it was necessary to make some difficult decisions about what to include and—unfortunately—what to leave out. No specialist on Browning or Tennyson may be happy with the limited number of selections on the many fine and influential poems by these two authors; nevertheless, the high school student or college undergraduate should find the entries included for these poets, as well as for Arnold and Hardy, sufficient to gain a sound introduction to these writers' art and thought. Generally, the principle of selection employed in this volume is a simple one. Whenever possible, criticism of poems by Tennyson, Robert Browning, Arnold, and Hopkins is selected from works published after 1970. Hence, a number of good critical sketches in which readers may find useful information are omitted. On occasion, however, a critic or a work has proven so seminal that references are included, even though the date of publication is much earlier in the century. One example is Jerome Hamilton Buckley's influential 1961 volume on Tennyson.

All criticism cited in this volume is contained in books or monographs. Considerable commentary is also available in scholarly journals. A good starting place for locating articles and notes is the *MLA International Bibliography*, published annually by the Modern Language Association. Victorian poets are listed alphabetically in the section titled "English Literature, 1800-1899." A second general listing may be found in the H. W. Wilson Company's *Humanities Index* (formerly *Social Sciences and Humanities Index*); this index is also issued annually. Other journals that routinely contain articles on nineteenth century poetry include *Critical Inquiry* (though the emphasis of most articles in this publication is on critical theory), *ELH, English Language Notes, Essays in Literature, The Explicator, Genre, Hopkins Quarterly, JEGP, Journal of Pre-Raphaelite Studies, Philological Quarterly, PMLA, SEL: Studies in English Literature, 1500-1900* (autumn issue), *Studies in Browning and His Circle, Tennyson Research Bulletin, Victorians Institute Journal, Victorian Newsletter, Victorian Periodicals Review, Victorian Poetry,* and *Victorian Studies.* Two other publications should be mentioned: *The Arnoldian,* which until 1986 was devoted to criticism of Matthew Arnold's poetry and prose, and *Browning Institute Studies,* which has expanded its scope and changed its name to *Nineteenth Century Culture.* An updated listing of journals containing articles on Victorian poetry is published biannually by the Modern Language Association: the *MLA Directory of Periodicals.*

General Studies

Altick, Richard D. *Victorian People and Ideas.* New York: W. W. Norton, 1973.
Indispensable guide to backgrounds for understanding the milieu in which Victorian poetry was produced. Lengthy explanation of the social class system and the rising influence of the middle class; also discusses influence of the rising number of literate citizens on popular literature. Explores intellectual and philosophical climate, especially utilitarian attitudes about public management, importance of laissez-faire approaches to business and government, and growing influence of socialism. Deals extensively with Victorian notions of religion and the conflicts of religion and science. Includes information about the Victorians' beliefs regarding the nature and function of the arts.

Armstrong, Isobel. *Language as Living Form in Nineteenth-Century Poetry.* Totowa, N.J.: Barnes & Noble, 1982.
Analysis of the way nineteenth century poets made use of language to create their distinctive impression of their world. Armstrong argues against the notion that most poetry of the Victorian period is simply self-expressive. Relies heavily on philosophical theories of G. F. W. Hegel and Karl Marx to establish an intellectual framework for evaluating Victorian poets' use of language. Introductory chapter provides especially valuable overview of Armstrong's thesis that Victorian poets were primarily interested in "making" works of art through language,

rather than simply copying from the works of others or slavishly
mimicking the external world.

_____,ed. *The Major Victorian Poets: Reconsiderations.* Lin-
coln: University of Nebraska Press, 1969.
Collection of essays specifically designed to answer charges by early
twentieth century critics that the work of Victorian poets is inferior to
that of their literary predecessors. Essayists attempt to "achieve a
clearer understanding of the nature of Victorian poetry" by giving
careful attention to representative works of both major and minor
figures. No comprehensive assessment of individual poets is provided;
rather, in each case, essays focus on those aspects of a poet's work
"where critical discussion seems most necessary" to correct previous
critical impressions.

Auerbach, Nina. *Woman and the Demon: The Life of a Victorian Myth.*
Cambridge, Mass.: Harvard University Press, 1982.
Thorough examination of the images of women in Victorian literature
and society; explores the many ways women were presented in literature, including their portrayal as victims, queens, angels, old maids,
and fallen women. Argues the conventional image of women as wives
and mothers is only one of many ways females took on life in literature
and affected the attitudes of Victorians. Believes women were powerful, even mythic, figures for nineteenth century readers. Includes
almost four dozen illustrations.

Ball, Patricia M. *The Heart's Events: The Victorian Poetry of Relationships.* London: Athlone Press, 1976.
Examination of a series of Victorian poems which exhibit what Ball
calls "the poetry of relationships"—ones that focus on love or friend-
ship between two clearly identifiable individuals (as opposed to generic expressions of these feelings). Shows how poets who explore
such relationships focus on conventional situations such as courtship
and marriage in an attempt to explain how love affects people in
everyday life. Focusing her analysis on works by Robert Browning,
Tennyson, Meredith, Arnold, Clough, and Coventry Patmore, Ball sees
the rise of this form of poetry as "a distinctly Victorian development."

Bloom, Harold, ed. *Pre-Raphaelite Poets.* Modern Critical Views. New
York: Chelsea House, 1986.
Collection of eighteen essays, most previously published in scholarly
journals or as parts of monographs, offering assessments of important

works by six writers associated with the Pre-Raphaelite movement in English letters: Dante Gabriel Rossetti, George Meredith, William Morris, Algernon Swinburne, Christina Rossetti, and Coventry Patmore. The volume's introduction offers an overview of the movement. Includes useful chronology and a bibliography of secondary sources.

Bradbury, Malcolm, and David Palmer, eds. *Victorian Poetry.* Stratford-on-Avon Studies 15. London: Edwin Arnold, 1972.
Collection of eleven essays focusing on Victorian writers' preoccupations with the past, with the idea of history, and with concepts of time. Essayists show how various poets and novelists retreat to the past to avoid complexities of modern life, while others confront contemporary issues directly. Includes discussion of works by Arnold, Robert Browning, Tennyson, the Pre-Raphaelites, Morris, and Hopkins; a concluding essay summarizes the various ways Victorians viewed history.

Brantlinger, Patrick. *The Spirit of Reform: British Literature and Politics, 1832-1867.* Cambridge, Mass.: Harvard University Press, 1977.
Collection of essays focusing on reform movements during almost four decades of great political and social turmoil in Britain. Argues throughout that Victorian writers saw literature as having the potential to assist in bringing about reform. Believes social reform actually ran counter to ideas of progress, which posited that society would need no intervention to become better. Comments on writers of imaginative literature and non-fiction; includes analysis of works by Matthew Arnold, the Brownings, and Tennyson.

Bratton, J. S. *The Victorian Popular Ballad.* Totowa, N.J.: Rowman & Littlefield, 1975.
Systematic study of a popular poetic form which thrived during the nineteenth century but which has received little critical attention. Discusses both literary and popular or folk ballads, devoting one or more chapters to writings about heroic figures, works distinctively propagandistic, and comic compositions sung in music halls and drawing rooms during the Victorian period. Throughout, Bratton examines both the technical qualities of the verse and the varied subject matter balladeers took up.

Buckler, William E. *The Victorian Imagination: Essays in Aesthetic Exploration.* New York: New York University Press, 1980.
Collection of essays examining the complex nature of Victorian literature and its resistance to monistic interpretation by twentieth century

critics. An introductory discussion explains how Carlyle and Tennyson were the "founders of Victorian literature," the first of a group of writers to undertake a "literary experiment" whose "desperate hope was the salvation of imaginative letters." Discusses the significance of Matthew Arnold as the preeminent critical voice of the age. Includes extensive commentary on works of Carlyle, Tennyson, Swinburne, Pater, and Hardy; useful for understanding the intellectual climate in which all Victorian poets worked.

Buckley, Jerome H. *The Triumph of Time: A Study of the Victorian Concepts of Time, History, Progress, and Decadence.* Cambridge, Mass.: Harvard University Press, 1966.
Studies the phenomenon new in the Victorian era: the "quite unprecedented awareness of time" and the effect of this awareness on individual life and society. Demonstrates how the age fostered the growth of interest in formal historical studies. Examines the ideas of progress and decadence, the Victorians' particular fascination with the past, and their concerns about both the present and the future. Makes liberal use of the poetry of Arnold, Robert Browning, Clough, Hopkins, Morris, Dante Gabriel Rossetti, Swinburne, and Tennyson to illustrate his thesis.

_____. *The Victorian Temper: A Study in Culture.* Cambridge, Mass.: Harvard University Press, 1951. Reprint 1969.
Influential study of the chief intellectual and social concerns of the Victorian age. Devotes chapters to examinations of religious attitudes, development of literature, and the rise of popular literary figures; also discusses issues involving morality and aesthetics, two areas of study Victorian artists and the populace in general came to see as mutually supportive and intertwined. Concludes with chapters on the reaction to Victorian attitudes about morality and literature by artists writing at the end of the century.

Chappel, J. A. V. *Science and Literature in the Nineteenth Century.* London: Macmillan, 1986.
Examines the development of the sciences in the nineteenth century and the impact of scientific inquiry on the literature of the period. Organized by scientific discipline; cites reaction of both poets and novelists to discoveries in astronomy, physics, chemistry, paleontology, geology, zoology, biology, anatomy, and physiology, as well as social sciences such as psychology, anthropology, ethnology, philology, and mythology. Includes a detailed chronology showing important

scientific milestones and literary publications. Also contains an extensive bibliography for further reading and research.

Christ, Carol T. *The Finer Optic: The Aesthetic of Particularity in Victorian Poetry.* New Haven, Conn.: Yale University Press, 1975.
Argues the Victorian poets, rejecting the neoclassic notion that greatness lies in aspiring to represent the ideal, focused their creative attention on the particular, that is, on individual representations of objects in nature. Shows how poets of the period transformed "mere particulars from portents of disorder and alienation into an aesthetic value, the means of a new kind of vision." Focuses analysis on three problems with which many poets of the period dealt: morbidity, the grotesque, and the "good moment." Includes extensive references to the works of Robert Browning, Hopkins, Dante Gabriel Rossetti, and Tennyson.

_____. *Victorian and Modern Poetics.* Chicago: University of Chicago Press, 1984.
Study intended to correct notions that there are few connections between modern poets and their Victorian predecessors. Claims both Victorians and moderns reacted against the extreme forms of subjectivism promoted by the Romantics. Examines the use of dramatic monologue, masks, and personas in both periods; discusses theories of the picturesque and of the image; comments on the use of myth and history in development of both Victorian and modern long poems. Analyzes the moderns' anti-Victorian stance. Focuses throughout on the works of Tennyson, Arnold, and Robert Browning, and on modern poets T. S. Eliot, Ezra Pound, and William Butler Yeats.

David, Deirdre. *Intellectual Women and Victorian Patriarchy.* Ithaca, N.Y.: Cornell University Press, 1987.
Study of three influential women writers of the Victorian period: Harriet Martineau, Elizabeth Barrett Browning, and George Eliot (Mary Ann Evans). Traces the struggles of women intellectuals to establish themselves as authorities within a society that devalued women's intellectual capacities. Especially useful for understanding how all women writers of the period overcame prejudices and reached their audiences with their writings. Chapters on Browning helpful in elucidating the special problems faced by the woman poet.

Dawson, Carl. *Victorian Noon: English Literature in 1850.* Baltimore: Johns Hopkins University Press, 1979.

Examination of the literature published during this watershed year in the Victorian era, a year which saw the publication of poems such as Tennyson's *In Memoriam*, Elizabeth Barrett Browning's *Sonnets from the Portuguese*, and Dante Gabriel Rossetti's "The Blessed Damosel," as well as Dickens' *David Copperfield*, Carlyle's *Latter-Day Pamphlets*, and Kingsley's *Alton Locke*. Provides exceptional insight into the intellectual climate which stimulated production of both popular and anti-establishment poetry.

Fletcher, Pauline. *Gardens and Grim Ravines: The Language of Landscape in Victorian Poetry.* Princeton, N.J.: Princeton University Press, 1983.
Study of the ways poets use landscape in their works; suggests their attitudes toward landscape reflect important values, especially as they respond to natural scenes or manmade natural landscapes. Special focus on the significance of gardens in the works of Tennyson, Robert Browning, Arnold, Swinburne, Dante Gabriel Rossetti, and Morris. Contains an extensive bibliography of secondary sources.

Fraser, Hilary. *Beauty and Belief: Aesthetics and Religion in Victorian Literature.* Cambridge, England: Cambridge University Press, 1986.
Analysis of the cultural and historical conditions underlying the Victorians' concerns about the relationship between religion, art, and aesthetics. Examines ways religious truths came to be expressed through poetry and the eventual rejection of poetry's moral role for society. Particularly useful for an understanding of the works of Arnold, Hopkins, and Wilde.

Harrison, Antony. *Victorian Poets and Romantic Poems: Intertextuality and Ideology.* Charlottesville: University Press of Virginia, 1990.
Study of several important poems by major figures of the Victorian period to show how these writers transformed previous works within the literary tradition to serve their own political or aesthetic purposes. Offers in the introduction a brief discussion of the methodology employed in analyzing individual works and a summary of theoretical principles on which this analysis is based. Includes examination of works by Arnold, Robert Browning, Tennyson, Dante Gabriel Rossetti, Christina Rossetti, Morris, and Swinburne. Compares poems by Victorians to those of their Renaissance or Romantic predecessors.

Hickok, Kathleen. *Representations of Women: Nineteenth-Century British Women's Poetry.* Westport, Conn.: Greenwood Press, 1984.

Examination of works by dozens of nineteenth century women poets to determine how their perception of women's role in society affected the production of poetry in the age. Includes many women poets popular in their own day but forgotten or ignored by later generations. Begins with an overview of ways women were presented in literature and follows with chapters on women depicted as daughters, wives, mothers, spinsters, workers, and "fallen"; concludes with a chapter on the "New Woman" and assessments of the careers of Elizabeth Barrett Browning and Christina Rossetti. Appendix provides short biographies of numerous minor Victorian women poets. Contains an excellent bibliography.

Houghton, Walter E. *The Victorian Frame of Mind 1830-1870.* New Haven, Conn.: Yale University Press, 1957.
Influential and comprehensive study of Victorians who made up the reading public for poets of the age. Discusses important concepts that dominated the age, such as the will to believe, dogmatism, and anti-intellectualism; also focuses on emotional attitudes such as anxiety and optimism and on the general moral character which pervaded the period, exhibited in such diverse traits as hero-worship and the worship of force, earnestness, enthusiasm, hypocrisy, love, a growing veneration of (or revulsion from) commercialism, and the importance of authority in governing individual lives.

Hughes, Linda K., and Michael Lund. *The Victorian Serial.* Charlottesville: University Press of Virginia, 1991.
Discussion of the importance of serialization in the presentation of long works to Victorian audiences. Includes substantial selections from nineteenth century sources to show how Victorians themselves viewed serialized novels and poems. Discusses factors contributing to readers' special affection for this form of presentation and examines the effect of having to extend one's engagement with a work over a long period. Concludes that serialization made "the relationship between life and literature" "more dynamic and intense." Includes an excellent bibliography of secondary sources.

Hunt, John Dixon. *The Pre-Raphaelite Imagination 1848-1900.* London: Routledge & Kegan Paul, 1968.
Examines the ideas of the Pre-Raphaelite Brotherhood as they developed in the 1840's and 1850's and were accepted and adapted during the remainder of the century. Places special emphasis on the survival of Pre-Raphaelite ideas in the 1890's. Begins with analysis of the

elements of Pre-Raphaelitism and follows with chapters on the Pre-Raphaelites' enthusiasm for the Middle Ages; their preoccupation with communicating the psychological aspects of character; their "search for a dialect of symbolism" which could convey the world beyond the material; their creation of an image of woman which became specifically associated with them and their works; and their focus on realistic description.

Johnson, Wendell Stacy. *Sex and Marriage in Victorian Poetry*. Ithaca, N.Y.: Cornell University Press, 1975.
Wide-ranging study of Victorian poets' attitudes toward topics such as sexuality, sexism, and relations between the sexes. Deals with psychological and political implications of this subject. Begins with an assessment of Victorians' public and private responses to sexual matters; devotes separate chapters to examination of works by Robert Browning and Tennyson which focus on marriage and divorce. Concludes with a comparison of Victorian and modern approaches to sexual matters.

Kaplan, Fred. *Sacred Tears: Sentimentality in Victorian Literature*. Princeton, N.J.: Princeton University Press, 1987.
Brief study of the Victorians' penchant for sentimentality, a feeling they valued and openly expressed. Provides an analysis of the eighteenth century philosophical background to this idea; explores the presence of sentimentality in works by Dickens and Thackeray in detail, but makes many observations of value to students of Victorian poetry. Includes a chapter on Carlyle, whose writings influenced virtually every other author of the period.

Kennedy, Judith, ed. *Victorian Authors and Their Works: Revision, Motivation, and Modes*. Athens: Ohio University Press, 1991.
Collection of essays focusing on textual criticism, detailing the importance of revision as it is accomplished by an author both during the composition process and after a work has been published. Includes an essay on Tennyson's poetry and references to the works of several other Victorian poets. Useful to gain an appreciation of the way friends, relatives, critics, and the general public influenced the production and revision of literary works, including poetry.

Kumar, Shiv K. *British Victorian Literature: Recent Revaluations*. New York: New York University Press, 1969.
Collection of thirty essays previously published in scholarly journals

or in important monographs, surveying all genres of Victorian literature. Several essays focus on the intellectual climate of the period and the ways Victorian authors communicated with their readers. Eleven essays discuss the work of Victorian poets, especially Tennyson. Contains a selected bibliography of sources for further study.

Landow, George. *Victorian Types, Victorian Shadows: Biblical Typology in Victorian Literature, Thought, and Art.* Boston: Routledge & Kegan Paul, 1980.
Study of the influence in the Victorian period of biblical typology, a method of interpretation whereby images of Christ are seen prefigured in Old Testament characters and texts. Claims both writers and readers were intimately familiar with the Bible; hence, authors could use a kind of shorthand to communicate important ideas by relying on readers' understanding of typology. Examines ways poets, novelists, and nonfiction writers used typology to create patterns of imagery and structure in their works.

Lang, Cecil Y. "Introduction." *The Pre-Raphaelites and Their Circle.* Boston: Houghton Mifflin, 1968.
Provides excellent overview of the Pre-Raphaelite movement, explaining its origins and its contributions to poetry and painting. Briefly sketches the roles of significant figures involved in the movement, focusing on the contributions of Dante Gabriel Rossetti. Assesses the characteristics of Pre-Raphaelitism as they appear in literature and art.

Levine, Richard A., ed. *Backgrounds to Victorian Literature.* San Francisco: Chandler Publishing Co., 1967.
Collection of critical essays offering an assessment of the intellectual, cultural, and political background of the period; many selections are excerpts from previously published studies. Includes commentary on religion and science, education, the role of the artist, the development of the historical consciousness, the rise of the study of economics, and several discussions of what "Victorianism" meant to people at different points during the century. Particularly helpful to students of poetry who wish to understand the external stimuli which influenced the production of art during the period. Very useful chronology of the years 1830-1901.

_____. *The Victorian Experience: The Poets.* Athens: Ohio University Press, 1982.
Essays by distinguished critics of Victorian literature providing general assessments of the work of several important nineteenth century poets.

In each the focus is on what makes reading the individual poet's work particularly valuable in the twentieth century. The editor's introduction explains how these essays are an antidote to overspecialized criticisms (especially new critical theory) which often fail to account for the value of the direct experience readers have in confronting Victorian poetry directly.

Lucas, John, ed. *Literature and Politics in the Nineteenth Century.* London: Methuen, 1971.

Collection of essays by noted critics of Victorian literature focusing on selected authors whose works address or are affected by political issues. All literary genres are considered; includes commentary on Tennyson, Arnold, Robert Browning, Clough, and Morris. Essays demonstrate how writers of both imaginative literature and nonfiction attempt to "interpret and render the actual political process" in their works.

McGhee, Richard D. *Marriage, Duty, and Desire in Victorian Poetry and Drama.* Lawrence: University Press of Kansas, 1980.

Focuses on the Victorians' preoccupation with the competing ideas of duty and desire: sees both poets and dramatists struggling to strike a balance between them. Notes how often artists turned to the institution of marriage both as a subject for exploring the tension between duty and desire, and as a metaphor for expressing larger concerns about the conflicts between these human tendencies. Reviews the works of ten major poets and dramatists to demonstrate the prevalence of Victorians' concern with the issue.

Mermin, Dorothy. *The Audience in the Poem: Five Victorian Poets.* New Brunswick, N.J.: Rutgers University Press, 1983.

Examines a particular group of poems popular in the Victorian period: those with a clearly identifiable auditor, whom the speaker in the poem addresses directly and from whom he or she takes cues in presenting and modifying the argument of the poem. Uses general description of the dramatic monologue as a starting point for discussion but expands analysis to emphasize the significance of the auditor. Reads these poems as attempts on the part of the poets to find acceptable ways of reaching their own audiences. Sees the impetus for creating this poetry in the Victorians' growing affection for the novel. Discusses works by Tennyson, Robert Browning, Arnold, Clough, and Meredith.

Miyoshi, Masao. *The Divided Self: A Perspective on the Literature of the Victorians.* New York: New York University Press, 1969.

Study of the ways Victorian writers dealt with "the self-division endemic to their times, and gave expression to it in their writing." Focuses on writers who were clearly aware of the competing forces that affected their psyches. Examines all literary genres; includes discussion of Tennyson and Matthew Arnold. Begins with an exploration of Romantic traditions that influenced the Victorians; concentrates on the mid-Victorians' method for showing "the problem of self-division." Concludes with a review of writers of the 1890's, who reacted against the earlier generation's attempts to compromise with the competing demands on the self.

Nichols, Ashton. *The Poetics of Epiphany: Nineteenth-Century Origins of the Modern Literary Movement.* Tuscaloosa, Ala.: University of Alabama Press, 1987.
Study of the way the notion of the epiphany, an illuminating moment of experience, became a source of poetic inspiration and was transformed into literature. Traces the development of the process from its origins with the Romantic poets through its use by twentieth century figures such as Wallace Stevens and T. S. Eliot. Claims the "literary epiphany develops in important ways during the Victorian period"; examines works by Robert Browning, Tennyson, and Hopkins to show how the techniques of developing meaning by transforming this momentary experience into art helped shape the poetry of these individuals and permanently influenced the production of poetry in the next century.

Reed, John R. *Victorian Conventions.* Athens: Ohio University Press, 1975.
Comprehensive study of dozens of conventions which shaped the lives and attitudes of Victorians and served as means of stylizing the representation of life in nineteenth century literature. In fifteen lengthy chapters, Reed treats subjects such as views of women and types of men; marriage, duelling, and attitudes toward death and dying; views of money, madness, gypsies, and orphans; uses of disguises; and ideas about memory, the occult, coincidence, and the motif of the return. Cites examples from many Victorian poets, especially Tennyson.

Richards, Bernard A. *English Poetry of the Victorian Period, 1830-1880.* London: Longmans, 1980.
Exceptionally useful introduction to the study of Victorian poetry. Organized thematically; addresses matters of both content and technique. Includes a chapter on the image of the poet and the function of

poetry, and two chapters on diction and versification. Separate chapters examine genres popular during the period; love poetry; the Victorians' interest in the past; domesticity; the elegiac impulse; satire; concern with nature and science; religion; art and culture. Detailed bibliographies covering general topics and individual authors.

Sambrook, James, ed. *Pre-Raphaelitism: A Collection of Critical Essays.* Chicago: University of Chicago Press, 1974.
Seventeen selections from members of the Pre-Raphaelite Brotherhood and critics of the nineteenth and twentieth centuries, explaining the premises which guided the development of the movement. Several contributors focus on achievements of individual artists such as Dante Gabriel Rossetti and William Morris. Introduction provides excellent detailed overview of the history of the Pre-Raphaelite movement and summarizes critical reactions from 1850 through 1970.

Schulz, Max F. *Paradise Preserved: Recreations of Eden in Eighteenth- and Nineteenth-Century England.* Cambridge, England: Cambridge University Press, 1985.
Examines various artistic renditions of paradise, both literary and pictorial, created over two centuries. Investigates Enlightenment, Romantic, and post-Romantic ideas of Eden; includes discussion of works by Victorian poets Tennyson, Patmore, and Dante Gabriel Rossetti, as well as painters J. M. W. Turner, Rossetti, and James McNeill Whistler. Especially helpful for understanding the close relationship between poetry and painting in the Victorian era.

Shaw, W. David. *The Lucid Veil: Poetic Truth in the Victorian Age.* Madison: University of Wisconsin Press, 1987.
Ambitious attempt to explore the "connection which exists between Victorian poetics and changing theories of language and knowledge." Examines metaphors used by Victorian poets, scientists, and literary figures to represent truth and humanity's developing notions of self-consciousness. Also discusses the growth of holistic theories of language and knowledge in the century. Discusses the impact on Victorian literature of agnosticism as a philosophical position; surveys the use of analogy, especially historical parallels, and the emergence of Hegelian methodology in shaping poetic vision. Cites throughout the works of both major and minor poets to illustrate the thesis.

Shmiefsky, Marvel. *Sense at War with Soul: English Poetics 1865-1900.* The Hague: Mouton, 1972.

Extensive examination of Victorian poetic theory as it was formulated in the latter half of the century. A brief overview of the main issues is followed by nine chapters focusing on critical works by important nineteenth century theorists, including Matthew Arnold, Algernon Swinburne, Gerard Manley Hopkins, William Butler Yeats, and Oscar Wilde. Reviews the way critics of the era wrestled with the problem of form versus content in both contemporary and earlier poetry.

Slinn, E. Warwick. *The Discourse of Self in Victorian Poetry.* Charlottesville: University Press of Virginia, 1991.
Examines Victorian long poems in light of philosophical concepts of the self and of discourse as the only form of knowing. Relies heavily on the work of Hegel and Jacques Derrida, stressing the shift in a belief in the possibility of transcendence to an acceptance of the notion that such a philosophical position is untenable because of the nature of language. Describes Victorian long poems as examples of poets' recognition of the inability to achieve absolute knowledge of the self. Includes analysis of Tennyson's *Maud*, Clough's *Amours de Voyage*, and Browning's *The Ring and the Book*. Two introductory chapters establish the theoretical groundwork for an analysis of these works.

Starzyk, Lawrence J. *The Imprisoned Splendor: A Study of Victorian Critical Theory.* Port Washington, N.Y.: Kennikat Press, 1977.
Critical assessment of Victorian aesthetic theory, examining its early chaotic state in which critics and poets alike struggled to disassociate themselves from well-defined Romantic notions about the role of the critic and the artist. Explores ways Victorian poets were able to make their work both artistically sound and socially meaningful in a world where discoveries in science called into question the value of all artistic endeavor. Especially valuable for understanding the artistic development of Arnold, Robert Browning, and Tennyson.

Stein, Richard L. *The Ritual of Interpretation: The Fine Arts as Literature in Ruskin, Rossetti, and Pater.* Cambridge, Mass.: Harvard University Press, 1975.
Examines the literary response to the fine arts during the nineteenth century, discussing ways Victorian writers used the arts as subjects for poetry and prose. Traces the roots of this impulse to use art as the subject for other forms of art to its classical, neoclassical, and Romantic roots. Describes how an understanding of this literary phenomenon sheds light on Victorian aesthetics.

Stevenson, Lionel. *The Pre-Raphaelite Poets*. Chapel Hill: University of North Carolina Press, 1972.

Comprehensive study of poets associated with the Pre-Raphaelite Brotherhood, focusing on the four major figures (Dante Gabriel Rossetti, Christina Rossetti, William Morris, and Algernon Charles Swinburne) and their collective influence on English poetry beginning in the middle decades of the nineteenth century. Examines their attack on Victorian hypocrisy, their uninhibited exploration of sexual issues, and their glorification of medieval and classical subjects and values. Traces their roots to Romanticism and to contemporary critics such as Carlyle and Ruskin; surveys their influence on modern poetry. Includes an extensive bibliography.

Tennyson, G. B. *Victorian Devotional Poetry*. Cambridge, Mass.: Harvard University Press, 1981.

Examines this special form of Victorian poetry, most of it written to express feelings about God and people's dependence on God. Intended not to revise critical opinion of individual poets, but rather to show how an understanding of devotional poetry leads to greater appreciation of Victorian intellectual life, society, and culture. Focuses on the works of John Henry Newman, John Keble, and Isaac Williamson. Tennyson includes a chapter on poets Christina Rossetti and Gerard Manley Hopkins.

Thesing, William B. *The London Muse: Victorian Poetic Responses to the City*. Athens: University of Georgia Press, 1982.

Extensive examination of the influence of city life, especially London, on British poets from William Blake to T. S. Eliot. Concentrates on works by more than twenty poets of the Victorian period, including Tennyson, Morris, Hopkins, Arnold, Patmore, and Thomson. Demonstrates how different writers made "social and political sense of the city"; explains why novelists became chief analysts and apologists for city life, as poets found treatment of urban subjects incompatible with their vision of the role of poetry.

Vicinus, Martha. *The Industrial Muse: A Study of Nineteenth Century British Working Class Literature*. New York: Barnes & Noble, 1974.

Critical analysis of literature produced by members of the working classes during the Victorian era. Examines impact of these writings on their primary audience, the lower classes. Displays differences between this literature and works normally studied by academics. Includes chapters on street literature, propaganda, and dialect writers;

another chapter examines work influenced by the Chartist movement. Discussion of poetry included in general analysis of major forms of working-class writing. Numerous illustrations; excellent bibliography of both primary and secondary sources.

Chapter 1
MATTHEW ARNOLD

General Studies

Allott, Kenneth, ed. *Matthew Arnold*. Writers and Their Background.
Athens: Ohio University Press, 1976.

Collection of ten lengthy essays focusing on Arnold's relationship to
and influence on the political, social, and artistic movements of his
time. Fraser Neiman provides a good overview of the poet's accomplishments. Two essays examine Arnold's poetry, another two review
his criticism; one surveys his relationship with the poet Arthur Hugh
Clough. Others discuss his social and political thought, his attitude
toward religion, and his use of the classics. Includes an excellent
chronology placing major events in Arnold's life and his publications
in context of the significant events of the century.

Allott, Miriam. "Matthew Arnold: 'All One and Continuous.'" In Richard
A. Levine, ed. *The Victorian Experience: The Poets*. Athens: Ohio
University Press, 1982.

General assessment of Arnold's status among his contemporaries and
in the twentieth century. Believes the body of his work reveals a
remarkably consistent temper, and a vision of how the world both is
and ought to be. Continuously compares him to George Eliot, and on
occasion to other contemporaries such as Tennyson, Robert Browning,
and Clough, to show how modern Arnold really is. Cites numerous
examples from Arnold's poems to illustrate ways he has captured the
modern temper.

apRoberts, Ruth. *Arnold and God*. Berkeley: University of California
Press, 1983.

Comprehensive study of Arnold's attitudes toward religion and his
numerous writings on the subject. Believes an examination of Arnold's
writings from a religious perspective reveals a sense of unity among
his disparate productions. Looks extensively at Arnold's prose works;
notes his heavy dependence on German scholarship, especially Higher
Criticism of the Bible. References to poetry are scattered throughout
the study.

Bloom, Harold, ed. *Matthew Arnold.* Modern Critical Views. New York: Chelsea House, 1987.
Nine essays, eight excerpted from longer works previously published, brought together to provide a representative sampling of what the editor judges "the best contemporary criticism of Arnold's work." Most give an overview of the poet's theories regarding poetry and culture, showing his ongoing fascination with and reliance on classical authors and biblical issues. Also includes extended analyses of "The Scholar-Gipsy" and "Empedocles on Etna."

Brick, Allan. "Equilibrium in the Poetry of Matthew Arnold." In Shiv Kumar, ed., *British Victorian Literature: Recent Revaluations.* New York: New York University Press, 1969.
Argues that Arnold, unlike his Romantic predecessors and Victorian contemporaries, is not an idealist; he does not believe people can transform the world through individual will. Rather, the world shapes individuals and determines their destiny. Reviews several of the poet's major lyrics to show how the central character is actually static and passive despite surface attempts to alter his or her state in life. True self-knowledge for these characters is "the discovery of the self vis-à-vis the outer world," which produces a state of equilibrium between action and isolation.

Buckler, William E. *On the Poetry of Matthew Arnold: Essays in Critical Reconstruction.* New York: New York University Press, 1982.
Believes Arnold's poetry has been misunderstood for more than a century because critics have seen it as largely autobiographical and limited to mere poeticizing of philosophical statements. Looks carefully at the entire corpus to reveal Arnold as "a dramatic and personative poet" similar in technique to Thomas Hardy. Devotes a lengthy chapter to the poet's early work; considers in a central chapter "Empedocles on Etna" and "Tristram and Iseult"; and includes a separate lengthy analysis of poetry written after 1853, when Arnold published his famous manifesto on the function of poetry.

Bush, Douglas. *Matthew Arnold: A Survey of His Poetry and Prose.* New York: Macmillan, 1976.
Summary judgment of Arnold's place in the history of letters. Claims he is the most important Victorian figure in criticism; his influence has shaped both poetry and criticism which has followed him. Includes separate chapters on Arnold's life, his poetry, his literary criticism, his writings about education, and his publications on religion. Sees the

poetry as representing a constant conflict between Romanticism and classicism.

Carroll, Joseph. *The Cultural Theory of Matthew Arnold.* Berkeley: University of California Press, 1982.
Attempts to establish and examine Arnold's sources for his critical theory; believes Arnold's criticism was systematic, founded on the notion that criticism should help "give shape and definition" to human experience. Sees the poet passing through four stages in his critical thought; his feelings of discontent with modern life are best expressed in the poetry he wrote as a young man. Traces Arnold's debt to English neoclassical thinkers of the eighteenth century and to German writers on cultural theory.

Collini, Stefan. *Matthew Arnold.* New York: Oxford University Press, 1988.
Modest study of Arnold's literary accomplishments. Argues Arnold has made the greatest lasting impact as a literary and social critic; his poetry is of less value. Devotes individual chapters to a brief biography, an analysis of Arnold's work as a poet, his literary criticism, his social commentaries, and his writings on religion; concludes with a review and assessment of Arnold's legacy. Includes brief summary of important critical studies of the poetry and prose.

Culler, A. Dwight. *Imaginative Reason: The Poetry of Matthew Arnold.* New Haven, Conn.: Yale University Press, 1966.
Comprehensive analysis of the canon of Arnold's poetry, focusing on the recurrent pattern underlying all of the poet's work. Sees Arnold following the cyclic pattern outlined in late eighteenth and early nineteenth century concepts of history, vivified in a symbolic landscape which includes for Arnold the Forest Glade, the Burning Plain, and the Glimmering Sea; these images suggest alternatively the passage of time, the growth and decay of faith, and progress through life. Claims all of Arnold's verse is essentially elegiac.

Dawson, Carl. *Matthew Arnold: The Poetry: The Critical Heritage.* London: Routledge & Kegan Paul, 1973.
More than five dozen excerpts from reviews, notices, essays, and correspondence by Arnold's contemporaries, offering a wide sampling of critical reactions to Arnold's poetry after its initial appearance and in the latter decades of the nineteenth century. Includes a number of

retrospectives written after the poet's death. Also contains a useful bibliography of secondary sources.

DeLaura, David J. *Hebrew and Hellene in Victorian England: Newman, Arnold, Pater*. Austin: University of Texas Press, 1969.
Explores the importance of Newman's thought and writings in shaping Arnold's and Pater's ideas about culture. Argues Newman was an important source for Arnold as he worked out his ideas about the conflict he saw in modern society between competing impulses, the Hebraic (a quest for rules and moral codes characteristic of the Judaeo-Christian tradition) and the Hellenic (the tendency toward openness of inquiry typified by the classical period). Sees Arnold secularizing Newman's ideas about religion to explain the phenomenon of culture. Important for understanding the background for Arnold's poetry and his decision to turn from composing poetry to writing social criticism.

_____. "Matthew Arnold and the Nightmare of History." In Malcolm Bradbury and David Palmer, eds. *Victorian Poetry*. Stratford-on-Avon Studies 15. London: Edwin Arnold, 1972.
Extensive analysis of Arnold's concept of history. Argues that Arnold rejects the optimism of Emerson, Carlyle, and Clough, consistently attempting to "salvage from the shipwreck of the past a coherent version of man's emotional and imaginative nature"; finds him "historical" in trying to locate the sources of modern malaise in the past. Discusses the poet's pessimistic reaction to the French Revolution of 1848. Believes Arnold eventually developed a theory of history which balances Christianity and "the Hegelian world-process."

Fletcher, Pauline. "Arnold: The Forest Glade." In *Gardens and Grim Ravines: The Language of Landscape in Victorian Poetry*. Princeton, N.J.: Princeton University Press, 1983.
Discusses in some detail Arnold's use of natural landscapes in his poetry, especially mountain landscapes and forest glades. Reviews the poet's debt to Wordsworth and explains how Arnold differed from his mentor in responding to nature. Sees the poet attaching symbolic significance to the landscape, creating in his works a recognizable symbolic pattern; natural settings offer retreats from the complexities of social life. Discusses more than a dozen poems.

Fraser, Hilary. "Criticism: John Ruskin and Matthew Arnold." In *Beauty and Belief: Aesthetics and Religion in Victorian Literature*. Cambridge, England: Cambridge University Press, 1986.

Claims Arnold's concern with objectivity and disinterestedness in his criticism is a mask for hiding his genuine doubts about the true nature of the self and the real psychological issues involved in religious belief. Investigates how much of Arnold's poetry is highly self-referential and how much of it seems to demand objectivity and commitment to living in the real world, while the tone of the works suggests the poet was uncertain about the philosophical position he was advocating so stridently.

Fulweiler, Howard D. *Letters from the Darkling Plain: Language and the Grounds of Knowledge in the Poetry of Arnold and Hopkins.* Columbia: University of Missouri Press, 1972.
Commentary on Arnold and Hopkins focusing on their special concern with the role of poetry in the modern world and the ability of language to be used in meaningful communication. Approximately half the study is devoted to an analysis of Arnold's works, illuminating his particular problems with identifying the proper role of the poet. Points out how Arnold uses romantic love and the struggles of lovers to communicate as an analogy for the larger problem of the disintegration of language and meaning in the nineteenth century.

Giddings, Robert, ed. *Matthew Arnold: Between Two Worlds.* Totowa, N.J.: Barnes & Noble, 1986.
Collection of six essays reviewing Arnold's engagement with his society and exploring the values which prompted him to write both poetry and criticism. An introduction provides an overview of Arnold's place in English intellectual tradition and his prescience in seeing the central problems which would plague society in the years to come.

Honan, Park. *Matthew Arnold: A Life.* New York: McGraw-Hill, 1981.
Comprehensive life study of the poet, based on a large collection of unpublished sources provided to the author by Arnold's family and many friends. Attempts to give biographical explanations for many of the poet's attitudes about poetry and society which appear in his published works. Explains how Arnold developed under the tutelage of a strong father and how he balanced his intellectual life and writings with the heavy demands placed on him by his work as a schools inspector.

Johnson, Wendell Stacy. *Sex and Marriage in Victorian Poetry.* Ithaca, N.Y.: Cornell University Press, 1975, pp. 57-71.
Cites Arnold as a poet who was less concerned with specific Victorian

attitudes about love and marriage than he was with exploring the impossibility of establishing any lasting relationship between individuals. Arnold's poetry is always concerned with the issue of isolation and with attempts by men and women to break through that state. Examines more than a dozen lyrics to demonstrate the consistency of Arnold's attention to the problem of individual isolation.

McGhee, Richard D. "Arnold and Clough." In *Marriage, Duty, and Desire in Victorian Poetry and Drama*. Lawrence: University Press of Kansas, 1980.

Argues all of Arnold's poetry is infused with the tension the poet felt in modern life: conflicting desires to participate in the chaos of the moment or withdraw in order to observe and comment on the human condition. Examines virtually all of Arnold's major poems to illustrate ways the poet dramatizes this theme. Suggests "The Forgotten Merman" is one of the poet's best shorter works. Analyzes *Empedocles on Etna* and *Tristram and Iseult* in some detail. Explains Arnold's changing notion of the *Zeitgeist*.

Machann, Clinton, and Forrest D. Burt. *Matthew Arnold in His Time and Ours*. Charlottesville: University Press of Virginia, 1988.

Fourteen essays by distinguished critics of Arnold's poetry and criticism, assessing the writer's place among his contemporaries and his influence on succeeding generations. Especially helpful for understanding Arnold's theory of poetry and the importance of poetry in shaping culture. Includes an excellent chapter on modernist elements in Arnold's poetry and commentary on the poems in numerous other essays.

Madden, William A. *Matthew Arnold: A Study of the Aesthetic Temperament in Victorian England*. Bloomington: Indiana University Press, 1967.

Study of the development of Arnold's aesthetic temperament. Highlights the importance of English and German Romantic writers. Argues Arnold's identification with this aesthetic tradition stood in sharp contrast to an equally compelling need to respond positively to the prevailing intellectual movements of his own time, which stressed civic involvement and moral earnestness. These competing ideologies produced a tension that fired Arnold's special creative genius and provided the unifying theme for all his works. In separate sections, discusses the poetry and the criticism; uses many less well known works to demonstrate the consistency of Arnold's aesthetic outlook.

Mermin, Dorothy. "Arnold." In *The Audience in the Poem: Five Victorian Poets*. New Brunswick, N.J.: Rutgers University Press, 1983.
In a study of dramatic poems in which auditors are present in the text, Mermin examines several of Arnold's works which fall in this genre. Believes Arnold was always concerned with the poet's ability to "speak to his audience," and with the audience's ability to understand. Discusses Arnold's continued worry about the obscurity of his works. Extensive analysis of "Resignation" and "The Buried Life"; briefer commentary on "Dover Beach."

Neiman, Fraser. *Matthew Arnold*. New York: Twayne, 1968.
Modest overview of Arnold's contributions to English letters and social criticism. Argues that, despite his diverse activities, Arnold is an "integrated personality" who presents a consistent view of the world. Organized chronologically to show the development of Arnold's thought. Includes a selected bibliography and a useful chronology. Excellent introduction to Arnold studies.

Riede, David G. *Matthew Arnold and the Betrayal of Language*. Charlottesville: University Press of Virginia, 1988.
Explores Arnold's attempts to find a language which would allow him to speak authoritatively. Believes the poet failed because he was always distrustful of his efforts and because the age in which he lived was beset by cultural upheaval. Relies heavily on poststructuralist theory to criticize Arnold's poetry; reviews all the major works and dozens of minor ones. Concludes Arnold ultimately failed in his attempt to speak with authority, but he is still an important figure in the history of letters.

Roper, Alan. *Arnold's Poetic Landscapes*. Baltimore: Johns Hopkins University Press, 1969.
Focuses attention on the way Arnold uses landscapes in his poems. Believes the poet is not as monolithic in his construct of landscape as other critics have argued. Further suggests that, like other writers, Arnold uses descriptions of natural settings to evoke human feelings and display aspects of human character. Devotes individual chapters to examinations of the poems in Arnold's 1849 and 1852 volumes; focuses attention in two other chapters on *Empedocles on Etna* and on the poems set in the Cumnor Hills.

Shaw, W. David. "Agnostic Theories of the Word: Arnold's Deconstruction"; "Arnold's Platonism: Analogies of Self and State." In *The Lucid*

Veil: Poetic Truth in the Victorian Age. Madison: University of Wisconsin Press, 1987.

Two essays describing Arnold's attitude toward the nature of language and the ability of human begins to apprehend reality. Places Arnold in the group of agnostic thinkers who want to revise conventional notions of God. Claims the poet was essentially a Platonist; demonstrates similarities between Arnold and his friend Benjamin Jowett, and between Arnold's writings and Plato's *Republic.* Cites several poems, especially "Rugby Chapel," as examples of Arnold's philosophical stance.

Stange, G. Robert. *Matthew Arnold: The Poet as Humanist.* Princeton, N.J.: Princeton University Press, 1967.

Attempts to provide a comprehensive reading of Arnold's poetry, eschewing extended exegesis of individual poems to concentrate on the major ideas which underlie all of the poet's works. Devotes chapters to analysis of Arnold's idea of poetry, his views on nature, his sense of the self, and his attitude toward love. Stresses the influence of Goethe page on Arnold's works, and the poet's consistent anti-Romantic stance.

Super, R. H. *The Time Spirit in Matthew Arnold.* Ann Arbor: University of Michigan Press, 1970.

Three lectures by the editor of Arnold's prose works focusing on the poet's ability to make sense of the main intellectual trends of his own day. Demonstrates Arnold's ability to apply his classical training on modern problems. Discusses the writer's relationship with the work of John Stuart Mill, Thomas Carlyle, and John Henry Newman. Includes useful discussion of *Empedocles on Etna* and "Stanzas from the Grand Chartreuse," as well as briefer comments on other poems.

Thesing, William B. "Matthew Arnold: The Promise of Urban Repose in the Future." In *The London Muse: Victorian Poetic Responses to the City.* Athens: University of Georgia Press, 1982.

Posits that unlike many of his contemporaries, Arnold was "seriously interested in describing the city" and found hope for the future of human beings as city-dwellers. Traces the poet's long-standing concern with city life through poems in all his published volumes. Notes how, as Arnold turned from more abstract to more concrete questions about human life, his interest in city life increased. Includes an analysis of "A Summer's Night," "The Buried Life," "Lines Written in Kensington Garden," and "The Future."

The Buried Life

Buckler, William E. *On the Poetry of Matthew Arnold: Essays in Critical Reconstruction.* New York: New York University Press, 1982, pp. 79-82.
Brief but insightful analysis of the dramatic qualities of the poem. Claims that in the work both the speaker and his female auditor are clearly identified. The speaker quickly establishes his chief concern: his obsession with his own identity, especially his inner life, which he tries to make apparent to both auditor and reader. Argues the speaker's repeated claims regarding his sensitive nature at first appeals to readers, but the vagueness of his pleas eventually raises doubts about his sincerity in the minds of more skeptical readers.

Fulweiler, Howard D. *Letters from the Darkling Plain: Language and the Grounds of Knowledge in the Poetry of Arnold and Hopkins.* Columbia: University of Missouri Press, 1972, pp. 49-50.
Brief commentary on the central themes of the poem. In it Arnold is attempting to formulate "a creative and inner theory of art." The poem is clearly about the failures of dialogue and hence a psychological exploration of the conflict between inner desires and external conventions; but it is also an examination of the difficulties faced by the creative imagination in the modern world.

Mermin, Dorothy. *The Audience in the Poem: Five Victorian Poets.* New Brunswick, N.J.: Rutgers University Press, 1983, pp. 92-98.
In a study of poems containing auditors present before the speaker in the poem and affecting his behavior and speech, Mermin examines this work to show how Arnold uses a female auditor at the beginning to dramatize the speaker's wish to communicate his innermost feelings to someone he loves. Argues the auditor seems to disappear after the opening lines, and the speaker continues as if talking to himself about the impossibility of being sincere with others. Compares the theme of "The Buried Life" to several others in Arnold's canon.

Riede, David G. *Matthew Arnold and the Betrayal of Language.* Charlottesville: University Press of Virginia, 1988, pp. 182-195.
Extremely detailed analysis of the language, diction, and rhetoric of the poem. Claims the poem is an effort "to find an entirely sincere poetic language"; the poet discovers it is not possible to use language to communicate genuine feeling. Discusses Arnold's subtle allusions to Wordsworth, to Milton, and to Coleridge's "Kubla Khan."

Roper, Alan. *Arnold's Poetic Landscapes*. Baltimore: Johns Hopkins University Press, 1969.

Claims in this poem Arnold means to focus readers' attention on "the possibility of meaningful communion in love." Describes the poetic techniques Arnold uses to present the reader with a stoic view of human existence. Concentrates on the various metaphors recurring throughout the poem. Notes how typically Arnoldian the concluding section of the work is, but believes the poet ultimately fails to achieve greatness because he is unable to present his philosophical ideas clearly through consistent use of poetic devices.

Stange, G. Robert. *Matthew Arnold: The Poet as Humanist*. Princeton, N.J.: Princeton University Press, 1967, pp. 168-179.

Cites the work as "the center of a constellation of poems" dealing with Arnold's "idea of the self." Detailed explication of the poem, focusing on the poet's use of imagery which projects the note of melancholy permeating the work. Claims Arnold makes clear distinctions between outer and inner selves; discusses the particular qualities of melancholy the poet experiences as he discovers the inability of the self ever to engage fully all of his innermost feelings.

Dover Beach

Buckler, William E. *On the Poetry of Matthew Arnold: Essays in Critical Reconstruction*. New York: New York University Press, 1982, pp. 102-107.

Challenges the traditional reading of the poem as a mere statement of Arnold's attitude toward modern life. Claims the speaker is a Romantic hero overwhelmed by his own despair; the image of Sophocles having had to bear the same burden suggests there is an alternative vision—a classical attitude of acceptance and understanding which "turns pathos into tragedy." Believes the final image of armies clashing by night is intended to recall the last battle of King Arthur, the medieval hero so admired by Romantic and post-Romantic writers.

Collini, Stefan. *Matthew Arnold*. New York: Oxford University Press, 1988, pp. 39-41.

Brief comments on the poem focus on Arnold's ability to sketch quickly in the opening lines the "mood of reflective sadness" characteristic of his best work. Notes how the speaker's invocation to his beloved that their love may provide solace is quickly overwhelmed by the image of battle at the close of the work. Also comments on the unusual structure, suggesting the poem is an early example of free verse.

Culler, A. Dwight. *Imaginative Reason: The Poetry of Matthew Arnold.* New Haven, Conn.: Yale University Press, 1966, pp. 39-41.
  Considers this poem a particularly good summary of Arnold's position on the modern condition. Focuses on the use of imagery, showing how the quality of the sea changes as the speaker moves from a lofty vantage point closer to the water; what appears calm from afar is actually discordant. Sees this as an imaginative movement "from the illusion of natural beauty to the tragic fact of human experience." Arnold's view is decidedly modern in that he sees humanity as alienated from traditional systems of belief.

Mermin, Dorothy. *The Audience in the Poem: Five Victorian Poets.* New Brunswick, N.J.: Rutgers University Press, 1983, pp. 83-84, 106-108.
  Brief analysis of a work Mermin calls "the most widely popular short poem of the Victorian period." Discusses the function of the auditor in the work, the woman whose presence before the male speaker prompts his conversation and allows him to feel that love is his refuge against an uncaring world in which faith has been lost. Believe the poem is emblematic of the Victorians' belief that a retreat into private relationships may be the only escape from insoluble modern social problems. Claims the tone of the poem, conversational rather than declamatory, makes its message especially powerful.

Riede, David G. *Matthew Arnold and the Betrayal of Language.* Charlottesville: University Press of Virginia, 1988, pp. 195-203.
  Careful analysis of the text to reveal a subtext which vitiates whatever solace Arnold's speaker may suggest as a possibility in faithless times. Demonstrates how the works of Wordsworth, Milton, and Shakespeare are alluded to and how these serve as a sobering background to the poem. Cites the work of numerous other critics whose interpretations of the poem support this reading.

Roper, Alan. *Arnold's Poetic Landscapes.* Baltimore: Johns Hopkins University Press, 1969, pp. 177-182.
  Believes this is Arnold's finest lyric because it renders human feelings through intense description of landscape. Unlike most of Arnold's best work, this poem achieves its effects through concentration of emotion achieved by providing deft descriptions; the poet relies heavily on adjectives to convey the significance of the moment. Offers careful

analysis of the language and descriptive scenes Arnold uses to create and sustain a mood throughout the work.

Empedocles on Etna

Buckler, William E. *"Tristram and Iseult* and *Empedocles on Etna."* In *On the Poetry of Matthew Arnold: Essays in Critical Reconstruction.* New York: New York University Press, 1982.

Asserts the poem is the century's finest statement on the condition of modernism; its vision of humankind is hopelessly dark, for Arnold suggests the conditions of human existence are timeless. Discusses the poet's construction of his story from the fragments available in classical sources. Also stresses the dramatic nature of the work. Briefly sketches the roles of Pausanias and Callicles. Concludes the poem is a profound critique of Romanticism.

Bush, Douglas. *Matthew Arnold: A Survey of His Poetry and Prose.* New York: Macmillan, 1976, pp. 56-62.

Examines the structure of the poem to show how Arnold uses the drama to vivify his ideas about the necessity for achieving self-understanding and for moderating one's emotions and desires. Singles out a number of passages for more extensive analysis, pointing out that some of Arnold's best writing and his most penetrating psychological insights appear in this poem.

Carroll, Joseph. *The Cultural Theory of Matthew Arnold.* Berkeley: University of California Press, 1982, pp. 1-15.

Claims the poem is Arnold's "most thorough exploration of the spiritual malaise" of modern life, which the poet saw as full of doubt and as a period in decline from earlier epochs of glory. Examines the character of Empedocles as Arnold creates him, skeptical and paralyzed by the world he sees around him. Discusses the prose outline Arnold wrote to summarize the ending of the work; notes how in the final soliloquy the poet fails to achieve his stated aim.

Collini, Stefan. *Matthew Arnold.* New York: Oxford University Press, 1988, pp. 34-38.

Brief commentary on the work Collini believes is a "brilliant dramatization of Arnold's own internal conflicts." Points out that, despite the poet's description of the work as a drama, it is actually a series of monologues. Pays special attention to the character of Empedocles, who tries to represent the stoic point of view in its best light; argues the hero is never really committed to the stoicism he preaches, however, since he is torn by conflicting ideas about commitment to the world versus a yearning to withdraw from its strife.

Fulweiler, Howard D. *Letters from the Darkling Plain: Language and the Grounds of Knowledge in the Poetry of Arnold and Hopkins.* Columbia: University of Missouri Press, 1972, pp. 35-42.
Considers the work Arnold's most direct expression of his doubts about the efficacy of poetry. Through the title character Arnold dramatizes his "loss of faith in the creative and validly communicative possibilities of art." Reviews the plot, highlighting the significance of Empedocles' lengthy sermon and the closing song of Callicles. Believes Empedocles' decision to commit suicide is a result of his realization that communication is impossible.

Harrison, Antony. "Arnold, Keats, and the Ideologies of *Empedocles on Etna.*" In *Victorian Poets and Romantic Poems: Intertextuality and Ideology.* Charlottesville: University Press of Virginia, 1990.
Claims in this poetic drama Arnold is heavily influenced by Keats, a poet he openly criticized. Traces the lengthy and subtle influence of this Romantic predecessor on Arnold's concept of the poet and his techniques. Cites ways Keats's view of the poet as one possessing "natural magic" forms the basis for Arnold's conception of Empedocles; calls the hero of the drama "a poet of natural magic vanquished by age." Notes how Arnold's dislike of Keats actually works to strengthen his sense of the value of poetry. Believes Arnold decided to exclude *Empedocles on Etna* from later editions of his poetry because he finally saw too much of Keats in the poem.

Neiman, Fraser. *Matthew Arnold.* New York: Twayne, 1968, pp. 71-74.
Brief review of Arnold's intentions for the poem, and a sketch of the main characters, Empedocles and Callicles. Argues Arnold may have failed to bring to fruition his grand design for the poem; he intended Empedocles to be a man who saw reality clearly and whole, a sight denied to most people. Points out parallels Arnold saw between his own age and Sicily during the fifth century b.c.

Riede, David G. *Matthew Arnold and the Betrayal of Language.* Charlottesville: University Press of Virginia, 1988, pp. 78-93.
Claims the poem dramatizes the difficulties Arnold had in finding "a firm basis for speech," an authoritative voice with which he could

address the world. Every speech in the poem is undercut by the one following it. Empedocles appears to be a most rational character, but his language is simply sterile. The poet sets up a dialogue between two seemingly opposite points of view, but actually Callicles and Empedocles are two sides of Arnold's divided self. Carefully examines the speeches and songs; demonstrates how neither Empedocles nor Callicles actually communicates with the other.

Roper, Alan. "Mount Etna." In *Arnold's Poetic Landscapes*. Baltimore: Johns Hopkins University Press, 1969.

Asserts this is Arnold's greatest poem, presenting "a total myth of Victorian England." Discusses ways Arnold modifies the historical Empedocles and his philosophy to suit a modern purpose. Believes this work is essentially different from others in the Arnold canon because it is based on a belief that humanity and nature are one; people can achieve real rest only when they recognize this symbiotic relationship. What Empedocles learns (and what drives him to suicide) is that the mind, his defining principle, is also his greatest impediment to achieving harmony with nature. Provides lengthy explanation of the appropriateness of the rather prosaic homily in the central section of the poem; also explains the function of Callicles' songs.

Suleri, Sara. "Entropy on Etna: Arnold and the Poetry of Reading." In Harold Bloom, ed. *Matthew Arnold*. Modern Critical Views. New York: Chelsea House, 1987.

Explores the notion that Arnold transforms philosophic beliefs into literary figures and texts, leaving it to the Wordsworthian "attentive reader" to extract the appropriate philosophy from the literary production. Believes "Empedocles on Etna" subverts the poet's idea that the classical world provided certainty, which the modern world lacks; because he learns while writing the poem that the classical world suffered from the same uncertainties as the age in which he lived, Arnold was forced to reject the work, displacing it from his canon. Claims the structure of the poem rests on the failure of dialogue between Empedocles and the other characters in the work.

Super, R. H. *The Time Spirit in Matthew Arnold*. Ann Arbor: University of Michigan Press, 1970, pp. 17-24.

Calls the poem Arnold's finest, in which he provides "an analysis of the spiritual state" of his century. Explains why Arnold rejected the poem in his 1853 Preface. Provides lengthy description of the poet's sources for the story. Notes how the addition of Callicles allows Arnold to achieve some balance between philosophical positions. Believes Arnold intends to mock the nineteenth century religious notions of a personal God and an afterlife which will make up for one's present wants.

Resignation

Riede, David G. *Matthew Arnold and the Betrayal of Language*. Charlottesville: University Press of Virginia, 1988, pp. 57-61.
Reads the poem as a rejection of Wordsworth's view of nature and of the poet's proper role. Arnold sets up a situation similar to that in Wordsworth's "Tintern Abbey" only to undercut the older poet's notion that nature is harmonious and the poet's role is to look deeply into Nature for her truths. Arnold believes the poet must be aloof and stoical and must look widely rather than deeply to discover truth.

Stange, G. Robert. *Matthew Arnold: The Poet as Humanist*. Princeton, N.J.: Princeton University Press, 1967, pp. 54-70.
Argues the poem is specifically Arnoldian in its celebration of the contemplative over the active life. Sees the concrete situation Arnold creates as an appropriate setting for the philosophical speculations which dominate the work; examines the conversation between the speaker and Faust. Concludes one of the major aims of the work is the explication of the proper role of the poet in society.

Rugby Chapel

Buckler, William E. *On the Poetry of Matthew Arnold: Essays in Critical Reconstruction*. New York: New York University Press, 1982, pp. 163-169.
Brief examination of Arnold's elegy for his father, explaining its genesis and describing the central structural principles on which the work is built. Believes it is chiefly a statement of the superiority of the classical worldview over the Romantic one; claims people can find hope only in themselves, not in nature. Makes careful distinctions between the poet and the speaker.

Culler, A. Dwight. *Imaginative Reason: The Poetry of Matthew Arnold*. New Haven, Conn.: Yale University Press, 1966, pp. 272-277.
Concentrates on the background to the poem's composition. Notes Arnold's strong feelings about the significance of his father's work in

shaping not only the poet's life but that of many young boys who attended Rugby. Cites Tom Hughes's *Tom Brown's School Days* and a review by FitzJames Stephen as the immediate stimuli for Arnold's poetic inspiration. Claims the aim of the work is to establish Dr. Arnold's reputation and his importance as both thinker and teacher.

Riede, David G. *Matthew Arnold and the Betrayal of Language.* Charlottesville: University Press of Virginia, 1988, pp. 156-160.

Believes Arnold's attempt to present a "saving vision of truth" causes him to use extremely strident rhetoric throughout the poem; contends the poet is never really convinced of the efficacy of the quest he describes, and never fully committed to the principles he claims are dramatized by his father's life. Believes that, despite his overt assertions about the Christian nature of his father's heroic efforts, Arnold is really expressing an agnostic point of view in the work.

The Scholar-Gipsy

Culler, A. Dwight. "The Scholar-Gipsy." In *Imaginative Reason: The Poetry of Matthew Arnold.* New Haven, Conn.: Yale University Press, 1966.

Extended analysis of what Culler considers Arnold's finest poem. Examines sources for Arnold's inspiration, especially Glanvill, a seventeenth century writer, and nineteenth century writings on mesmerism. Explains how Arnold transforms Glanvill's Renaissance Oxford scholar into a Romantic hero whose quest for knowledge is paralleled by the poet's quest for his proper role. Demonstrates Arnold's reliance on Romantic dream vision; covers in detail the five-part structure of the work. Explicates the curious ending in which Arnold uses the Tyrian trader as a symbol of "ancient civilization" which refuses to be corrupted by the modern world.

Drew, Philip. "Matthew Arnold and the Passage of Time: A Study of *The Scholar-Gypsy* and *Thyrsis.*" In Isobel Armstrong, ed. *The Major Victorian Poets: Reconsiderations.* Lincoln: University of Nebraska Press, 1969.

Claims "The Scholar-Gipsy" and "Thyrsis" are among the poems in which Arnold combines serious purpose and superb writing. Believes the two are actually parts of a single poem whose subject is an exploration of the concepts of mutability and time. In "The Scholar-Gipsy" Arnold examines the question of a young man's proper re-

sponse to the contagion of modern life, which saps creativity. Traces
the movement of the poem, showing how Arnold outlines the difficulty
of achieving noble action in the modern world. Concludes the note of
melancholy which characterizes the work is meant to mirror the sad
state of contemporary life.

Knight, G. Wilson. "The Scholar-Gipsy." In Harold Bloom, ed. *Matthew Arnold*. Modern Critical Views. New York: Chelsea House, 1987.

Systematic attempt to explain the relevance of the final stanzas of the
poem. Notes that Arnold makes additional references to Tyrian characters, citing the mention of Dido earlier in the work. Claims the central
interest in the poem is in the contrast of Eastern and Western modes of
thinking; the Scholar-Gipsy is a combination of these divergent worldviews. Believes Arnold is cautioning his readers about western ideology, which has squeezed out the mystical beliefs of the Eastern
tradition; these are also valuable to humanity's understanding of itself
and the world.

Madden, William A. *Matthew Arnold: A Study of the Aesthetic Temperament in Victorian England*. Bloomington: Indiana University Press,
1967, pp. 65-69.

Notes the nostalgic tone which dominates the poem; sees Arnold
presenting the conflict between a past golden age and modern times.
The speaker in the poem envies the life of the Scholar, and urges him
to avoid the encroaching demands of modern civilization; the story of
the Tyrian sailor at the end of the poem is offered as an example for
the Scholar and for those who, like him, long for a simpler life. Argues
the poem offers little hope for people to succeed in avoiding the
frustration of modern life; the overriding tone of the work is one of
melancholy.

Riede, David G. *Matthew Arnold and the Betrayal of Language*. Charlottesville: University Press of Virginia, 1988, pp. 134-147.

Acknowledges the poem is normally linked to the Romantic phase of
Arnold's career. Notes how heavily the poet relies on literary tradition
(especially Milton) for creating character and setting; points out how
bleak his language becomes when he discusses modern life. Believes
the Gipsy is not a fit hero, since he achieves success only by escaping
from society; the closing lines about the Tyrian trader simply reinforce
the antisocial attitude promoted by the poem. Considers the real
achievement of the work its display of "the purposeless multitudous-
ness of modern life."

Roper, Alan. *Arnold's Poetic Landscapes*. Baltimore: Johns Hopkins University Press, 1969, pp. 209-224.

Argues this poem is one of Arnold's best. Reviews the readings of Leavis, Knight, Dyson, and Culler to show how the poem has inspired varying interpretations. Provides detailed explication of individual stanzas to explain ways Arnold dramatizes his central concern: the "contrast between the active and reflective lives." The poem allows readers to "test the validity of the contemplative life" against the vigorous commercial life Arnold saw around him. The Scholar becomes a symbol of the alternative which is both attractive and yet ultimately unattainable. Explains why the figure of the Tyrian trader at the end of the poem is an appropriate closing image, suggesting the necessity for action as well as the rejection of modern commercialism.

Sohrab and Rustum

Buckler, William E. *On the Poetry of Matthew Arnold: Essays in Critical Reconstruction*. New York: New York University Press, 1982, pp. 149-154.

Sees the poem as Arnold's attempt to write "truly worthy poetry"; briefly traces its history of composition. Believes the poet has succeeded in constructing a highly complex narrative poem and in transforming the story of Sohrab and Rustum into a compelling account which recalls the antipathies of classicism and Romanticism while simultaneously creating an existential parable of human beings' struggle to find meaning in life.

Culler, A. Dwight. "Sohrab, Balder, Merope." In *Imaginative Reason: The Poetry of Matthew Arnold*. New Haven, Conn.: Yale University Press, 1966.

Explains how the poem exemplifies the new poetic credo Arnold sets forth in the Preface to his 1853 volume; it is action-centered, highly structured, dependent on the ancients for subject matter and technique. Describes the action of the work, noting its parallels to *Empedocles on Etna*; both works involve a conflict between father and son. Shows how Arnold's many similes work together to create a "symbolic topography" within the poem. Concludes, however, that the work focuses too much on resolving a conflict that is not sufficiently dramatized.

Fulweiler, Howard D. *Letters from the Darkling Plain: Language and the Grounds of Knowledge in the Poetry of Arnold and Hopkins*. Columbia: University of Missouri Press, 1972, pp. 83-85.

Believes the poem is significant in the poet's canon not because Arnold succeeds in creating a great, objective poem but because the work is an illustration of his state of mind at the time of composition. Arnold enjoyed creating the work because it served as a statement of the direction his writing would take: away from self-analysis through creative art toward his public role as a critic.

Madden, William A. *Matthew Arnold: A Study of the Aesthetic Temperament in Victorian England.* Bloomington: Indiana University Press, 1967, pp. 27-33.

Reads the poem as an objectification of Arnold's attempt to come to grips with the legacy of his father and all Dr. Arnold stands for. Discusses the particular appeal of the source of the story; Arnold was fascinated with Eastern philosophy and its belief in intuitive apprehension as an alternative to Western rational thought. Describes the central conflict between Rustum and the son he does not recognize as emblematic of Arnold's own intellectual conflict with the image of his father, whose "ethical bias" stands in sharp contrast to Arnold's own "aesthetic temperament." The work suggests Arnold saw his father as responsible for the poet's eventual decision to give up writing poetry in favor of social and cultural criticism.

Riede, David G. *Matthew Arnold and the Betrayal of Language.* Charlottesville: University Press of Virginia, 1988, pp. 102-109.

Focuses on Arnold's successes and failures in trying to compose a poem in the grand style he describes in his famous 1853 Preface to his poems. Believes Arnold is unsuccessful in producing a work that is truly Homeric, even though his subject has epic qualities; claims the poet relies too heavily on imitation of other poetry. Any success the work does enjoy stems from the distance Arnold is able to establish between his readers and the experiences he describes.

Roper, Alan. *Arnold's Poetic Landscapes.* Baltimore: Johns Hopkins University Press, 1969, pp. 242-246.

Believes this poem deserves the label "academic"; claims it holds for contemporary readers little more than antiquarian interest in many ways. Like many of his works, "Sohrab and Rustum" displays Arnold's dependence on landscape description to reinforce the dramatic situation and reveal character. Argues the poem is tragic rather than epic, despite Arnold's attempts to link his tale to that genre. The central interest in the work lies in the "tragically fateful dichotomy" between individual fulfillment and social responsibility.

Stanzas from the Grand Chartreuse

Buckler, William E. *On the Poetry of Matthew Arnold: Essays in Critical Reconstruction.* New York: New York University Press, 1982, pp. 107-116.

Carefully explicates a poem which deals with "the stinging distresses of modern life." Focuses attention on the speaker, whose journey to the monastery represents a retreat from the modern world but offers no corrective for its ills. Believes the poem's ultimate message is that the spirit of an age can be fatal to individual human achievements; throughout the poem Arnold contrasts the sages of one period with those of other ages to heighten the differences between his own time and that of past centuries.

Carroll, Joseph. *The Cultural Theory of Matthew Arnold.* Berkeley: University of California Press, 1982, pp. 25-30.

Sees the poem as Arnold's attempt to create an aesthetic object out of his distress over modern life. The heroic action to which the narrator is encouraged is a moral and contemplative one: the rejection of the modern world, in the way the monks have, in favor of a faith which unfortunately cannot hold off the ravages of contemporary life. The grief Arnold feels for the passing of the Age of Faith is real, but it cannot be transformed into any useful action.

Culler, A. Dwight. *Imaginative Reason: The Poetry of Matthew Arnold.* New Haven, Conn.: Yale University Press, 1966, pp. 26-28.

Reads the poem as a symbolic attempt to return to a time of childhood or innocence, both suggested by medieval Christianity, or to the state of idealism sought by Romantic poets. The graphically accurate opening stanzas describing the literal ascent to the monastery call to mind the struggle to rise to some ideal state above the fray of modern times; the speaker learns the futility of finding stability and certainty in the modern world.

Madden, William A. *Matthew Arnold: A Study of the Aesthetic Temperament in Victorian England.* Bloomington: Indiana University Press, 1967, pp. 69-75.

Claims that "Stanzas" holds "the greatest biographical interest of all of Arnold's poems of nostalgia." Concludes the poem's central concern is not in nostalgia for lost religious faith, but rather in a longing for freedom from internal tensions generated by feelings of alienation from both the lost world of the past and the lost time of one's youth, when hope dominates an individual's life. Believes Arnold is positing that the Victorian intellectual has neither the optimism of Romantic philosophers nor the faith of an earlier Christianity to bolster him in times of emotional distress.

Roper, Alan. *Arnold's Poetic Landscapes.* Baltimore: Johns Hopkins University Press, 1969, pp. 237-241.

Links this poem with others in which Arnold discusses false hopes that keep human beings from confronting their existence and coming to genuine self-understanding. The speaker attempts to develop self-awareness by relating to the landscape surrounding the monastery, and within its walls. Considers this poem the "most consistently and overtly escapist" in Arnold's canon. Believes the poet fails to establish the analogy between the speaker and the monks, though he argues force-fully for parallels; unlike the speaker, the monks continue to have faith in a creed that modern people cannot accept.

Super, R. H. *The Time Spirit in Matthew Arnold.* Ann Arbor: University of Michigan Press, 1970, pp. 24-27.

Considers the poem one of Arnold's most complex analyses of the state of religion in the nineteenth century. Cites the genesis for several of the poem's lines in the Yale manuscripts of Arnold's notes and writings. Pays special attention to parallels between the poem and Carlyle's writings, especially his 1831 essay "Characteristics." Believes Arnold's reference to the speaker wandering between two worlds is a metaphor describing the spiritual state of England in his own time.

Stanzas in Memory of the Author of "Obermann"

Buckler, William E. *On the Poetry of Matthew Arnold: Essays in Critical Reconstruction.* New York: New York University Press, 1982, pp. 82-91.

Describes the work as "an elegiac action poem" in which the author creates a separate persona who explores the nature of life and literature and whose discoveries are worthy of note by readers. Carefully distin-guishes between Arnold and the speaker in the poem; Arnold has the speaker come to some understanding about himself and about the value of life through his contact with Sénancour's novel. Believes the speaker finally realizes that living life through literature is not as satisfying as confronting experience directly.

Culler, A. Dwight. *Imaginative Reason: The Poetry of Matthew Arnold.* New Haven, Conn.: Yale University Press, 1966, pp. 121-132, 236-237. Discusses the background of the poem, especially Arnold's heavy debt to Romantic ideology. Also notes the personal quality of the work, which was written while Arnold was still enamored with the woman he calls Marguerite in his poetry. Claims the poet celebrates Obermann as the greatest of the Romantics; though Arnold is attracted to him, in this poem he makes a conscious break with Obermann and the ideology he represents. Also suggests this poem is an example of the way Arnold uses the elegy as a form for expressing "spiritual repudiation."

Madden, William A. *Matthew Arnold: A Study of the Aesthetic Temperament in Victorian England.* Bloomington: Indiana University Press, 1967, pp. 43-54, 112-113. Argues this poem reveals much about Arnold's personal struggle to reconcile his desires to adopt the Romantic aesthetic in a world where such values are not held in high esteem. The speaker of the poem attributes his frustration to the age in which he has been raised; the contemporary world has stifled all attempts at the development of a higher sensitivity. The speaker must ultimately reconcile himself to living in the "mere bustle" of the modern world while somehow "preserving an inward sanctuary of silent attachment to the deeper movement of life itself."

Neiman, Fraser. *Matthew Arnold.* New York: Twayne, 1968, pp. 62-64. Brief discussion of the background of the work, noting Arnold's debt to George Sand and Charles Sainte-Beuve for introducing him to the work of Sénancour. Believes Arnold saw in Sénancour's hero a symbol of "the integrity necessary for the quest" to find a way to live in a fragmented modern world. Claims Arnold finally discovers that overcoming the malaise of modern times is virtually impossible.

Roper, Alan. *Arnold's Poetic Landscapes.* Baltimore: Johns Hopkins University Press, 1969, pp. 233-235. Brief sketch of the poem, comparing it with "Obermann Once More" (a poem written years afterward) to show Arnold's later work has less vigor and originality than earlier poems. In these "Stanzas," Arnold manages to use natural landscape as a way to describe the personal characteristics of his subject, the poet who stands with Wordsworth and Goethe as a pillar of Romanticism. Nevertheless, this poem is judged less successful than "The Scholar-Gipsy," largely because its stanzaic pattern is at odds with the seriousness of the poem.

Stange, G. Robert. *Matthew Arnold: The Poet as Humanist*. Princeton,
   N.J.: Princeton University Press, 1967, pp. 70-75.
   Classifies the poem as one of several in which Arnold discusses the
   idea of poetry. Reviews Arnold's fascination with Étienne Sénancour,
   to whom the poem is dedicated. Arnold finds the novelist an apt
   representative of a kind of artist who understands the world in which
   he lives and suffers from a dark melancholy as a result of his deep-felt
   sense of isolation. Arnold rejects this Romantic view of the artist.

Thyrsis

Culler, A. Dwight. *Imaginative Reason: The Poetry of Matthew Arnold*.
   New Haven, Conn.: Yale University Press, 1966, pp. 250-264.
   Notes the similarities between the poem and "The Scholar-Gipsy," but
   believes this work must be read independently so there is no undue
   biographical influence. Describes background to composition, noting
   Arnold's volatile relationship with Clough, the immediate subject of the
   work. Argues the poem is a highly structured elegy which contains a
   mini-elegy within it; though the death of Clough is the occasion for the
   poem, Arnold is really interested in exploring the way idealism is lost
   with the passage of time. The signal elm tree which he discovers at the
   climax of the poem is a reassurance that such ideals are recoverable.

Drew, Philip. "Matthew Arnold and the Passage of Time: A Study of *The
   Scholar-Gypsy* and *Thyrsis*." In Isobel Armstrong, ed. *The Major
   Victorian Poets: Reconsiderations*. Lincoln: University of Nebraska
   Press, 1969.
   Includes "Thyrsis" and "The Scholar-Gipsy" in a short list of great
   poems in which Arnold achieves serious purpose and mastery of poetic
   style. Argues "Thyrsis" is actually a continuation of the argument first
   posed in "The Scholar-Gipsy"; in this elegy for Clough, Arnold examines the proper response of middle-aged man to the loss of youthful
   ideals. Claims the discovery of the signal elm is a recognition that,
   while ideals may not be realizable in life, they are still worthwhile as
   antidotes to the malaise of modern life.

Riede, David G. *Matthew Arnold and the Betrayal of Language*. Charlottesville: University Press of Virginia, 1988, pp. 147-156.
   Reads the poem as an attempt to justify the poetic quest for meaning
   and authority. Discusses Arnold's efforts to establish the work within

the tradition of the elegy. Believes the poet fails to confront experience directly; instead, he derives his most sincere statements about the world from other poetry. Criticizes Arnold for his use of the signal elm tree as a symbol of permanence. Feels Arnold's logic is flawed, in that he praises "wandering" but wants to hang on to some sort of permanent truth.

Roper, Alan. *Arnold's Poetic Landscapes.* Baltimore: Johns Hopkins University Press, 1969, pp. 224-229.
Claims the poem is an extension of the argument in "The Scholar-Gipsy" about the necessity for reaching some form of certitude in a changing world. Believes Arnold is not quite successful in achieving his purpose because his central symbol, the signal elm tree, cannot be made into an image of permanence. Carefully explicates the action of the poem to demonstrate how the poet argues for his own version of certainty, one tempered heavily by skepticism and resignation that genuine certainty may not be attainable.

Tristram and Iseult

Buckler, William E. *"Tristram and Iseult* and *Empedocles on Etna."* In *On the Poetry of Matthew Arnold: Essays in Critical Reconstruction.* New York: New York University Press, 1982.
Considers this poem one of Arnold's most ambitious undertakings, linking it with others written at mid-century by Tennyson and Robert Browning which signal the creation of "a new poetry." Claims that, like "Empedocles on Etna," this work offers "a heartbreaking vision of man in his universe." Discusses Arnold's recasting of the medieval tale to meet his specifically modern purposes. Extensive analysis of Iseult of Brittany, whose character the poet transforms from its medieval sources.

Culler, A. Dwight. *Imaginative Reason: The Poetry of Matthew Arnold.* New Haven, Conn.: Yale University Press, 1966, pp. 140-152.
Careful analysis of the poem's structure, with special attention paid to the concluding section. Sees Tristram's choice between the two Iseults as being one between passion and calm. Notes how the three parts are written in three different styles to mirror the themes highlighted in each. Discusses Arnold's use of the children and the hunter on the arras in the final section of the poem.

Fulweiler, Howard D. *Letters from the Darkling Plain: Language and the Grounds of Knowledge in the Poetry of Arnold and Hopkins.* Columbia: University of Missouri Press, 1972, pp. 66-79.

Believes this is Arnold's finest statement about the inability of art to provide meaningful consolation to humankind. Examines the three principal figures in the work, noting how much symbolic significance the poet invests in his hero. Claims the poem promotes passivity and acceptance over activity; attempts at romantic love are doomed in this hostile world. Extensive discussion of Part III, which focuses on Iseult of Brittany's story of Merlin and Vivien, a tale which glosses the tragedy of Tristram and his ill-fated love.

Johnson, Wendell Stacy. *Sex and Marriage in Victorian Poetry.* Ithaca, N.Y.: Cornell University Press, 1975, pp. 65-68.

Brief analysis of the poem, showing how Arnold's interest in this well-known love story lies primarily in the death scene. Summarizes each of the poem's three sections; notes how the poet uses the final section to provide an oblique commentary on the poem's meaning. Believes Arnold chooses the story of Tristram and Iseult not because it deals with love or infidelity, but because it shows how, no matter what the circumstances that create a passionate relationship, love is ultimately doomed to fail.

Riede, David G. *Matthew Arnold and the Betrayal of Language.* Charlottesville: University Press of Virginia, 1988, pp. 125-134.

Calls the work Arnold's "most ambitious attempt to write a full-scale traditional romance." Points out parallels to other romances, especially those by Keats. Demonstrates how characters in Arnold's poem, notably Iseult of Brittany, have parallels in other literary works, especially Victorian works, not in life. Sees Arnold struggling throughout to make sense of the relationship between life and art.

Roper, Alan. *Arnold's Poetic Landscapes.* Baltimore: Johns Hopkins University Press, 1969, pp. 166-173.

Extensive analysis of the function of landscape and the seasonal cycle in the poem. Claims the landscape "provides external equivalents to inner qualities and moods and to human situations"; it serves as "a vehicle for psychological definition" in a poem concerned principally with exploring human passion in various forms: love, ambition, and remorse. Points out the static quality of many of the scenes, and the poet's reliance on contrasts (spring versus winter, heat versus cold) to dramatize the plight of the lovers. Explains the function of the Merlin and Vivien interlude.

Stange, G. Robert. *Matthew Arnold: The Poet as Humanist.* Princeton, N.J.: Princeton University Press, 1967, pp. 254-257.
Extensive discussion of the work Stange calls "the most brilliant of Arnold's poems on love." Reviews the sources for Arnold's portrait of the lovers. Explains how the poet expanded the role of Iseult of Brittany to achieve a balance between the competing forces of love within the work. Briefly compares the poem with Wagner's operatic version of the story. Discusses the significance of the huntsman's role in elucidating the theme. Abbreviated review of previous criticism. Concludes with sympathetic analysis of Arnold's ending for the poem.

Chapter 2
ELIZABETH BARRETT BROWNING

General Studies

Cooper, Helen. *Elizabeth Barrett Browning, Woman and Artist*. Chapel Hill: University of North Carolina Press, 1988.
Comprehensive feminist study of Browning's oeuvre, examining the development of the poet's distinctive poetic voice. Also discusses how an understanding of Browning's work leads to new appreciation of Victorian poetics. Posits that Browning saw herself as developing a distinctly female voice in her works, and consciously sought to rival male writers of her day. Examines individual works in their cultural context. Devotes individual chapters to volumes published in 1838, 1844, and 1850; to *Casa Guidi Windows*; and to *Aurora Leigh*.

——————. "Working into Light: Elizabeth Barrett Browning." In Sandra M. Gilbert and Susan Gubar, eds. *Shakespeare's Sisters: Feminist Essays on Women Poets*. Bloomington: Indiana University Press, 1979.
Surveys Browning's development as a feminist poet whose work exhibits women's struggle to free themselves from patriarchal tradition. Argues Browning was continuously preoccupied with three subjects: art, politics, and motherhood. Reviews dozens of her works to highlight her concern for the victimization of women and men's attempts to silence them, and with social injustices perpetrated on women and children. Quotes liberally from the poet's letters to support claims about her ideology.

David, Deirdre. "Elizabeth Barrett Browning: 'Art's a service.'" In *Intellectual Women and Victorian Patriarchy*. Ithaca, N.Y.: Cornell University Press, 1987.
Discusses Browning's career as a poet, which culminates in the publication of *Aurora Leigh*. Examines literary influences on her, which tended to be male-dominated. Searches through Browning's earlier poems to show how ideas which come to full bloom in *Aurora Leigh* are first seen in these works. Judges Browning to be less stridently feminist than some of her contemporaries; believes her poetry, espe-

cially *Aurora Leigh*, actually supports the Victorian patriarchal notion that the proper role for a woman is to be man's helpmate.

Forster, Margaret. *Elizabeth Barrett Browning: A Biography*. London: Chatto & Windus, 1988.
Comprehensive study of Browning's life, greatly expanding other accounts of her early years and her daily routine at home with her father and siblings before she married Robert Browning. Integrates brief commentary on the poems into a detailed look at the key events in Browning's life. Depends heavily on letters and diaries for insight into the poet's character. Includes photographs and artwork illustrations, and a brief chronology.

Hickok, Kathleen. "Elizabeth Barrett Browning." In *Representations of Women: Nineteenth-Century British Women's Poetry*. Westport, Conn.: Greenwood Press, 1984.
Overview of Browning's career, focusing on feminist traits throughout her canon. Explicates several early lyrics to show how the poet handled conventional representations of women as wives and mothers. Notes the frequent occurrences of social protest in Browning's poetry, especially in "The Runaway Slave at Pilgrim's Point" and "Lady Geraldine's Courtship." Concludes with an extended analysis of *Aurora Leigh*, in which Browning portrays all three classes of Victorian women and explores the role each plays within nineteenth century society; believes in this poem Browning took considerable risk in defying conventions of subject matter and presentation to speak out on behalf of women.

Johnson, Wendell Stacy. *Sex and Marriage in Victorian Poetry*. Ithaca, N.Y.: Cornell University Press, 1975, pp. 53-57.
Brief commentary on Browning's attitude toward marriage. Suggests both her poetry and her comments in letters to friends present a more skeptical view than might be suggested by her own life experiences. Cites *Aurora Leigh* as the best example of the poet's view of problems with marriage. Provides a brief plot summary of the work; suggests that even though the work ends with a marriage, the harsh treatment of women throughout the poem is a reminder of the drawbacks to their conventional role.

Leighton, Angela. *Elizabeth Barrett Browning*. Bloomington: Indiana University Press, 1986.
Feminist reassessment of Browning's corpus. Admits Browning was

not a strident proponent of women's rights, but reads her poetry as a "political instrument of change": through her works she crusades for a change in attitudes toward women. Acknowledges the greatest literary influence on Browning was the work of Romantic poets, especially Wordsworth, but argues the strongest single influence was her father. Most of the poet's works are attempts to speak out to establish the place of women in a patriarchal society. Devotes chapters to exploring ways Browning develops a distinctly female voice speaking through her poetry, and to discussions of *Sonnets from the Portuguese* and *Aurora Leigh*.

McGhee, Richard D. "Elizabeth Barrett Browning and Oscar Wilde." In *Marriage, Duty, and Desire in Victorian Poetry and Drama.* Lawrence: University Press of Kansas, 1980.

Argues Browning's poetry "celebrates the liberating power of love and marriage"; devotes some attention to the Brownings' love letters to show the poet's concern for the conflict she felt in her personal life between her desire for union with her future husband and her duty to obey her father. Discusses *The Seraphim* and other poems in her early volumes, *Sonnets from the Portuguese*, *Casa Guidi Windows*, and *Aurora Leigh.*

Mander, Rosalie. *Mrs. Browning: The Story of Elizabeth Barrett.* London: Wiedenfeld & Nicolson, 1980.

Biography written for the general reader, focusing on Browning's development as a poet; details her harsh home life before her marriage to Robert Browning and describes in some detail their courtship and elopement. Also chronicles the Brownings' extensive travels. Integrates brief commentary about the poet's work into the biographical narrative. Contains an appendix on *Aurora Leigh* and one on the career of the Brownings' only son.

Mermin, Dorothy. *Elizabeth Barrett Browning: The Origins of a New Poetry.* Chicago: University of Chicago Press, 1989.

Carefully researched, penetrating study of Browning's canon, aimed at demonstrating how she became "the first woman poet in English literature." Shows how Browning was forced to reshape the male tradition she inherited and to look outside that tradition to find models for her art. Organized biographically to illustrate the close relationship of life and experiences to Browning's art. Includes individual chapters on each of the poet's major volumes, and a selected bibliography of primary and secondary sources.

Radley, Virginia L. *Elizabeth Barrett Browning*. New York: Twayne, 1972.
Study intended for the general reader, providing brief biographical
sketch, and summaries of Browning's major works and many of her
minor poems. Attempts to demonstrate reasons Browning was held in
high esteem by her contemporaries, including the great male literary
figures of the period. Proceeds chronologically through the published
volumes. Contains separate chapters on *Sonnets from the Portuguese*
and *Aurora Leigh*. Includes bibliography of secondary sources and a
detailed chronology.

Stephenson, Glennis. *Elizabeth Barrett Browning and the Poetry of Love*.
Ann Arbor, Mich.: UMI Research Press, 1989.
Claims the revival of interest in Browning brought on by the feminist
movement has not brought renewed interest in her love poetry. Argues
Browning is a major feminist voice in exploring the role of the woman
in love relationships and "the question of woman's voice in love
poetry." Sketches the importance of Felicia Hemans and Letitia Lan-
don in Browning's development as a woman poet. Examines the early
ballads and lyrics; explores Browning's techniques in "Lady Geraldine's Courtship," *Sonnets from the Portuguese*, and *Aurora Leigh*, as
well as selections from later poetry.

Aurora Leigh

Brantlinger, Patrick. "Liberal Individualism: The Brownings." In *The
Spirit of Reform: British Literature and Politics, 1832-1867*. Cambridge, Mass.: Harvard University Press, 1977.
Discusses the poem as an example of Barrett Browning's treatment of
political subjects. Sees Romney as an extremist reformer bent on
imposing grand schemes for social betterment upon society. Aurora is
a strong counterbalance to her impetuous cousin; she sees that his
schemes do not address individual needs. Argues the union of the two
at the end of the poem is not meant to symbolize a simple fusion
between the poetic spirit and the spirit of social reform, since Romney
is clearly not presented as equal in intellectual stature or strength of
character with Aurora.

Cooper, Helen. "Woman and Artist, Both Complete: *Aurora Leigh*." In
Elizabeth Barrett Browning, Woman and Artist. Chapel Hill: Univer-
sity of North Carolina Press, 1988.
Extended feminist analysis demonstrating how Browning establishes

an authentic female poetic voice within the patriarchal tradition she inherited. Discusses early reviews by Browning's contemporaries. Examines the structure of the work and provides detailed study of Aurora's relationship with Romney and with Marian Erle. Suggests the ending, in which Aurora and Romney are reconciled, is not simply conventional but rather is a radical reversal in which the male becomes muse for the female poet.

David, Deirdre. "Elizabeth Barrett Browning: 'Art's a service.'" In *Intellectual Women and Victorian Patriarchy*. Ithaca, N.Y.: Cornell University Press, 1987.
Lengthy analysis of the poem, comparing it to other works in Browning's canon. Claims the work is less feminist and revolutionary than other critics have argued. Detailed examination of the imagery, prosody, and structure; extensive discussion of Browning's handling of the "fallen woman" theme. Concludes Browning's chief interest lies in exploring the place of poetry and the poet in the modern world.

Gilbert, Sandra M., and Susan Gubar. *The Mad Woman in the Attic: The Woman Writer and the Nineteenth Century Literary Imagination*. New Haven, Conn.: Yale University Press, 1979, pp. 575-580.
Brief analysis stressing the feminist qualities of the work. Argues Browning adopts an "aesthetic of service," tracing the development of her heroine from self-indulgent would-be poet to mature writer and wife, willing to put aside personal satisfaction for larger social aims. Short plot summary; notes parallels to *Jane Eyre* and other works by Victorian women writers. Also comments about Browning's influence on Emily Dickinson.

Leighton, Angela. "'If orphaned, we are disinherited': The Making of the Poet"; "'Come with me, sweet sister': The Poet's Last Quest." In *Elizabeth Barrett Browning*. Bloomington: Indiana University Press, 1986.
Two chapters provide detailed analysis of the poem's plot, structure, and themes. Believes Browning's heroine engages in two mythic quests: first for the absent father, whom she must exorcise if she is to speak in her own voice about contemporary social concerns; and second for a sister, whom she finds in Marian Erle, the "fallen woman" whom Browning portrays with great sympathy. Considers the poem Browning's greatest achievement. Challenges other feminist readings which do not recognize the importance of the father figure, whose presence was personally significant to Browning.

Mander, Rosalie. *Mrs. Browning: The Story of Elizabeth Barrett*. London: Wiedenfeld & Nicolson, 1980, pp. 95-102, 131-140.

Briefly describes the publication history and critical reception of the work by Browning's contemporaries. Suggests some autobiographical genesis for certain characters and incidents. Believes the poem is a "feminist epic" only "in an individual sense"; Aurora wants personal emancipation as a woman poet, but she does not struggle for larger social reforms. Provides extensive plot summary to show how Browning develops her self-willed female artist-hero.

Mermin, Dorothy. *"Aurora Leigh."* In *Elizabeth Barrett Browning: The Origins of a New Poetry*. Chicago: University of Chicago Press, 1989.

Describes the work's affinities with other poems and with nineteenth century novels by women. Sees the poem as an epic in which the heroine is like a questing knight; the traditional quest for love is paralleled, however, by "the daughter's quest for the mother." Explores autobiographical aspects of the heroine and her relationship to other women writers of the period. Sees Browning dealing throughout with the role of poetry as a weapon against social ills; this creates some tension, since the traditional role for women is domestic. Concludes with a sampling of the reaction to the work by Browning's contemporaries.

Radley, Virginia L. *"Aurora Leigh*: The Artist as Woman."* In *Elizabeth Barrett Browning*. New York: Twayne, 1972.

Provides a modest plot summary of this lengthy verse novel, setting forth clearly the heroine's growing social conscience, her awareness of her proper role as a poet, and her love for her cousin Romney. Follows with a brief evaluation of the work's artistic merits: summarizes critical opinions of Browning's contemporaries, notes the presence of many passages of intense realism and those of strong social commentary, but finally judges the poem of only modest value as a work of art.

Stephenson, Glennis. "Love and Life: The Expansion of Boundaries in *Aurora Leigh*." In *Elizabeth Barrett Browning and the Poetry of Love*. Ann Arbor, Mich.: UMI Research Press, 1989.

Detailed examination of this verse novel explores Browning's development of the woman artist and her role in society. Sees the poem as a story of "a woman's growth toward new understanding and acceptance of love" and the heroine's quest to reconcile her need for love with her equally compelling desire to fulfill her artistic impulses. Lengthy character analysis of both Aurora and Romney to show how

Browning works out her themes. Criticizes contemporary feminist critics for overrating Aurora's rejection of Romney's initial marriage proposal; argues Browning is insisting that conventional attitudes about social relationships, which confine women to roles as mother and wife, must change if women are to be able to fulfill themselves as individuals.

Sonnets from the Portuguese

Cooper, Helen. *Elizabeth Barrett Browning, Woman and Artist*. Chapel Hill: University of North Carolina Press, 1988, pp. 98-110.
Discusses the background of the sonnets, which were not originally written for publication; sees Browning striking out against her father and against the patriarchal tradition in literature which valued women only as objects, not as authors. Sees a "confident female poetic 'I'" emerging from the sequence as Browning progresses from the opening sonnets where the speaker is a female object of desire to the concluding poems in which she is free to express her own desires. Examines several of the individual poems to show the development of the poet's voice.

Leighton, Angela. "'How do I love thee?': The Woman's Right to Say." In *Elizabeth Barrett Browning*. Bloomington: Indiana University Press, 1986.
Sketches the biographical background of the sequence. Argues Browning is not merely interested in expressing her feelings for her husband, an accomplished poet in his own right, but wishes instead to establish a woman's right to speak out boldly in literature. Her use of the sonnet tradition, a male-dominated art form, is especially noteworthy. Notes ways Browning deals with the object of her desire, her husband, without dehumanizing him. Carefully explicates several sonnets to demonstrate the poet's ability to reverse the conventions of the form, making the woman an active speaker rather than the object of desire.

Martin, Loy D. *Browning's Dramatic Monologues and the Post-Romantic Subject*. Baltimore: Johns Hopkins University Press, 1985, pp. 168-173.
Discusses the sonnet sequence as a dramatic monologue in the special context in which it is defined in Martin's study; claims the sequence contains many elements traditionally associated with the genre, including an implicit dialogue with an auditor whose reaction influences

the progress of the work. Believes Elizabeth Barrett resurrected the sonnet sequence as an appropriate "enclosing fiction" within which she could explore "the day-to-day vacillations" of her feeling for Robert Browning.

Mermin, Dorothy. "Courtship, Letters, *Sonnets from the Portuguese*." In *Elizabeth Barrett Browning: The Origins of a New Poetry*. Chicago: University of Chicago Press, 1989.
Reads the *Sonnets* as a companion piece to the letters in which Browning expressed her feelings for the man who would become her husband. Explains why the form is appropriate for the poet's psychological musings and how Browning put this form to best use in displaying her strongly felt desire for her beloved. Shows how Browning transformed the conventional sonnet sequence, doubling both principal figures so there is an effect of seeing two speakers and two beloveds. Explicates numerous individual lyrics to demonstrate the poet's methodology. Offers suggestions to explain why readers find these intensely autobiographical poems uncomfortable.

Radley, Virginia L. "Parnassus Attained: *Sonnets from the Portuguese*." In *Elizabeth Barrett Browning*. New York: Twayne, 1972.
Suggests an understanding of biographical background is helpful to appreciate the intensity of these poems, though they can be read without knowledge of the poet's life. Sees Browning speaking "the universal language of love" through her highly individualized work. Careful analysis of the individual sonnets, showing how the poet displays the growth of her love for her future husband. Sees the pattern as a dramatization of the Platonic ideal outlined in the *Symposium*, in which love ascends from lower to higher orders. Also examines Browning's letters to demonstrate how personal sentiments are transformed into the individual lyrics which make up the sonnet sequence.

Stephenson, Glennis. "Space and Distance: The Dramatization of Desire in *Sonnets from the Portuguese*." In *Elizabeth Barrett Browning and the Poetry of Love*. Ann Arbor, Mich.: UMI Research Press, 1989.
Argues that to fully appreciate these sonnets, readers must get beyond their autobiographical nature. Browning is using the sonnet tradition and its conventions "to delineate a form of love quite different from that which the conventions typically suggest." Inverting the normal pattern, Browning explores the love relationship from the woman's point of view; the woman is not merely a passive object, however, but

a full participant in the relationship, having desires of her own. Looks carefully at individual sonnets within the sequence to illustrate Browning's method of reversing the male-dominated sonnet tradition. Discusses the sensual language and sexual imagery that permeates the sequence.

Chapter 3
ROBERT BROWNING

General Studies

Armstrong, Isobel. "Browning and the 'Grotesque' Style." In Isobel Armstrong, ed. *The Major Victorian Poets: Reconsiderations*. Lincoln: University of Nebraska Press, 1969.
Believes "grotesque" is a term misapplied to Browning's poetry; actually the poet's complicated syntax and style is intended to reveal "the structure of experience as a fluid, unfinished process." Examines *Sordello*, "By the Fire-side," and "Caliban Upon Setebos" to show how the poet involves the reader in the process of constructing experience. Also uses minor poems, and some considered failures, to show the pervasiveness of Browning's method.

_____, ed. *Robert Browning*. Writers and Their Background. Athens: Ohio University Press, 1975.
Eleven essays by distinguished critics of Browning, collectively providing a sense of the poet's interests and accomplishments. The writers deal with Browning's attitude toward Romanticism; his views of history; his understanding and use of philosophy, politics, painting, and music; and his development of the dramatic monologue. Includes a useful essay describing available scholarship on the poet and his works, as well as a selected bibliography of secondary sources.

Bloom, Harold, ed. *Robert Browning*. Modern Critical Views. New York: Chelsea House, 1985.
Nine essays by Browning scholars, most excerpted from previously published studies, focusing on the poet's literary accomplishments. Includes discussions of Browning's use of the dramatic monologue and analyses of "Caliban Upon Setebos," "Love Among the Ruins," "Mr. Sludge, the Medium," "Childe Roland to the Dark Tower Came," and "Cleon." Also contains brief chronology and bibliography of secondary sources.

Bloom, Harold, and Adrienne Munich, eds. *Robert Browning: A Collection of Critical Essays*. Englewood Cliffs, N.J.: Prentice-Hall, 1979.
Collection of nine essays, five done originally for this volume, exam-

ining the many facets of Browning's poetic career. Most offer general
assessments of the poet's technique, especially his use of the dramatic
monologue, illustrating their conclusions with examples selected from
many of the poet's works. Also contains a brief lyric composed for the
volume by poet Richard Howard. Includes a brief chronology and
selected bibliography.

Brantlinger, Patrick. "Liberal Individualism: The Brownings." In *The
Spirit of Reform: British Literature and Politics, 1832-1867*. Cambridge, Mass.: Harvard University Press, 1977.
Discusses Browning's iconoclastic view of history. Finds his "sense of
history" is "inadequate" because the poet is too intent on individual
eccentricities to fully comprehend the significance of larger historical
forces. Believes Browning's interest in the psychological dimensions
of character leads him into historical inaccuracies and to inadequate
appreciation of parallels and contrasts between past and present. Instead of focusing on historical processes, the poet mines the past as if
it were merely a storehouse of individual experiences from which he
can construct his art. Finds Browning's view of historical processes
consistently negative.

Burrows, Leonard. *Browning the Poet: An Introductory Study*. Nedlands,
W. Australia: University of Western Australia Press, 1969.
Overview of the poet's chief works, intended for a general audience.
Examines thirty works in some detail, concentrating on dramatic
poems because Browning's particular strengths lie in these. Focuses
on explication of individual works rather than elucidating general
principles about Browning's oeuvre. Pays special attention to language, rhythm, and other poetic devices.

Collins, Thomas J. *Robert Browning's Moral-Aesthetic Theory, 1833-
1855*. Lincoln: University of Nebraska Press, 1967.
Systematic analysis of the development of Browning's ideas about the
nature and purpose of art, and the function of the artist, during the early
decades of his career. Traces the poet's growing fascination with the
idea that imperfection is an inherent quality of whatever is best in the
real world. Includes chapters on *Pauline, Paracelsus, Sordello, Bells
and Pomegranates*, and *Men and Women*.

Cook, Eleanor. *Browning's Lyrics: An Exploration*. Toronto: University
of Toronto Press, 1974.
Extensive analysis of virtually all of Browning's major lyrics and

dozens of minor ones. Examines works in each of the poet's major collections. Looks carefully at the poet's imagery, finding repeated patterns that link the individual poems and provide readers a portrait of the author's complex mind. Develops an outline of Browning's poetics. Serves as a handbook to the shorter works.

Crowell, Norton B. *The Convex Glass: The Mind of Robert Browning.* Albuquerque: University of New Mexico Press, 1968.
Systematic attempt to answer charges of earlier critics that Browning was a shallow thinker. Devotes chapters to examining Browning's ideas on the problem of evil; his attitudes toward individualism; his optimism; his concept of truth, especially as it is exemplified in *The Ring and the Book*; and his intellectual links with the philosophical position now known as Christian Existentialism. Argues throughout that Browning is "a respectable thinker" with great abilities as a poet, possessing "luminous insight into life and the soul of man."

Drew, Philip. *An Annotated Critical Bibliography of Robert Browning.* New York: Harvester Wheatsheaf, 1990.
Very useful sourcebook identifying both primary and secondary sources. Lists original publications, reprints, and collected editions of Browning's works. Includes a section cataloging bibliographies, concordances, and handbooks. Also provides annotations on principal biographies and general studies, as well as brief synopses of criticism of dozens of Browning's works. Contains an annotated listing of the poet's published letters.

_____, ed. *Browning: A Collection of Critical Essays.* Boston: Houghton Mifflin, 1966.
Nineteen essays and excerpts, reprinted from monographs and journals, offering an assessment of the poet and his works; includes selections from important nineteenth century critics as well as numerous studies by influential twentieth century scholars. Ten selections provide overviews of Browning's accomplishments and review his use of various poetic devices; nine focus on individual poems, including "Pauline," "Mr. Sludge, the Medium," and "A Grammarian's Funeral."

_____. *The Poetry of Browning: A Critical Introduction.* London: Methuen, 1970.
Studious, detailed analysis of the Browning corpus; claims several critical positions developed during the previous seventy years are decidedly erroneous. Believes "the distinctive qualities of Browning

as a Victorian poet" are of great value. Challenges the notions that the poet created works which were "wilfully difficult" and that his poetry is consistently optimistic. Reviews the pronouncements of important Browning critics and sketches a plan for future Browning studies.

Erickson, Lee. *Robert Browning: His Poetry and His Audiences*. Ithaca, N.Y.: Cornell University Press, 1984.

Detailed examination of Browning's attempt to create poems which would speak to the kinds of audiences he felt would read his works sympathetically. Claims the poet found in Elizabeth Barrett a perfect reader whose love for him created the kind of circumstances which make poetry possible. Also examines ways the protagonists in Browning's poetry seek to identify and correspond with their stated and implied audiences. Surveys works from the every period of the poet's life, devoting two chapters to the important volume of major dramatic monologues, *Men and Women*.

Fletcher, Pauline. "Browning: The Human Landscape." In *Gardens and Grim Ravines: The Language of Landscape in Victorian Poetry*. Princeton, N.J.: Princeton University Press, 1983.

Sees Browning as fundamentally different from other important Victorian poets in his use of landscape; unlike his contemporaries, he always subordinates landscape description to characterization. When he does focus on landscape, Browning animates the natural world, often giving natural settings anthropomorphic qualities. Reviews several poems to illustrate ways Browning uses landscapes to highlight internal character traits. Concludes with a more extensive analysis of "Childe Roland to the Dark Tower Came."

Flowers, Betty S. *Browning and the Modern Tradition*. London: Macmillan, 1976.

Examines various ways Browning's poetry influenced poets of the twentieth century, especially those writing in the early decades. Focuses on the stylistic aspects of the poetry; shows how Browning served as a precursor to the moderns in his interest in the poem as object; his particularly modern approach to subject matter, attending more to the process of revealing the commonplace in new ways; his use of common diction and his interest in words themselves; his employment of the dramatic method; his attention to the structural elements of his works, which often parallel musical compositions; and his affinities with prose writers. Ranges widely among modern poets to show the extent of Browning's influence.

Gibson, Mary Ellis, ed. *Critical Essays on Robert Browning*. New York: G. K. Hall, 1992.

Collection of thirteen essays, most reprinted from journals and longer scholarly studies, representing an important sampling of Browning criticism published between 1980 and 1990. Selections focus on ways readers have interpreted Browning and ways the poet has had an impact on his own and subsequent generations. Also includes analyses of the influence of cultural criticism on readers' appreciation of Browning's art. Gibson's introduction provides an insightful analysis of the history of Browning criticism.

_____. *History and the Prism of Art: Browning's Poetic Experiments*. Columbus: Ohio State University Press, 1987.

Careful analysis of the poet's understanding of history and his use of history in his poetry. Believes Browning is essentially contextualist in creating art out of historical materials. Organized topically to focus attention on subjects such as the importance of historical perspective, the use of irony, patterning within the poems, and the role of the poet. Concentrates discussion on monologues featuring historical figures and on *The Ring and the Book* and *Sordello*.

Gridley, Roy. *Browning*. London: Routledge & Kegan Paul, 1972.

Study intended for general readers, placing the poet and his works in historical context. Measures Browning's achievements in light of the cultural and intellectual traditions he inherited and which he influenced during his lifetime. Individual chapters examine the poet's early life, then focus on each decade from the 1830's through the 1880's. Brief analyses of the major poems included throughout. A final chapter surveys Browning's influence on twentieth century poets.

Hair, Donald S. *Browning's Experiments with Genre*. Toronto: University of Toronto Press, 1972.

Examines Browning's work with various poetic genres: dramatic, lyric, and narrative. Throughout, shows how the poet, like many of his contemporaries, adapted and combined traditional formats to stimulate response in his readers. Aims to illustrate the structure and character of Browning's works and to show how he used various genres to explore essentials of human character. Devotes chapters to the early poems, the plays, the poems of mid-career, and *The Ring and the Book*.

Harper, J. W. "'Eternity Our Due': Time in the Poetry of Robert Browning." In Malcolm Bradbury and David Palmer, eds. *Victorian Poetry*.

Stratford-on-Avon Studies 15. London: Edwin Arnold, 1972.
Explores the poet's lifelong concern with the question of time and its effects upon individuals and the human race. Offers commentary on more than a dozen works, including "Porphyria's Lover," "Johannis Agricola in Meditation," *Pauline*, *Sordello*, and *The Ring and the Book* to show how Browning attempted to erase the ravages of time on conceptions of human character; through his poetry he sought to reveal the essential truths about individuals whose stories had been obscured or revised as time passed.

Harrold, William E. *The Variance and the Unity: A Study of the Complementary Poems of Robert Browning*. Athens: Ohio University Press, 1973.
Studies poems which Browning intended to be viewed as complementary. Argues these various pairs or larger groups are designed to allow readers to achieve a deeper understanding of overarching themes because they generate recognition through numerous intertextual parallels. Considers more than ten pairs of shorter poems and several longer works in which complementary perspectives are emphasized, especially *Pippa Passes*, *James Lee's Wife*, and *The Ring and the Book*.

Honan, Park. *Browning's Characters: A Study in Poetic Technique*. New Haven, Conn.: Yale University Press, 1961.
Extensive analysis of many of the major poems, focusing on the dramatic, prosodic, and verbal techniques Browning uses to illuminate the memorable characters in his works. Traces the development of technique in the early poems, explains how Browning's dramatic monologues function, explores several "character revealing techniques" in twenty important poems, and examines the portrayal of character in two sections of *The Ring and the Book*.

Hudson, Gertrude Reese. *Robert Browning's Literary Life: From First Work to Masterpiece*. Austin, Tex.: Eakin Press, 1992.
Lengthy analysis of the relationship between Browning and his readers, especially his reviewers, during the decades between the publication of his first work and the appearance of *The Ring and the Book*. Carefully studies the influence of popular and critical opinion on the poet, who was intensely interested in attracting a large audience. Explains how contemporary ideas about poetry had significant negative influence on Victorian readers' willingness to accept Browning's work.

Jack, Ian. *Browning's Major Poetry*. Oxford: Clarendon Press, 1973.
Extensive scholarly study of the poet's career and accomplishments, intent on establishing Browning as a major Victorian poet. Organized chronologically, with chapters devoted to *Pauline, Paracelsus, Sordello*, the early lyrics, poems of mid-career, those published in *Men and Women, Dramatis Personae*, and *The Ring and the Book*; dismisses later work as inconsequential. Believes Browning had established his aim as a poet before he married Elizabeth Barrett, but her influence and support allowed him to achieve mastery of his profession.

Johnson, Wendell Stacy. "Marriage and Divorce in Browning." In *Sex and Marriage in Victorian Poetry*. Ithaca, N.Y.: Cornell University Press, 1975.
Claims Browning is always concerned with the importance of individual freedom; the poet sees love and marriage as offering the possibility for creativity, but also the opportunity for manipulation and entrapment. Argues that love and marriage are treated differently in each of Browning's major volumes; examines *Pippa Passes*, selected poems from *Men and Women* and *Dramatis Personae*, and *The Ring and the Book* to illustrate the variety of attitudes expressed by the poet throughout his career.

King, Roma A., Jr. *The Focusing Artifice: The Poetry of Robert Browning*. Athens: Ohio University Press, 1968.
Offers an introductory analysis of the entire Browning corpus, consciously extending critical inquiry beyond the dramatic monologues. Focuses on four works "most crucial to understanding Browning's central aim, the exploration of the concept of self": *Sordello, The Ring and the Book, Fifine at the Fair*, and *Parleyings with Certain People of Importance* (each from different periods in Browning's career). Includes a chapter on *The Ring and the Book* and analyses of several dozen additional poems, showing how Browning creates in his poetry a medium for finding meaning in human life without traditional aids such as religious faith.

Korg, Jacob. *Browning in Italy*. Athens: Ohio University Press, 1983.
Aims at illuminating Browning's poems by examining them in light of the poet's experiences in Italy. Explains how Browning's years of traveling and living there influenced his general development and shaped his ideas about the nature of poetry. Includes biographical information as well as literary analysis. Pays particular attention to the influence of Italian surroundings and culture on *Sordello, Pippa*

Passes, the poems published in *Men and Women* and *The Ring and the Book*. Illustrated.

Kumar, Shiv. "The Moment in the Dramatic Monologues of Robert Browning." In Shiv Kumar, ed. *British Victorian Literature: Recent Revaluations*. New York: New York University Press, 1969.
Discusses the importance of "the moment," a crucial epiphanic point in individual human life, as a central concern in Browning's major monologues. At this important juncture in an individual's experience, the significance and worth of life become apparent to both character and reader. Briefly discusses ten important monologues to illustrate the poet's method of dramatizing the process by which his characters try to fix that moment against the onslaught and flux of passing time.

Lawson, E. LeRoy. *Very Sure of God: Religious Language in the Poetry of Robert Browning*. Nashville, Tenn.: Vanderbilt University Press, 1974.
Extensive analysis of Browning's religious beliefs as exhibited primarily in his poetry but also in his correspondence. Discusses the context in which the poet makes references to the deity; attempts to define the level of orthodoxy Browning displays in his statements about God. Relies heavily on twentieth century theologians for the theoretical framework of the study. Claims Browning believed strongly in God and that his faith is characterized by "simplicity and economy."

Litzinger, Boyd, and K. L. Knickerbocker, eds. *The Browning Critics*. Lexington: University Press of Kentucky, 1967.
Twenty-two articles and excerpts from longer scholarly studies display the complexity of Browning's achievement and offer insight into the history of Browning criticism; includes both laudatory and deprecatory evaluations. Several essays give general evaluations of the poet's merits; a number concentrate on individual works, including *The Ring and the Book*, "My Last Duchess," and "Bishop Blougram's Apology." Contains very useful bibliography of Browning criticism to 1965.

Litzinger, Boyd, and Donald Smalley, eds. *Browning: The Critical Heritage*. New York: Barnes & Noble, 1970.
Collection of reviews, notes, letters, and excerpts by Browning's contemporaries about each of his major volumes. Valuable as a source for determining what nineteenth century readers thought of the poet's works and for gaining a sense of the growth of Browning's reputation

in his own time. Includes a brief chronology, information on the sale of Browning's works, and a selected bibliography.

McGhee, Richard D. "Browning." In *Marriage, Duty, and Desire in Victorian Poetry and Drama*. Lawrence: University Press of Kansas, 1980.
Focuses on similarities between Browning's aim in his poetry and that of the philosopher Søren Kierkegaard: to investigate the efficacy of Christianity in modern times. Believes most of Browning's major poems deal with the growth of individual characters who are forced to make choices about how they will live; argues the poet's characters usually begin with an awakening of aesthetic sensibility, and those readers see as honorable move beyond that level to ethical awareness. Discusses several poems as examples of Browning's method, including *The Blot on the 'Scutcheon, Pippa Passes*, "Fra Lippo Lippi," *The Ring and the Book*, and "Fifine at the Fair."

Melchiori, Barbara. *Browning's Poetry of Reticence*. London: Oliver & Boyd, 1968.
Focuses on several of the poet's works to show ways he reveals something of himself to readers. Believes Browning uses history as a convenient mask to cover his own feelings; he selects little-known characters so he can manipulate them more freely. Includes chapters on "The Bishop Orders His Tomb," "Caliban Upon Setebos," and "Childe Roland." An introductory essay sketches Browning's use of history and several rhetorical techniques for which he is commonly faulted.

Mermin, Dorothy. "Browning." In *The Audience in the Poem: Five Victorian Poets*. New Brunswick, N.J.: Rutgers University Press, 1983.
Discusses dramatic monologues by Browning in which the poet makes specific references to an auditor whose presence in the work helps define the central character in whom readers' special interest lies. Claims Browning is interested in the power of speech and its effect on those who hear it; this relationship is similar to the one between the poet and his readers. Believes Browning was always concerned with finding responsive readers, and uses poems with auditors as a way of testing out his own power to reach various kinds of people. Examines more than a dozen monologues, including "My Last Duchess" and "Fra Lippo Lippi"; various sections of *The Ring and the Book*; and four later poems.

Millgate, Michael. *Testamentary Acts: Browning, Tennyson, James, Hardy*. Oxford: Clarendon Press, 1992.

Discusses ways the aging Browning sought during the 1870's and 1880's to shape his reputation and to determine how he would be viewed by posterity. Examines his relationships with his publisher and with friends; concentrates on his continuing dialogue with his son, Robert Weideman Barrett Browning, who did much to perpetuate the legendary love affair of his parents. Useful in understanding how a poet's reputation and biography is shaped.

Pearsall, Robert Brainard. *Robert Browning*. Boston: Twayne, 1974.
Modest study of the poet's life and works, offering general readers an overview of Browning's chief concerns and accomplishments. Comments on every major work; attempts to place each in the context of the poet's career. Includes chapters on *Dramatis Personae* and *The Ring and the Book*. Includes a short chronology and selected, annotated bibliography of secondary sources.

Raymond, W. O. "The Jewelled Bow: A Study of Browning's Imagery and Humanism." In Shiv Kumar, ed. *British Victorian Literature: Recent Revaluations*. New York: New York University Press, 1969.
Examination of Browning's penchant toward transcendentalism, following the lead of Shelley, and his "ethical humanism," which held strong sway with him throughout his life. Discusses the influence of Shelley, noting many points at which the two poets differ. Sees Browning focusing on the development of individuals who must achieve perfection by working in an imperfect world. The poet's brand of humanism does not negate his belief in God's presence in the world. Concludes the poet's fascination with "the warp and woof of the colored strands of human experience" is the source of his special poetic genius.

Ryals, Clyde de L. *Becoming Browning: The Poems and Plays of Robert Browning, 1833-1846*. Columbus: Ohio State University Press, 1983.
Focuses on the poet's development of irony as a tool for presenting his characters and themes. Elaborates on his notions about the "principle of becoming," an idea at odds with notions of philosophical stasis at the heart of classical theories of human nature; believes Browning saw change as not only inevitable but often without purpose. Shows how he rebels against Romantic predecessors. Explains his preoccupation with the poet's role as a revealer of fact and a constructor of truth.

_____. "Browning's Irony." In Richard A. Levine, ed. *The Victorian Experience: The Poets*. Athens: Ohio University Press, 1982.
Attempts to illuminate the source of Browning's particular form of

irony, which requires readers to see two equally compelling but antithetical ways of judging truth. Focuses on early works to show how the poet developed the form of dramatic poetry that permitted him to explore a subject from various viewpoints simultaneously. Believes all of Browning's work is informed by the poet's conviction that it is impossible for human beings to be totally objective in their search for truth.

_____. *Browning's Later Poetry, 1871-1889.* Ithaca, N.Y.: Cornell University Press, 1975.
Directs critical attention at works contained in more than a dozen volumes Browning published during the last two decades of his life. Concentrates analysis on the structure of these works, examining ways themes and ideas are presented to readers. Argues much can be learned about the poet from an understanding of these works.

Shaw, W. David. "Browning and Bradley on Re-Presentation"; "Liberal Hermeneutics: Browning, Jowett, Strauss"; "Browning and Schleiermacher: The Analogy of Dependence"; "Browning and F. H. Bradley: The Progress of Ethics"; "Beyond Schleiermacher: Browning and the Double Trinity." In *The Lucid Veil: Poetic Truth in the Victorian Age.* Madison: University of Wisconsin Press, 1987.
Five short essays, and commentary in two others, focusing on Browning's ideas about the nature of truth and the poet's ability to represent reality. In two of these, Browning is shown as dramatizing in his poems the philosophical positions espoused by F. H. Bradley, nineteenth century England's most prominent Hegelian philosopher. Another discusses the poet's use of ideas about truth derived from the writings of biblical critic David Friedrich Strauss and the liberal theology of Benjamin Jowett. Three discuss his debt to the philosophy of Friedrich Schleiermacher. In a long essay on Hegelian aesthetics, Browning's "Saul" is used to show how it is possible to receive God's gifts.

_____. *The Dialectical Temper: The Rhetorical Art of Robert Browning.* Ithaca, N.Y.: Cornell University Press, 1968.
Looks carefully at Browning's rhetorical skills, including both figures of speech and logical devices used by the poet to engage readers and instruct them. Claims Browning is most successful when he elevates himself above pure subjectivity and engages in dialectical presentation of ideas, taking on different positions, examining them, then moving beyond them. Focuses on early works and those of Browning's mid-career, culminating in a lengthy analysis of *The Ring and the Book.*

Tucker, Herbert F., Jr. *Browning's Beginnings: The Art of Disclosure*.
Minneapolis: University of Minnesota Press, 1980.
Argues Browning was intensely interested in the possibilities for
human experience; as a result, much of his poetry takes as its theme
"the difficulties and rewards of initiation," as "beginnings" open up
new possibilities for the future. Shows how this attitude explains
Browning's belief in the value of the incomplete as a desirable alter-
native to the finality of perfection, which implies closure and stasis.
Focuses primarily on early poetry; includes chapters on *Pauline*,
Paracelsus, *Sordello*, and the dramatic lyrics and monologues. Uses
theories of Barbara Herrnstein Smith (on poetic closure), Harold
Bloom (on poetic argument), and Jacques Derrida (on deconstruction)
to illuminate Browning's ideas about the nature and function of poetry.
Extensive notes and bibliography.

Andrea del Sarto

Burrows, Leonard. *Browning the Poet: An Introductory Study*. Nedlands,
W. Australia: University of Western Australia Press, 1969, pp. 187-200.
Contrasts this poem with "Fra Lippo Lippi," the companion poem
Browning paired with this one in *Men and Women*. Discusses the muted
tone, imagery, and rhetoric, all of which create the precise portrait of
Andrea's character which the poet sought. Provides extensive para-
phrase of the poem, showing how the poet reveals nuances of character
through the monologue.

Erickson, Lee. *Robert Browning: His Poetry and His Audiences*. Ithaca,
N.Y.: Cornell University Press, 1984, pp. 165-170.
Brief analysis of Browning's enigmatic hero, whose love for his
unfaithful wife adversely affects his ability as an artist. Notes how
images of enclosure dominate the poem, as Andrea feels closed in and
unable to reach his wife to gain her sympathy; ironically, he is a master
of form in his painting, skilled at enclosing his subjects but unable to
give them life. Suggests readers normally judge Andrea harshly, but he
deserves sympathy because of his great passion for his wife.

Hassett, Constance W. *The Elusive Self in the Poetry of Robert Browning*.
Athens: Ohio University Press, 1982, pp. 89-96.
Calls Andrea Browning's "master" of "strategic self-indictment."
Though he seems to possess an understanding of his limitations as an
artist and husband, his timidity makes him stop short of genuine

self-knowledge. He uses his overt self-effacement to ward off the necessity of confronting the idea that he may really lack the imagination necessary to be a great artist. Also discusses the role of Lucrezia in the poem.

Honan, Park. *Browning's Characters: A Study in Poetic Technique.* New Haven, Conn.: Yale University Press, 1961, pp. 156-158, 270-271.
Brief examination of Browning's skillful use of Andrea's wife Lucrezia as the auditor for the painter's monologue. Suggests the young wife is a reflection of her husband's aspirations and his character: like his paintings, she has a quality of surface perfection about her that masks her moral deficiencies. Andrea's pleas for his wife not to leave him reflect his anguish over the "soulless facility of his work." Also discusses several prosodic techniques Browning uses to establish the pace of the poem; notes how the "phonetic quality" of the verse helps retard the tempo of the work, reflecting the painter's "quiet despair."

Jack, Ian. *Browning's Major Poetry.* Oxford: Clarendon Press, 1973, pp. 224-234.
Discusses the sources of Browning's inspiration; notes how closely he follows the account of the historical Andrea in Giorgio Vasari's biography. Examines Andrea's character flaws, remarking how, from the very beginning of the monologue, the painter realizes he is a failure both as a husband and as an artist. Briefly sketches the chief characteristics of Andrea's wife Lucrezia. Compares the painter to Fra Lippo Lippi, highlighting the contrasts between two men who aspire to the same standards as artists.

King, Roma A., Jr. *The Focusing Artifice: The Poetry of Robert Browning.* Athens: Ohio University Press, 1968, pp. 103-104.
Abbreviated summary of the poem's central theme: the tragedy of the failed artist. Shows how Andrea gradually comes to realize the extent of his artistic failure despite his technical skills, and the extent to which he has failed in his married life as well. Claims Andrea is a tragic character because he realizes the possibilities he is missing.

Korg, Jacob. *Browning in Italy.* Athens: Ohio University Press, 1983, pp. 117-123.
Claims the central conflict in the poem is the "choice between life and art"; Andrea is "deficient as an artist because he is deficient as a man." Describes Browning's sources for his portrait of Andrea, tracing them to the distorted view of the painter in Giorgio Vasari's *Lives* of the

Italian painters. Explains how the poet uses Vasari's account, and his own ideas derived from viewing Andrea's paintings, to formulate an idea of the painter's uxorious nature.

Martin, Loy D. *Browning's Dramatic Monologues and the Post-Romantic Subject.* Baltimore: Johns Hopkins University Press, 1985, pp. 139-149.
Analysis of this monologue as an example of the consequences of willful isolation. Believes Andrea is unable to open himself to his wife, despite his repeated attempts to communicate with her verbally, because he has already shut himself off from relevant interchange by treating her as simply one of his possessions; his is a "hermetic mind incapable of meaningful intercourse." Reviews Browning's extensive use of images of enclosure and possession.

Melchiori, Barbara. "A French Source for 'Andrea Del Sarto' in De-Mussett"; "The Portrait of Lucrezia." In *Browning's Poetry of Reticence.* London: Oliver & Boyd, 1968.
Outlines the parallels between Browning's poems and a play about Andrea del Sarto by the French playwright Alfred de Musset. Describes how Browning may have been familiar with the play. Notes how closely the poet's introduction of the cousin whom Lucrezia loves follows the description of the lover introduced in de Musset's play but missing from Giorgio Vasari's biography of Andrea, the principal source for Browning's story. A second short essay describes Browning's knowledge of portraits of Andrea and his wife.

Ormond, Leonee. "Browning and Painting." In Isobel Armstrong, ed. *Robert Browning.* Writers and Their Background. Athens: Ohio University Press, 1975.
Comments on this poem in an essay examining Browning's fascination with Italian painters. Discusses the poet's extensive reliance for details in the poem on Giorgio Vasari's biography of del Sarto in his *Lives* of the Italian painters. Briefly comments on Browning's attitude toward Andrea, whom he believes was tormented by his second-class status as a painter, inferior to Raphael and Michelangelo, and frustrated by his inability to hold on to the love of a woman he adores.

Shaw, W. David. *The Dialectical Temper: The Rhetorical Art of Robert Browning.* Ithaca, N.Y.: Cornell University Press, 1968, pp. 145-155.
Harsh assessment of a character Shaw describes as having an overdeveloped aesthetic sense but an underdeveloped ethical dimension.

Claims the real auditor in the poem is not Lucrezia but Andrea himself; the painter uses his speech as self-justification for his failures, blaming his wife for his own shortcomings. He is unable to be truly self-aware and engage in genuine self-criticism. Points out parallels between Andrea and Browning.

Tucker, Herbert F., Jr. *Browning's Beginnings: The Art of Disclosure.* Minneapolis: University of Minnesota Press, 1980, pp. 194-201.
Presents a strong case to show how the hero of the poem wills his own failure by limiting himself to doing only what he knows he can do successfully, never striving for greatness. Investigates the psychology of Andrea as a man who understands himself fairly well, recognizes his faults, but overcompensates for his shortcomings by failing to strike out boldly either as a painter or as a husband. Shows how the poet employs rhetoric and imagery to vivify his portrait of the melancholy painter.

Bishop Blougram's Apology

Crowell, Norton B. *The Convex Glass: The Mind of Robert Browning.* Albuquerque: University of New Mexico Press, 1968, pp. 98-128.
Detailed analysis of the poem which, in Crowell's view, features one of Browning's greatest villains. Argues that, contrary to earlier claims by some critics, the Bishop's contention that human beings' only moral limits are those they set for themselves are not views held by the poet. Carefully explicates Blougram's argument to point out its many casuistries and its distortions of ideas Browning himself held in high esteem.

Drew, Philip. *The Poetry of Browning: A Critical Introduction.* London: Methuen, 1970, 122-143.
Engages in analysis of the poem to show how a reader may understand the difficulty Browning had in establishing characters who are convincing on the surface but whose attitudes and values were not those held by the poet. Briefly summarizes three critical essays which reach different conclusions about the poet's attitude toward the Bishop. Examines in detail the entire monologue to show the fallacies and inconsistences in Blougram's argument.

Erickson, Lee. *Robert Browning: His Poetry and His Audiences.* Ithaca, N.Y.: Cornell University Press, 1984, pp. 183-187.
Judges this poem the best in the Browning canon at "dealing directly with the contemporary problem of man's faith in God." The Bishop

uses his position in the Catholic Church as an official mediator between human beings and God to gain power over others. Sees Blougram as a master manipulator who understands the impact of statements of Faith on different audiences; though not admirable for his personal qualities, the Bishop must be recognized for his ability to control his auditors.

Gibson, Mary Ellis. *History and the Prism of Art: Browning's Poetic Experiments.* Columbus: Ohio State University Press, 1987, pp. 204-213.
Examines the character of Blougram to explain what appear to be inconsistencies in Browning's portrait of the Bishop. Believes it is possible to "construct a consistent reading" by noting the ironies which result from Blougram's absolutism and by recognizing the distinctions between Blougram's office in the Church and his personal character. Suggests that, while Blougram is clearly modeled on Cardinal Wiseman, it is impossible to find a historical parallel for Gibadibs, the auditor.

Gridley, Roy. *Browning.* London: Routledge & Kegan Paul, 1972, pp. 82-86.
Browning's brief analysis of the character of the Bishop, whose quick wit and intelligence seem incompatible with his adherence to Roman Catholicism. Describes the contemporary nature of the work. Cites several reviews which suggest the notoriety the poem achieved when it first appeared. Cites the important contrasts between Blougram and Gibadibs, whom Gridley calls "the most fully drawn listener" Browning created in his early monologues.

Jack, Ian. *Browning's Major Poetry.* Oxford: Clarendon Press, 1973, pp. 201-208.
Discusses Browning's source for the poem, commenting on the poet's negative feelings for Catholics and for Bishop Wiseman, the real-life model for Blougram. Claims that, despite some commentators' arguments to the contrary, the work is a satire; Browning is more concerned with exposing the sham of the Bishop's arguments than with exploring his character. Also comments on the epilogue and on parallels between Gibadibs and Browning's friend Alfred Domett.

Mermin, Dorothy. *The Audience in the Poem: Five Victorian Poets.* New Brunswick, N.J.: Rutgers University Press, 1983, pp. 58-63.
Examines Browning's development of the Bishop as a clever villain who works hard to convince the auditor present in the poem of his

sincerity. Considers Blougram persuasive but ultimately unsuccessful in winning over the reader, who sees him for what he is. Argues this poem, like "Mr. Sludge, the Medium," is about sincerity, a topic of great interest to the Victorians. Examines other Victorians' attitudes toward the subject, especially Carlyle's ideas; notes how Blougram tries to make light of the value of sincerity because he is incapable of being sincere.

Shaw, W. David. *The Dialectical Temper: The Rhetorical Art of Robert Browning.* Ithaca, N.Y.: Cornell University Press, 1968, pp. 203-212.
Careful analysis of the rhetoric employed by Bishop Blougram to win over the journalist Gibadibs to an understanding of the true nature of faith. Offers a surprisingly sympathetic portrait of a character often denigrated by other critics. Argues the poem is Browning's attempt to offer a systematic definition of faith; believes the Bishop, not the journalist, comes closer to understanding what faith entails because he does not demand exclusionary alternatives for every seemingly contradictory circumstance in life.

The Bishop Orders His Tomb at St. Praxed's Church

Burrows, Leonard. *Browning the Poet: An Introductory Study.* Nedlands, W. Australia: University of Western Australia Press, 1969, pp. 104-115.
Explicates the action of the poem, focusing on ways Browning highlights the ironic nature of the Bishop's dying instructions to his kinsmen. Discusses the Bishop's insistence on dictating what his heirs will do for him. Explores the poet's ability to dramatize the incoherent ramblings of a man close to death. Also examines devices Browning uses to achieve unity in the work. Concludes the poem's ironies are complex, since the Bishop is certainly not admirable but his feeble deathbed protests evoke readers' sympathy.

Gridley, Roy. *Browning.* London: Routledge & Kegan Paul, 1972, pp. 60-64.
Brief but insightful commentary on the character of the Bishop. Discusses Browning's negative feelings toward the Catholic Church and the topicality of the poem, which appeared in the same year John Henry Newman converted to Roman Catholicism. Claims the dying Bishop's chief fault is his inability to distinguish between sensual and spiritual realms. He is at times a laughable figure, but at other times he evokes sympathy. Shows how the Bishop fits E. M. Forster's definition of a

round character; the poem shows Browning's affinities to realistic novelists.

Hassett, Constance W. *The Elusive Self in the Poetry of Robert Browning.* Athens: Ohio University Press, 1982, pp. 74-80.
Points out Browning's continuing interest in deathbed scenes, which offer the best opportunity for individuals to come to genuine under-standing of themselves. Believes the Bishop is afforded this opportu-nity but fails to realize or acknowledge his faults. Instead, he focuses attention on objects, exhibiting his cupidity and sensuality. Believes readers come to understand the truth even though the Bishop dies not recognizing his moral failure.

Honan, Park. *Browning's Characters: A Study in Poetic Technique.* New Haven, Conn.: Yale University Press, 1961, pp. 218-219, 236-237, 281-284.
Brief explication of the Bishop's use of language within the poem; focuses on the variations in meaning associated with his use of the word "God" and his constant mentioning of concrete objects which are distinctly sensual, offering an ironic contrast with his professed spiri-tualism. Discusses ways the Bishop's syntax helps reveal something of his character as well: the frequent occurrence of incomplete sen-tences, filled with worldly thoughts, presents to readers a more accurate portrait of the speaker than do his infrequent and unconvincing prot-estations about religious concerns.

Jack, Ian. *Browning's Major Poetry.* Oxford: Clarendon Press, 1973, pp. 198-201.
Brief commentary attesting to the subtlety with which Browning handles his subject. Acknowledges the poet does not care for the values to which his subject clings; notes the skill Browning demonstrates in representing the words of the dying man. Cites other writers who have been similarly interested in last thoughts. Notes how much ill-directed attention has been focused on finding the real-life model for the Bishop's tomb; a great irony of the work is that, though ordered, the tomb is never built.

King, Roma A., Jr. *The Focusing Artifice: The Poetry of Robert Browning.* Athens: Ohio University Press, 1968, pp. 78-80.
Modest summary of the Bishop's character; considers him incapable of nobility and lacking in real insight. Only upon his deathbed does he begin to realize how ineffectual he has been and how little real

influence he has over others. Sees the poem characterized by the contrast between the Bishop's vision for his tomb and the actual edifice being erected for his eventual interment.

Korg, Jacob. *Browning in Italy*. Athens: Ohio University Press, 1983, pp. 60-62.
Brief commentary on a work Korg calls "the most significant poem resulting from the 1842 journey" Browning made to Italy. Describes the actual church which serves as the setting for the work. Discusses Ruskin's praise for the poem but notes that other critics have claimed Browning imposes Victorian view on his Renaissance character.

Melchiori, Barbara. "Where the Bishop Ordered His Tomb." In *Browning's Poetry of Reticence*. London: Oliver & Boyd, 1968.
Examines several works that may have provided inspiration for Browning's portrait of the Bishop's tomb. Cites the critical debate over the historical models for the tomb. Suggests many points of his description come from the writings of Gérard de Lairesse, an architect whose works the poet read frequently and which inspired some details in "Childe Roland." The description offers a moral commentary on the speaker: the tomb is a living monument to the Bishop's punishment for his sins.

Shaw, W. David. *The Dialectical Temper: The Rhetorical Art of Robert Browning*. Ithaca, N.Y.: Cornell University Press, 1968, pp. 104-111.
Pairs the character of the Bishop with the Duke of Ferrara in "My Last Duchess": both are sensualists whose view of life is incomplete and abhorrent to the poet. Carefully examines the language of the poem and the many rhetorical devices, especially alliteration, to show how Browning presents the Bishop as a man intent on sensual gratification and unconcerned about the spiritual aspects of life. Suggests the ending is a masterful stroke which keeps the Bishop from appearing as a tragic figure. Considers the work "as perfect a poem as any Browning wrote."

Caliban Upon Setebos

Burrows, Leonard. *Browning the Poet: An Introductory Study*. Nedlands, W. Australia: University of Western Australia Press, 1969, pp. 202-220.
Links the poem with several others in which Browning shows an interest in ways people justify themselves and their beliefs. Compares the poem to "Mr. Sludge, the Medium" and "Prince Hohenstiehl-Schwangau," other works featuring characters the poet seems to hold

up for particular criticism. Shows how Browning preserves the essence
of Shakespeare's Caliban. Extensive discussion of the theological
implications of Caliban's musings. Also discusses the satiric nature of
the poem. Claims the work is "a wonderfully inventive and playfully
entertaining display of the comic imagination."

Drew, Philip. *The Poetry of Browning: A Critical Introduction*. London:
Methuen, 1970, pp. 150-154.
Examines the poem in detail to explain why it appears to be difficult.
Suggests Browning is arguing against all forms of anthropomorphism
in conceiving of the deity; the poet believes that God is beyond humankind's ability to conceive of that and any vision human beings may
construct will of necessity be debased. Most views held by Browning's
contemporaries omit the quality of love from God's attributes; through
the poem Browning is suggesting nineteenth century men and women
should have advanced beyond primitive notions of the Creator.

Erickson, Lee. *Robert Browning: His Poetry and His Audiences*. Ithaca,
N.Y.: Cornell University Press, 1984, pp. 217-220.
Brief comments on a poem Erickson considers the finest among those
published in *Dramatis Personae*. Discusses Caliban's understanding
of Setebos, a god he pictures in his own image; believes Browning
intended readers to see the limitation of a vision which allows individuals to envision themselves as the center of the universe.

Gridley, Roy. *Browning*. London: Routledge & Kegan Paul, 1972, pp.
114-117.
Brief account of the reaction by Browning's contemporaries to the
beast-man who speaks in the poem. Describes the intellectual climate
of the mid-nineteenth century, when discussions of evolution bred
strong emotional responses among many of the poet's readers and
critics. Claims Browning found fault with the process of "natural
theology," whereby people came to a knowledge of God by studying
the world around them; his portrait of Caliban satirizes this ideology.

Jack, Ian. *Browning's Major Poetry*. Oxford: Clarendon Press, 1973, pp.
263-268.
Calls the poem an argument within a dramatic framework: Browning
wishes to explore humanity's futile attempts to comprehend the nature
of God. The work is a "brilliant exploration of the primitive mind in
its attempts to fathom the unfathomable." Briefly compares the poem
to other theological arguments. Notes Browning's fascination with his

main character, who "made a deep appeal to Browning's imagination." Shows how the poet satirizes systems of natural theology.

King, Roma A., Jr. *The Focusing Artifice: The Poetry of Robert Browning.* Athens: Ohio University Press, 1968, pp. 123-124.
Brief sketch of Browning's method of handling two distinct tasks in this poem: the development of a most unattractive subhuman figure who would nevertheless engage readers' sympathy, and the completion of a satire on natural theologians whose ideas rose to prominence in the late eighteenth and early nineteenth centuries. Considers the poem "a triumph of the dramatic method," in which Browning is able to use character study and commentary on the religious issue to reinforce each other in a work that is "richly and ironically complex."

Melchiori, Barbara. "Upon 'Caliban Upon Setebos.'" In *Browning's Poetry of Reticence.* London: Oliver & Boyd, 1968.
Calls the poem an experiment based on Darwinian theory of evolution: Browning uses the figure of Caliban, a primitive man, to explore ways humanity's notion of God may have evolved. Points out the poet's dependence on biblical allusions and his repeated use of sexual imagery. Discusses the anthropomorphic nature of Caliban's idea of God. Claims the work is a superb example of the possibility for psychoanalysis which Darwin's theory of evolution makes possible.

Shaviro, Steven. "Browning Upon Caliban Upon Setebos." In Harold Bloom, ed. *Robert Browning.* Modern Critical Views. New York: Chelsea House, 1985.
Uses psychological theories of Freud and Nietzsche to examine the character of Caliban and to explain his preoccupation with and hatred of Setebos. Like the reader, Caliban seeks constantly to interpret: his text is the world around him, of which he desperately tries to make sense. Argues Caliban is fixated upon Setebos, who is a form of superego; the monster directs his aggression against the creator as a means of asserting his freedom.

Shaw, W. David. *The Dialectical Temper: The Rhetorical Art of Robert Browning.* Ithaca, N.Y.: Cornell University Press, 1968, pp. 193-203.
Detailed analysis of the rhetoric and logic of Caliban's assessment of his unhappy lot. Argues that, like many individuals in extreme circumstances, Caliban finds himself driven to posit his opposite as the perpetrator of his misfortune. Shows how, throughout the monologue, the animal-like narrator struggles to understand what God must be like.

Childe Roland to the Dark Tower Came

Bloom, Harold. "Testing the Map: Browning's *Childe Roland.*" *A Map of Misreading*. New York: Oxford University Press, 1975.
Extended reading of the poem to illustrate Bloom's concept of "misprision," the struggle poets undertake to circumscribe tradition and differentiate themselves from their predecessors. Discusses the psychological and rhetorical dimensions of the poem; argues Roland's quest is one doomed to failure. Compares the hero to the modern poet struggling to find his own voice free of influence of strong poetic predecessors. Claims Shelley is the poetic father-figure Browning is striving to surpass.

Burrows, Leonard. *Browning the Poet: An Introductory Study*. Nedlands, W. Australia: University of Western Australia Press, 1969, pp. 161-169.
Focuses on Browning's use of scenery and setting, which Burrows says is intended to highlight the poet's unusual hero. Discusses the effectiveness of the opening, which brings readers immediately into the action; also explores the poet's use of cacophony and dissonance in the work. Examines the enigmatic ending, which has puzzled and frustrated many critics, especially Browning's contemporaries, who tended to allegorize Roland's story and found it hard to establish a consistent reading.

Erickson, Lee. *Robert Browning: His Poetry and His Audiences*. Ithaca, N.Y.: Cornell University Press, 1984, pp. 147-150.
Abbreviated analysis of the poem's central character, whom Erickson calls "a mad quester after fame." Considers Roland a paranoid figure whose attempts to communicate with the natural world simply produce a series of nightmare visions. Reviews the ambiguous ending of the poem, which has caused critics to wonder if Roland dies upon reaching the Dark Tower or lives to recount his experience.

Flowers, Betty S. *Browning and the Modern Tradition*. London: Macmillan, 1976, pp. 25-27, 69-70.
In a general discussion of Browning's concern for creating poetry out of distinct images and mythical materials, Flowers compares "Childe Roland" with T. S. Eliot's *The Waste Land* to show how the two poems are similar in presenting stories whose narratives are seemingly incomplete. Concludes if meaning is to be gleaned from either poem, it "is not to be found in the narrative or didactic content, but suspended within the structure of imagery."

Jack, Ian. *Browning's Major Poetry*. Oxford: Clarendon Press, 1973, pp. 179-194.

Summarizes the enduring fascination the poem has held for critics; points out the many enigmatic elements which prompt varying reactions. Describes the literary sources which inspired the poet; cites *Pilgrim's Progress* as a particularly relevant source. Argues for the dramatic unity of the poem; claims readers' interpretations of the success or failure of Roland to achieve his quest arise from their understanding of the significance of the nightmare landscape through which he must pass.

King, Roma A., Jr. *The Focusing Artifice: The Poetry of Robert Browning*. Athens: Ohio University Press, 1968, pp. 91-93.

Brief analysis of this enigmatic quest-poem which dramatizes an internal spiritual journey toward self-realization. Explains how the poem's imagery externalizes this mental process. Believes Browning displays an ironic reversal of the traditional heroic quest; in this work the central character moves "from conqueror to victim" as the medieval quest "is transformed into a modern spiritual pilgrimage."

Martin, Loy D. *Browning's Dramatic Monologues and the Post-Romantic Subject*. Baltimore: Johns Hopkins University Press, 1985, pp. 179-192.

Psychological exploration of the poem using criteria established in earlier chapters which define the genre of the dramatic monologue; establishes the limits of psychological interpretation of the poem. Considers the dramatic monologue an appropriate form for capturing dreams and giving them form; uses this notion to explain why Browning is able to transform his own dream into this poem. Believes "Childe Roland to the Dark Tower Came" is essentially "an interpretation of a dream about the loss of human communication" in which the poet, through his protagonist, explores "the terror of loneliness."

Melchiori, Barbara. "Browning's 'Waste Land'"; "The Tapestry Horse." In *Browning's Poetry of Reticence*. London: Oliver & Boyd, 1968.

Explores the implications of the nightmarish quality of the work. Reviews other critics' interpretations of these scenes. Points to the writings of architect Gérard de Lairesse as one source. Believes the poem is an anomaly in the poet's canon, because Roland fails in his quest. Associates this failure with Browning's fear that he might fail as an artist. Includes an appendix dealing with the origins for the "stiff blind horse" which appears on the landscape.

Shaw, W. David. *The Dialectical Temper: The Rhetorical Art of Robert Browning*. Ithaca, N.Y.: Cornell University Press, 1968, pp. 126-135. Describes the poem as Browning's best attempt to dramatize the process of spiritual growth. Sees the poet making effective use of dramatic techniques to display the dialectical movement of the hero as he confronts and rejects various philosophical positions. Believes much of the action in the poem occurs within the knight's imagination. Compares the hero of the work to Shakespeare's King Lear.

Cleon

Gridley, Roy. *Browning*. London: Routledge & Kegan Paul, 1972, pp. 79-82.
Brief sketch of the poem's title character. Believes Cleon is arrogant, proud, and not open to Christian revelation. He represents a certain nineteenth century attitude which Browning disliked: the notion that the present civilization has progressed beyond all others. Cleon expresses the same feelings about first century Greece and is blind to the message of Christ. Despite his feelings of superiority about his age, he has a deep sense of unfulfillment and anxiety.

Harrison, Antony. "'Cleon' and Its Contexts." In *Victorian Poets and Romantic Poems: Intertextuality and Ideology*. Charlottesville: University Press of Virginia, 1990.
Discusses the poem as Browning's entry in the mid-nineteenth century debate on the nature and function of contemporary poetry. Points out its affinities with Arnold's *Empedocles on Etna*; both poems attack the trend in poetry exemplified by the Spasmodics, whose works were popular in the middle decades of the century. Notes Browning's frequent references to "joy" in the poem; shows how these references establish links between "Cleon" and other works, notably *Empedocles on Etna* and Wordsworth's "Ode: Intimations of Immortality."

Honan, Park. *Browning's Characters: A Study in Poetic Technique*. New Haven, Conn.: Yale University Press, 1961, pp. 129-130, 161-165.
Directs attention to the dramatic situation Browning creates in the poem: Cleon's work on an epistle to the monarch Protos gives him ample opportunity to explain himself and his ideas to that potentate without the physical presence of Protos to deter his honesty or overawe him. Because he is not intimidated, his carefully crafted explanation

of his ideology reveals Cleon's intellectual deficiencies as well as his strengths: his egocentricity emerges from this letter.

Jack, Ian. *Browning's Major Poetry*. Oxford: Clarendon Press, 1973, pp. 239-243.
Believes the source of the poem lies in Browning's reading of Matthew Arnold's *Empedocles on Etna*. Sketches similarities between the title characters but argues Browning does not sympathize with his creation, despite the many fine passages he writes to describe Cleon's world. Quotes liberally from the text to show how the poet paints an unsympathetic portrait of his subject; considers Cleon's attitude is close to that of many twentieth century readers. Judges the poem as not one of Browning's best.

King, Roma A., Jr. *The Focusing Artifice: The Poetry of Robert Browning*. Athens: Ohio University Press, 1968, pp. 106-108.
Brief commentary focusing on the psychological dimensions of the work. Sees Cleon struggling to resolve a series of tensions which trouble him as he grows increasingly aware that all he values is fragile and transient. He is unable to reconcile the contraries of life and unable to accept the alternative the new religion, Christianity, offers as a way to achieve some form of resolution. Sees the special strength of the poem in Browning's ability to vivify "the immediate sense of Cleon's frustration."

Lawson, E. LeRoy. *Very Sure of God: Religious Language in the Poetry of Robert Browning*. Nashville, Tenn.: Vanderbilt University Press, 1974, pp. 113-116.
Brief analysis of the title character, whose insistence in finding an empirical foundation for the existence of God causes him to dismiss the message St. Paul brings to the region. Though supremely talented, Cleon remains unfulfilled. Believes Browning uses this character to point up the inadequacies of nineteenth century science, which demanded empirical evidence for all belief; Lawson feels the poet is willing to accept "the necessarily contingent character of faith."

Shaw, W. David. *The Dialectical Temper: The Rhetorical Art of Robert Browning*. Ithaca, N.Y.: Cornell University Press, 1968, pp. 177-184.
Discusses the dilemma Cleon faces as he is confronted with ideas which challenge his deepest beliefs. Describes the three-part movement of the work, showing how the speaker defends Greek art and philosophy. Also describes his attitude toward death and immortality;

Cleon comes to realize that, when he has learned enough to lead a full
life, he will be too old to do so. Suggests Browning is mocking
rationalist philosophy in his portrait of Cleon.

Tucker, Herbert F., Jr. "Cleon Orders His Urn." In *Browning's Beginnings:
The Art of Disclosure.* Minneapolis: University of Minnesota Press,
1980.
Examines the title character as an example of the kind of artist Browning rejected: one intent on perfection, bent on being judged a great
writer whose works are the fulfillment and high point of literary
tradition. Explores the psychological dimensions of such a person who
rejects growth, demands closure, and denies the possibility of a future
for art. Believes Browning created Cleon as an antithesis to his own
theory that great art always has about it something of the unfinished,
and always presages something which will follow and build upon it.

An Epistle of Karshish

Collins, Thomas J. *Robert Browning's Moral-Aesthetic Theory, 1833-
1855.* Lincoln: University of Nebraska Press, 1967, pp. 136-140.
Links this poem with "Cleon" as one in which Browning examines the
"significance of the coming of Christ as a historical event." Explicates
the text to highlight Karshish's curiosity and to show the irony of his
revelations about Lazarus, whose rising from the dead is recounted as
but one of several medical oddities discovered among the Jewish
people. Karshish's speculations about the possibility of God's coming
to live among men, and the implications of that event, provide the
central question over which Browning wishes readers to ponder.

Gridley, Roy. *Browning.* London: Routledge & Kegan Paul, 1972, pp.
76-79.
Brief sketch of the poem's plot; remarks on the character of the Arab
physician whose openness to new experiences leads him into confusion
as he tries to make sense out of the story of Lazarus' claim to have been
raised from the dead. Karshish is a rationalist and hence cannot accept
the notion that God has intervened in the world's activities. Abbreviated discussion of the religious controversies which prompted Browning to write his poem.

Hassett, Constance W. *The Elusive Self in the Poetry of Robert Browning.*
Athens: Ohio University Press, 1982, pp. 82-85.

Brief discussion of the reason Karshish is unable to accept Lazarus' story of resurrection. Points out the physician's long prologue and his inconsequential conclusion, which frame the central issue. His training as a doctor makes him unable to allow for the possibility of an extraordinary explanation of Lazarus' return from the dead. Believes the poem exhibits a paradox of human character which Browning understood well: "a man's vested interest in his own expertise may be a source of self-division."

Jack, Ian. *Browning's Major Poetry*. Oxford: Clarendon Press, 1973, pp. 234-239.
Considers the poem an attempt to explore one of the more important controversies of the nineteenth century: the facts surrounding the nature of Christ. Believes the work engenders "a double psychological interest," both in the character of the risen Lazarus and in the imaginative but skeptical Karshish. Describes ways Browning sketches his generally sympathetic portrait of the Arab physician. Judges the poem successful because Browning is able to generate thoughts about the religious mystery of the Incarnation without resorting to "direct theological argument."

King, Roma A., Jr. *The Focusing Artifice: The Poetry of Robert Browning*. Athens: Ohio University Press, 1968, pp. 109-111.
Describes the psychological turmoil of the speaker, an Arab man of science, as he relates in his an epistle to his mentor the strange experience he has had on a visit to Palestine: an encounter with Lazarus, who claims to have been raised from the dead. Though Karshish tries to write with scientific dispassion, emotion predominates in his report. He professes skepticism about what he has been told but remains open-minded about the possibility that this God who raised Lazarus may indeed be real.

Shaw, W. David. *The Dialectical Temper: The Rhetorical Art of Robert Browning*. Ithaca, N.Y.: Cornell University Press, 1968, pp. 170-177.
Describes Browning's method of dramatizing the "conflict between science and religion in the soul of a skeptical physician." Acknowledges the central interest in the work is not in the debate over Lazarus' story about his resurrection from the dead but in Karshish's presentation of the story to his auditor. Believes Karshish is won over by the possibility that Lazarus is telling the truth, but his representation of Lazarus as mad vitiates his argument.

Fra Lippo Lippi

Burrows, Leonard. *Browning the Poet: An Introductory Study*. Nedlands,
  W. Australia: University of Western Australia Press, 1969, pp. 170-187.
  Argues Browning makes masterful use of comic traditions to create a
  work which explores with great seriousness notions about reality and
  about God. Quotes liberally from the text to illustrate the poet's ability
  to create both setting and dramatic tension. The monk's justification of
  the realism of his painting is a metaphor for Browning's defense of his
  dramatic poems. Fra Lippo claims his realism is actually endorsed by
  God, because it is based on the notion that humankind is both body and
  soul, and both deserve celebration.

Erickson, Lee. *Robert Browning: His Poetry and His Audiences*. Ithaca,
  N.Y.: Cornell University Press, 1984, pp. 174-179.
  Short commentary about the poem's exploration of "the proper relationship between life and art." Summarizes the action of the work,
  emphasizing ways Fra Lippo defines himself by his actions both as an
  artist and as a seeker after life's pleasures. Notes the use of images of
  entrapment and moonlight throughout the poem.

Gridley, Roy. *Browning*. London: Routledge & Kegan Paul, 1972, pp.
  91-96.
  Considers the poem Browning's justification for realism in art. Claims
  it is also a study of the way a person's life is shaped by external
  forces and circumstances. Fra Lippo's monologue is an extended self-
  justification, in which he makes an eloquent defense of his love of
  nature and the physical world. Notes how much the poem affected
  other artists and how much Browning himself loved the work.

Hair, Donald S. *Browning's Experiments with Genre*. Toronto: University
  of Toronto Press, 1972, pp. 107-110.
  Focuses on the ironies in the poem. The monk is "aware of the discrep-
  ancy between his view of life and art"; he represents the "confident
  new outlook" of the Renaissance. Notes the comic aspects of Fra
  Lippo's exchange with the watchmen, pointing out the serious tone of
  the monk's discussion of art. Fra Lippo is convinced great art must take
  into account both the fleshly and the spiritual sides of human nature.

Hassett, Constance W. *The Elusive Self in the Poetry of Robert Browning*.
  Athens: Ohio University Press, 1982, pp. 130-137.
  Argues Fra Lippo's reaction to his arrest seems out of proportion to the

external circumstances; believes the "forces that frustrate" him are "psychological, not socio-economic." Despite his strong appeal for the right to express the new realism which characterizes his paintings, Fra Lippo cannot shake the notion that there is merit in the tradition which is represented for him by the Prior.

Jack, Ian. *Browning's Major Poetry*. Oxford: Clarendon Press, 1973, pp. 213-224.
Extensive examination of the sources for Browning's portrait of the monk; concentrates on the poet's use of Giorgio Vasari's *Lives* of the Italian painters and cites commentary by Johnstone Parr and Mrs. Jameson on the historical Fra Lippo. Believes Browning manipulates history to highlight the "fascinated delight" the monk "takes in the human scene." Browning's Fra Lippo is "vivacious" and possesses a strong imagination; he takes great delight in the natural world. Considers the poet sympathetic toward this artist who celebrates human life.

King, Roma A., Jr. *The Focusing Artifice: The Poetry of Robert Browning*. Athens: Ohio University Press, 1968, pp. 105-106.
Believes the speaker in the poem, though glib in his explanation of his apparent transgression against monastic rules, does not achieve complete success in resolving the dilemma he faces between the spiritual and sensual sides of his personality. Notes how Browning dramatizes Fra Lippo's dilemma through a series of paradoxes. Though readers eventually come to sympathize with the artist-monk, Fra Lippo's final position is not one of triumph but only of compromise: his "penance," a portrait of the Virgin, includes a sensuous young lady.

Korg, Jacob. *Browning in Italy*. Athens: Ohio University Press, 1983, pp. 108-116.
Sees the central conflict in the poem as that of a mind caught "between its own convictions and the commands of authority." Claims Browning's monk believes art must be aesthetically pleasing as well as spiritually uplifting. Explains how the poet developed his ideas about Fra Lippi's attitudes toward art, first through written sources such as Giorgio Vasari's *Lives* of the Italian painters, then through viewing paintings by Fra Lippo and others; describes a number of these paintings. Includes photographs of paintings discussed in the text.

Martin, Loy D. *Browning's Dramatic Monologues and the Post-Romantic Subject*. Baltimore: Johns Hopkins University Press, 1985, pp. 86-91.

Focuses on the opening lines of the monologue to show how Browning establishes a power relationship between Fra Lippo and the constable who arrests him and how the friar manages to overcome his initial position of dependence. Explains how Browning manipulates language to bring about the transformation of this power relationship so the monk becomes the dominant figure in the scene.

Shaw, W. David. *The Dialectical Temper: The Rhetorical Art of Robert Browning.* Ithaca, N.Y.: Cornell University Press, 1968, pp. 155-163.
Calls Browning's monk a "comic philosopher" who appears at first to be merely a seeker after sensual gratification but whose argument displays his genuine sense of the religious element in people's lives. Demonstrates how the monologue actually functions as a Socratic dialogue, moving from an initial false position about the nature of reality toward a more accurate appreciation of the balance between sensual and spiritual aspects of human personality.

Tucker, Herbert F., Jr. *Browning's Beginnings: The Art of Disclosure.* Minneapolis: University of Minnesota Press, 1980, pp. 201-208.
Sees Browning's artist-friar as emblematic of the poet himself: like his creator, Fra Lippo avoids the entrapments of formal systems, opting instead to find meaning in the experiences of life as he comes upon them in all their variety. Reads the poem as a commentary on the poet's search to establish a philosophical ground for his approach to art and to life: for Browning, meaning does not derive from preconceived systems, nor can it be grasped in its entirety. As one lives, one creates meaning by living and doing. The artist creates works which suggest meaning but never "fix" it; great art engages the art of the past in order to create new forms to suggest new possibilities for meaning.

A Grammarian's Funeral

Burrows, Leonard. *Browning the Poet: An Introductory Study.* Nedlands, W. Australia: University of Western Australia Press, 1969, pp. 120-130.
Detailed analysis of the "counterbalancing ironies" of the poem. Describes the scholar's heroic quest to master all knowledge but acknowledges the limited accomplishments which actually mark his career. Comments on the attitude of the disciples who carry the Grammarian to his grave. Compares this portrait with those offered by George Eliot in *Middlemarch* and Yeats in "The Scholar." Believes the Grammarian represents both the excitement and the dangers of scholarly pursuits.

DeLaura, David J. "Ruskin, Arnold, and Browning's Grammarian: 'Crowded with Culture.'" In John Clubbe and Jerome Meckier, eds. *Victorian Perspectives: Six Essays*. London: Macmillan, 1989.
Discusses Browning's heavy debt to Ruskin for the ideas about the Middle Ages and the Renaissance which inform the poet's portrait of the Grammarian. Also examines Browning's use of the term "culture" as it had been defined by Arnold in the Preface to Arnold's 1853 volume of poems. Attempts to explain why modern readers find the Grammarian simultaneously repellant and attractive, while feeling uneasy about the attitude of the Grammarian's disciples toward their preceptor.

Jack, Ian. *Browning's Major Poetry*. Oxford: Clarendon Press, 1973, pp. 168-174.
Offers a sympathetic reading of the poem, claiming Browning intends for readers to admire the scholar's pursuit of knowledge. Compares the work to passages in the poetry of Alexander Pope and the commentary of Samuel Johnson on scholars but thinks Browning did not share the eighteenth century's disdain for what was perceived as pedantry. Believes the meter and rhythm suggest a "celebratory and triumphal" note which calls forth admiration for the Grammarian.

Shaw, W. David. *The Dialectical Temper: The Rhetorical Art of Robert Browning*. Ithaca, N.Y.: Cornell University Press, 1968, pp. 81-86.
Points out critical problems involved in monologues in which one character provides readers a view of another. Believes the Grammarian is actually a laudable figure; his disciple, who serves as speaker in the poem, is too preoccupied by his own sensual world to see the admirable qualities of his professor. The Grammarian has seen the inadequacy of defining the fulfillment of life as simply satisfying sensual pleasures. Nevertheless, Browning does not fully sympathize with the Grammarian either.

My Last Duchess

Burrows, Leonard. *Browning the Poet: An Introductory Study*. Nedlands, W. Australia: University of Western Australia Press, 1969, pp. 115-120.
Believes Browning intended the Duke to serve as a representative figure from the Renaissance. Explicates the poem in detail to show how the carefully controlled tone and repeated understatement reveal the Duke's real nature. Points out the many ways the Duke exhibits his

penchant for control, his cruelty, and his egotism. Concludes Browning
wanted readers to judge the Duke harshly as "an arrogant, coldblooded,
cruel tyrant."

Flowers, Betty S. *Browning and the Modern Tradition.* London: Macmillan, 1976, pp. 105-107.
Brief analysis of the poem highlighting ways Browning creates the
"double view" of the Duchess: the one the Duke wants his auditor to
have (a fickle, silly, ungrateful girl) and the one the poet wants his
readers to see (a generous, openhearted, appreciative young woman).
Explains how Browning's creation of the dialogue helps him achieve
the effect he seeks.

Gibson, Mary Ellis. *History and the Prism of Art: Browning's Poetic
Experiments.* Columbus: Ohio State University Press, 1987, pp. 184-
189.
Brief, perceptive review of previous criticism and assessment of those
qualities of the Duke which intrigue readers. Believes readers' fascination with the amoral and self-centered speaker arise from the different perspectives they have about events and objects described by the
Duke. The poem is full of dissonance, created by the Duke's insistence
on making the emissary see things from his point of view. Concludes
with a discussion of the significance of the statue of Neptune mentioned at the end of the poem.

Gridley, Roy. *Browning.* London: Routledge & Kegan Paul, 1972, pp.
57-60.
Abbreviated commentary focusing on Browning's ability to create a
sense of realism within the work. Believes this occurs because the poet
includes a specific auditor within the work; the Duke is able to
manipulate the emissary's behavior and anticipate his thoughts.
Through his speech the Duke reveals the essentials of his character: he
is a man obsessed by things. Suggests the Duke represents "the
dehumanizing forces at work in the 1840s." Compares the poem to
Browning's later work, "The Flight of the Duchess."

Harrold, William E. *The Variance and the Unity: A Study of the Complementary Poems of Robert Browning.* Athens: Ohio University Press,
1973, pp. 37-51.
Examines the work in relationship to "Count Gismond," a poem
considered complementary to "My Last Duchess." Focuses attention

on the two main characters, showing how Browning's portraits of the Duke and the Countess offer readers a well-rounded view of the villain who reveals himself or herself through language. Demonstrates similarities in structure, satiric tone, social conventions, and character development. Considers the Duke a master of rhetoric whose carefully planned explanation of the Duchess' history allows him to attain mastery over her now that she is dead.

Jack, Ian. *Browning's Major Poetry*. Oxford: Clarendon Press, 1973, pp. 91-95.
Points out a possible source for Browning's inspiration, focusing on works in Tennyson's 1842 volume which were dramatic in nature and which contain circumstances similar to the one depicted in this poem. Notes how fascinated Browning was with what he found in Tennyson's poetry. Briefly addresses the issue of the poet's use of insanity as a possible excuse for the Duke's behavior, but points out the many ways Browning convinces readers the Duke is in control of the situation.

Langbaum, Robert. "The Dramatic Monologue: Sympathy vs. Judgment." In Harold Bloom, ed. *Robert Browning*. Modern Critical Views. New York: Chelsea House, 1985, pp. 28-31.
Believes the poem is an excellent example of Browning's ability to create sympathy in readers for characters who may, under other circumstances, incite moral outrage. Claims readers are overwhelmed by the Duke's egoism and grandeur; the Duke is so absorbed in telling the envoy about himself that he is unconcerned if he is revealing the Duchess' good nature. Readers are too busy trying to understand such a character to make moral judgments about him.

Martin, Loy D. *Browning's Dramatic Monologues and the Post-Romantic Subject*. Baltimore: Johns Hopkins University Press, 1985, pp. 96-102.
Discusses the way Browning uses language and sentence structure to withhold and only gradually reveal details about the Duke which lead readers to a final estimate of his character. Both past and future are implied in the Duke's monologue, in which he dominates the present and directs the action of the auditor viewing the Duchess' portrait; through this historical context readers come to understand what the Duke has done and will do and hence can reach judgment of his moral worth. Believes the conventional idea that the Duke should be condemned because he treats others as objects to be controlled and possessed is accurate.

Ryals, Clyde de L. *Becoming Browning: The Poems and Plays of Robert Browning, 1833-1846*. Columbus: Ohio State University Press, 1983, pp. 149-155.
Claims the poem is simultaneously subjective and objective. Disagrees with critics who find the Duke calculating; believes instead his speech to the envoy is an example of "feedback phenomenon": he is compelled to keep talking because he feels the urge to justify (perhaps to himself) what he has done. Explains Browning's use of rhymed couplets as an ironic device reminding readers they are reading a work of art.

Shaw, W. David. *The Dialectical Temper: The Rhetorical Art of Robert Browning*. Ithaca, N.Y.: Cornell University Press, 1968, pp. 92-104.
Considers the Duke Browning's greatest creation. Challenges earlier readings of the poem as incomplete. Argues the Duke is involved in high drama, treating life as if it were a play; his inability to control the Duchess forces him to have her killed. The Duke's explanation of his actions is yet another well-produced drama. Claims the Duke is a superb example of Freud's classic obsessive neurotic personality.

Tucker, Herbert F., Jr. *Browning's Beginnings: The Art of Disclosure*. Minneapolis: University of Minnesota Press, 1980, pp. 177-183.
Argues Browning's Duke is constantly searching to understand his Duchess, whose activities seem inexplicable to one accustomed to relying on tradition and form as ways of fixing meaning and significance to life's occurrences. The Duke's comments about the Duchess to the visiting ambassador show how much he is haunted by his inability to make sense of the woman he eventually had to put away. Also offers an interesting analogy between the Duke and many readers of Browning's poetry, who become angry when Browning's works do not lend themselves to fixed, reductive interpretation.

Pippa Passes

Flowers, Betty S. *Browning and the Modern Tradition*. London: Macmillan, 1976, pp. 130-132, 150-154.
Uses examples from this poem to show how Browning's techniques of composition presage those of twentieth century poets. Examines dramatic techniques the poet employs in this work but explains how Browning violates the strict conventions of the drama when doing so serves his purpose. Also explores the structure of the poem, noting its complexity and symmetry as Browning experiments with a variety of

verse forms. Follows with a discussion of the way modern poets such as T. S. Eliot and W. B. Yeats use similar techniques.

Gridley, Roy. *Browning*. London: Routledge & Kegan Paul, 1972, pp. 43-48.

Considers the poem an example of the poet's "indirect, oblique commentary upon the cultural crises of his time and place." Compares it to Elizabeth Barrett Browning's "The Cry of the Children," which has a similar theme: oppression of the young. Describes Pippa's interactions with the characters whose stories are hidden from her. Believes Browning wants his readers to see many ironic circumstances which indicate all is not right in the world; Pippa does not necessarily bring about good by her passing, though she does bring change.

Hair, Donald S. *Browning's Experiments with Genre*. Toronto: University of Toronto Press, 1972, pp. 50-56.

Discusses the ironic nature of the poem; points out that, despite the naïvely optimistic nature of Pippa's song, there is a certain degree of truth in the notion that, from God's point of view, the events of the individuals whose lives the little girl touches are being governed by a higher power. Describes each of the four episodes in which people are touched by Pippa's song.

Harrold, William E. *The Variance and the Unity: A Study of the Complementary Poems of Robert Browning*. Athens: Ohio University Press, 1973, pp. 23-35.

Focuses on the structural devices which unite the disparate stories. Notes how the various points of view, characterization, and imagery contribute to a representation of truth which Browning favored over a straightforward presentation. Examines the function of the Prologue and the "talks by the way" which offer commentary illuminating the stories of the four sets of individuals Pippa encounters on her walk through the city. Also discusses the appropriateness of the imagery.

Honan, Park. *Browning's Characters: A Study in Poetic Technique*. New Haven, Conn.: Yale University Press, 1961, pp. 79-92.

Briefly traces the development of the poem following Browning's failure to produce drama acceptable for the Victorian stage. Examines the rhyme and rhythm of the work to show how much freedom of expression Browning achieved by abandoning traditional dramatic verse forms: through these variations the poet is able to highlight differences in character. Examines the main characters in each of the four sections of the poem.

Johnson, Wendell Stacy. *Sex and Marriage in Victorian Poetry*. Ithaca, N.Y.: Cornell University Press, 1975, pp. 188-193.
Focuses on three of the four sections in the poem which clearly deal with love; concentrates on the first and second parts, wherein Browning treats directly relationships between lovers both in and out of marriage. Notes how, ironically, Pippa actually accomplishes something worthwhile by her singing; these couples are able to salvage some good from their relationships by taking forceful, creative action as a result of the inspiration they receive by hearing Pippa's song.

King, Roma A., Jr. *The Focusing Artifice: The Poetry of Robert Browning*. Athens: Ohio University Press, 1968, pp. 45-55.
Argues the work has several important dramatic qualities even though Browning never intended it for the stage. Discusses the significance of Pippa as a force linking the disparate episodes in this closet drama. Concludes her function is to cause characters to make choices and thereby redeem themselves from indecision. Examines the structure of the work, noting its similarities to nineteenth century melodrama. Believes the first of the four stories is most interesting and succeeding stories are anticlimactic.

Korg, Jacob. "The First Italian Tour: *Sordello* and *Pippa Passes*." In *Browning in Italy*. Athens: Ohio University Press, 1983.
Describes how Browning's visit to Asolo on his first tour in Italy inspired the poem and provided significant elements of plot, characterization, and theme. Claims the poet is successful in identifying with the common people of Italy and transforming their lives into poetry. Explains how scenes and events in the poem are accurate descriptions of places and customs in Italy.

Litzinger, Boyd, and Donald Smalley, eds. *Browning: The Critical Heritage*. New York: Barnes & Noble, 1970, pp. 70-77.
Excerpts from three reviews by contemporaries of the poet, published immediately after the poem's appearance; all three give a sense of how Victorian readers responded to Browning's unusual poetic experiment. Also includes a letter to Browning by Thomas Carlyle, full of advice to the young poet about the significance of his vocation as a writer.

Riede, David G. "Generic and Poetic Authority in *Pippa Passes.*" In Mary
Ellis Gibson, ed. *Critical Essays on Robert Browning.* New York: G. K.
Hall, 1992.
Examines the poet's experimentation with genre in a work Riede
describes as a "medley" combining lyric and dramatic elements; also
explores the political subtext of the work. Claims there is no moral
center in the poem; though Pippa seems to function in that role, much
of what she does is actually misinterpreted or misunderstood by the
characters she supposedly influences. Browning is demonstrating in
the poem his strong aversion to any form of authority, even that of the
poet.

Ryals, Clyde de L. *Becoming Browning: The Poems and Plays of Robert
Browning, 1833-1846.* Columbus: Ohio State University Press, 1983,
pp. 119-137.
Reads the poem as Browning's effort to show how the poet may touch
the lives of others. Examines the four stories of characters who hear
Pippa to show the "psychic necessity of dialogue and relationship" in
human society. Explores each story in some detail. Believes the failure
of dialogue in these episodes reflects the more general breakdown in
human relationships. Briefly discusses the artifice of the poem's structure; suggests Browning is following Dickens in positing the importance of coincidence and chance in human endeavors.

Shaw, W. David. *The Dialectical Temper: The Rhetorical Art of Robert
Browning.* Ithaca, N.Y.: Cornell University Press, 1968, pp. 45-53.
Believes Browning's overt use of stage devices obscures his significant
achievement: the creation of characters whose ability to engage sympathetically with others' points of view enables them to rise above the
crises they face when Pippa passes them on her journey. Pippa represents the artist, whose special ability is to bring out the goodness
inherent in the characters Browning highlights in the four sections of
the poem.

The Ring and the Book

Altick, Richard D., and James F. Loucks. *Browning's Roman Murder
Story: A Reading of "The Ring and the Book."* Chicago: University of
Chicago Press, 1968.
Claims to be "the first full-length study" of Browning's poem "as a
work of literary art." Introductory chapters review the poet's purpose

in composing the poem and survey its overall design as a series of monologues. Individual chapters devoted to the nature of truth and humankind's apprehension of reality; the power of language; the problems of ethical relativism; the importance of allusion and metaphor; and the significance of comedy within what seems to be a tragic story. Argues the poem's critical concerns are with people's ability to know what is right and to act ethically.

Armstrong, Isobel. "*The Ring and the Book*: The Uses of Prolixity." In Isobel Armstrong, ed. *The Major Victorian Poets: Reconsiderations.* Lincoln: University of Nebraska Press, 1969.
Defends the work as a long poem, showing how prolixity is an advantage for making readers participants in uncovering the truth and coming to understand it more deeply than they might in a shorter work. Offer an extensive analysis of both the language and structure of the poem, focusing on monologues of the Pope and Guido. Concludes the work "sustains itself by virtue of repetition rather than in spite of it."

Brady, Ann P. *Pompilia: A Feminist Reading of Robert Browning's "The Ring and the Book."* Athens: Ohio University Press, 1988.
Detailed analysis of Browning's heroine as a character in the feminist tradition, a woman both "brave" and "self-directed," struggling to survive in a patriarchal society which treats women like chattel. Believes Caponsacchi and the Pope are the only male characters to see Pompilia's real value as a person. Considers Browning iconoclastic in supporting such a feminist view, since he did not behave in his own life in this fashion and since nineteenth century Britain was clearly patriarchal.

Buckler, William E. *Poetry and Truth in Robert Browning's The Ring and the Book.* New York: New York University Press, 1985.
Monograph attempting to redirect readers' attention away from prior critical readings toward the poem itself. Suggests that in an effort to categorize the work into one of a variety of preconceived critical formulas, earlier scholars missed the excitement of the reading experience which makes the poem great literature. Following the lead of Henry James, who captured the feeling in an early essay on the work, describes in nine chapters the monologues which make up the total poem. Shows how Browning creates the sense of seventeenth century Italy and sets each character's version of truth and morality against others' views; no external standards of morality inform the work.

Crowell, Norton B. "*The Ring and the Book*: Browning's Concept of Truth." In *The Convex Glass: The Mind of Robert Browning*. Albuquerque: University of New Mexico Press, 1968.
Systematic review of criticism focusing on the relationship of Browning's poem to the story the poet found in *The Old Yellow Book*. Points out early critics' obsession with determining the historical accuracy of the tale. Investigates both the works of critics and the text of the poem to determine the poet's understanding of the concept of truth; argues Browning was concerned throughout *The Ring and the Book* with defining this elusive concept, one which individuals could grasp only partially at best.

Erickson, Lee. "*The Ring and the Book*." In *Robert Browning: His Poetry and His Audiences*. Ithaca, N.Y.: Cornell University Press, 1984.
Chapter examining the work still considered one of the finest long poems in the language. Focuses on ways Browning idealized the story he found in *The Old Yellow Book*; methods the poet uses to accommodate his readers, especially the rhetorical strategies he employs in his opening monologue; the "larger social implications" of the unusual form Browning adopts to tell his story; and the poem's relationship to the epic tradition.

Gridley, Roy. "The Eighteen-sixties II: *The Ring and the Book*." In *Browning*. London: Routledge & Kegan Paul, 1972.
Acknowledges the poem's epic qualities. Describes the genesis of the work, and speculates about the poet's reasons for shaping the poem as he did. Explains Browning's methodology, noting his primary interest is in the psychological dimension of the story. Briefly reviews each of the twelve monologues, noting public reaction to the work as it appeared in installments. Sees the poet representing an optimistic belief that, through poetry, the truth can be revealed.

Hair, Donald S. "*The Ring and the Book*." In *Browning's Experiments with Genre*. Toronto: University of Toronto Press, 1972.
Focuses on the structure of the poem and on Browning's use of narrative, lyric, and dramatic elements to tell his story. Briefly explains how each genre is used to sketch the outline of the tale. Sees the central monologues organized in three groups: the first monologue in each group is satiric, the second romantic and comic, the third a combination of literary modes. Reviews each of the twelve monologues, focusing on the principal argument and structure to show how each reshapes the

central issue and advances toward Browning's ultimate goal: an understanding of the truth beyond the facts of Pompilia's murder.

Hughes, Linda K., and Michael Lund. *The Victorian Serial*. Charlottesville: University Press of Virginia, 1991, pp. 89-108.
Discusses the impact of the poem on its first readers, who obtained the work in four monthly installments. Claims serialization added a balance to the poem's "impetus toward circularity and simultaneous perception" by forcing readers to apprehend the tale linearly, that is, through time. Notes strong parallels between the poem and a courtroom trial, where truth emerges gradually. Analyzes the impact of each monologue on nineteenth century readers, relying on published reviews by Browning's contemporaries. Especially detailed discussion of Pompilia's character.

Jack, Ian. "*The Ring and the Book*." In *Browning's Major Poetry*. Oxford: Clarendon Press, 1973.
Reviews Browning's efforts to get others to write about the Franceschini murder before he took up the story. Discusses the structure to show how Browning attempts to provide a stereoscopic view of the truth; offers brief summaries of each of the twelve monologues, focusing on the revelation of character which emerges in the poet's presentation of events through these men and women. Faults Browning for simplicity of characterization; claims the poem may be the best Victorian long poem, but it is inferior to some of Browning's shorter works.

Johnson, Wendell Stacy. *Sex and Marriage in Victorian Poetry*. Ithaca, N.Y.: Cornell University Press, 1975, pp. 225-242.
Believes the poem can be read as an investigation of love and marriage. Discusses each of the twelve monologues which make up the work to show how individual speakers view marriage. Notes how those characters for whom the reader feels little sympathy generally regard women as chattel and men as superior partners in the marriage relationship. Argues that, when one focuses on the theme of marriage, Pompilia's testimony becomes critically important: she points out "the radical contrast between the ideal and the reality of marriage." Concludes Browning is uncertain about the possibility of "honest sexual love."

Killham, John. "Browning's 'Modernity': *The Ring and the Book*, and Relativism." In Isobel Armstrong, ed. *The Major Victorian Poets: Reconsiderations*. Lincoln: University of Nebraska Press, 1969.

Refutes claims by twentieth century critics that the poem presents a relativist view of truth. Examines several earlier studies to show how each is flawed in concluding Browning was suggesting through his multiple perspectives that truth is not absolute. Argues in *The Ring and the Book* Browning takes a decidedly moral stance, assuming the guilt and innocence of his villains and protagonists. Sees the poet "committed to faith in God" and soundly convinced of the value of suffering and passion.

King, Roma A., Jr. "Immortal Nakedness: *The Ring and the Book.*" In *The Focusing Artifice: The Poetry of Robert Browning*. Athens: Ohio University Press, 1968.
Outlines the background of the work's composition. Discusses Browning's aim in creating a poem from an old court case, noting how he saw his task as giving human significance to the story. Believes the poet's chief goal is to examine the ways human beings can achieve some sense of personal worth in a world where traditional creeds have proven ineffectual. Abbreviated sketches of monologues dealing with the speakers representing the Roman citizenry and monologues of the lawyers. More extensive analysis of Guido, Caponsacchi, the Pope, and Pompilia, characters who achieve some form of self-realization in the poem.

Korg, Jacob. "London and *The Ring and the Book.*" In *Browning in Italy*. Athens: Ohio University Press, 1983.
Describes the composition process in some detail. Focuses attention on the poem's frame, in which Browning, speaking in his own voice, explains his aims and methodology. Extensive discussion of the poet's use of the landscapes and cityscapes of Italy which served as inspiration for the work. Also examines in detail the transformations Browning made to characters and incidents from *The Old Yellow Book* and other written sources. Includes separate sections focusing on characters, imagery, and the use of art and artists in the poem.

Lawson, E. LeRoy. *Very Sure of God: Religious Language in the Poetry of Robert Browning*. Nashville, Tenn.: Vanderbilt University Press, 1974, pp. 118-127.
Discusses the poem as the best example of Browning's assertion that faith is necessary to comprehend fully the truths of existence. Briefly sketches the poet's conception of the work; notes how early in the composition process he saw this Roman murder story as "an allegory of man's apprehension of the truth." Points out various ways the

speakers in the monologues represent the story; concentrates on the Pope's determination of truth, because he goes beyond the facts and trusts his intuition to make a judgment about truth.

Litzinger, Boyd, and Donald Smalley, eds. *Browning: The Critical Heritage*. New York: Barnes & Noble, 1970, pp. 284-353.
Excerpts from eighteen reviews which appeared in British and American periodicals shortly after publication of the various parts of the work; collectively these give a sense of the public reaction to the poem, whose initial publication in installments affected contemporary readers' opinions in a way different from the effect the poem has had on people who read it as a completed work. Also includes excerpts from letters by the English poet Swinburne and the American Sidney Lanier, and a lengthy negative assessment by Alfred Austin, who angered Browning by his criticisms.

McGhee, Richard D. "Browning." In *Marriage, Duty, and Desire in Victorian Poetry and Drama*. Lawrence: University Press of Kansas, 1980.
Careful examination of several key monologues in the poem to highlight the importance of choice for the central characters in this work. Argues both the aesthetic and ethical dimensions of human conduct prove inadequate for a character like Pompilia, who finds solace only in religion. Notes how Browning indicts both society and the established Church throughout the work. Examines Guido's two speeches, as well as those by Caponsacchi, Pompilia, and the Pope, to show the existential nature of human life.

Pearsall, Robert Brainard. *Robert Browning*. Boston: Twayne, 1974, pp. 106-121.
Summarizes the biographical background of the poem's composition, describing Browning's excitement at discovering *The Old Yellow Book*, in which the murder of Pompilia is described. Provides a précis of the story. Includes commentary on each of the monologues, in which the citizenry of Rome and the central characters in the tale explain their versions of what happened and why.

Shaw, W. David. "The Union of the Subject and the World." In *The Dialectical Temper: The Rhetorical Art of Robert Browning*. Ithaca, N.Y.: Cornell University Press, 1968.
Provides extensive analysis of Browning's rhetorical devices, which vivify his characters and present what Shaw calls a kaleidoscopic

vision of truth. Brief commentary on the monologues by Roman citizens. More detailed discussion of those Shaw groups under the title "Legal Rhetoric": the monologues of Guido and the two lawyers. Parallel examination of the monologues Shaw describes as using "The Rhetoric of Religion": those of Pompilia, Caponsacchi, and the Pope. Believes Browning's underlying aim is to show how the poet reveals his vision of truth to his readers.

Sullivan, Mary Rose. *Browning's Voices in "The Ring and the Book": A Study of Method and Meaning*. Toronto: University of Toronto Press, 1969.

Attempts a comprehensive assessment of Browning's method of presentation. Acknowledges the repetitive nature of the work; focuses on differences among the speakers. Looks at each monologue systematically, examining nine formal characteristics: the speaker, the addressee, the larger audience, the speaker's motive, the tension created by the circumstances of the speech, the tone, the mode of address, the facts revealed, the opinions expressed. Concludes Browning found this method the best way of demonstrating the complexity of discovering truth.

Sordello

Collins, Thomas J. "*Sordello*: To Rifle a Musk-Pod." In *Robert Browning's Moral-Aesthetic Theory, 1833-1855*. Lincoln: University of Nebraska Press, 1967.

Lengthy examination of a work Collins admits is especially difficult to understand. Discusses the function of Browning's complex narrative structure; briefly reviews previous critical studies. A long section explores the poem's central themes, identifying causes for Sordello's isolation and his failure to effect change through his art or through his actions; a second discusses the proper role of the poet and poetry. Concludes with an explanation of Browning's decision, made clear in *Sordello*, to champion suffering humanity in his works.

Erickson, Lee. *Robert Browning: His Poetry and His Audiences*. Ithaca, N.Y.: Cornell University Press, 1984, pp. 48-64.

Discusses the many difficulties readers face in struggling through Browning's complex narrative. Traces the development of Sordello's character, noting how, through him, Browning dramatizes the types of poets and the ways they reach their audiences. Concludes the poet's experiment in *Sordello* was too radical for his Victorian reading public. Provides useful summary of the political background and references for further study of this topic.

Flowers, Betty S. *Browning and the Modern Tradition*. London: Macmillan, 1976.

Throughout her study Flowers uses this poem as a principal example of Browning's poetic techniques. Among the topics discussed are Browning's use of color; the dense structure, which relies heavily on historical details not always familiar to the reader; Browning's attitudes toward his readers; the poet's use of imagery and his experimentation with point of view; and his attempts to condense the text through a variety of poetic devices. Throughout, Flowers compares Browning's methods with those of modern poets such as Ezra Pound and T. S. Eliot.

Froule, Christine. "Browning's *Sordello* and the Parables of Modernist Poetics." In Mary Ellis Gibson, ed. *Critical Essays on Robert Browning*. New York: G. K. Hall, 1992.

Addresses the difficulties readers have had in making sense of the poem. Suggests the work offers its own explanation for the poet's intentional obscurity; much of the narrative "concerns Sordello's effort to define his relationship to his audience." Discusses Browning's attitude toward the historical Sordello and toward Dante, the other great figure alluded to in the poet's extended analysis of the nature and function of poetry. Believes Browning is closer to Sordello than to Dante in holding that poetic authority cannot be too closely tied to the authority of Church or State.

Hair, Donald S. *Browning's Experiments with Genre*. Toronto: University of Toronto Press, 1972, pp. 26-42.

Discusses Browning's adoption of the form of the popular romance to take advantage of the public's love for that type of poetry. Explains the function of the poet as both narrator and commentator, who at times advances the story and at other times digresses to explain its significance. Analyzes the problems Browning discovers in combining narrative and dramatic elements in a poem which attempts to explore the nature of poetry itself.

Jack, Ian. "*Sordello*." In *Browning's Major Poetry*. Oxford: Clarendon Press, 1973.

Discusses Browning's fascination with the figure of Sordello and his sources for the story; also sketches the impact of a poem about Sordello by Mrs. William Busk which appeared in 1837. Summarizes the action of each book within the work, tracing Browning's development of a poet-hero with whom he is obviously in sympathy. Believes the work's obscurity is due in part to the length of time the poet took to complete the poem.

King, Roma A., Jr. *The Focusing Artifice: The Poetry of Robert Browning.* Athens: Ohio University Press, 1968, pp. 19-28.
Believes the poem is a key one in the Browning canon. Argues the poet's chief interest is in showing the complexities of a character who is developing, not static, seeking to define himself and justify his actions without appealing to a higher authority or relying on notions of absolute truth. Discusses the complex relationship between the speaker of the poem and Sordello, the work's principal subject. Acknowledges the exceptional obscurity of the narrative.

Korg, Jacob. "The First Italian Tour: *Sordello* and *Pippa Passes*." In *Browning in Italy*. Athens: Ohio University Press, 1983.
Claims in *Sordello* the poet attempts to disguise the personal voice by placing his ideas in the character of the thirteenth century poet. Stresses the importance of Dante as a source of Browning's inspiration. Traces the composition process, showing how the focus of the poem changed as Browning became more familiar with the historical background. Discusses some of the personal experiences the poet had while in Italy which become fictionalized in the poem. Explains how Browning's views of history are Victorian in outlook, but his ideas about poetry expressed in *Sordello* have medieval and Renaissance roots.

Lucas, John. "Politics and the Poet's Role." In *Literature and Politics in the Nineteenth Century*. London: Methuen, 1971, pp. 24-29.
Has high praise for Browning's attempt to explore in *Sordello* the proper relationship of the poet to society. Claims the central theme of the work is "the problem of how the poet is a communicator and whether communication can ever be socially meaningful." Sees Browning's poet-hero as committed to living out the heroism he celebrates in his work; Browning ultimately argues that only by achieving a certain detachment from the world's events can the poet "become true to himself and his vision."

Ryals, Clyde de L. *Becoming Browning: The Poems and Plays of Robert Browning, 1833-1846*. Columbus: Ohio State University Press, 1983, pp. 66-118.

Lengthy discussion of the poem as an example of Romantic irony. Describes the composition process and the genre of the work. Examines Browning's concept of the narrator and the narrator's relationship to the poem's subject. Sketches Sordello's life story as Browning presents it, explaining reasons for the hero's shift from poet to political activist. Discusses the "dialogic mode of production" which contributes to the complex structure but which serves well Browning's purposes as an ironist.

Shaw, W. David. *The Dialectical Temper: The Rhetorical Art of Robert Browning*. Ithaca, N.Y.: Cornell University Press, 1968, pp. 22-39.
Careful examination of the many reasons the poem is a failure. Attributes most defects to the poet's insistence on taking a subjective stance, speaking directly to readers and ignoring conventional rhetorical devices. Examines the role of Sordello as a poet within the poem. Believes the poem provided Browning a lesson in composition that would serve him well when he adopted the dramatic monologue as his preferred form for poetry.

Chapter 4
ARTHUR HUGH CLOUGH

General Studies

Biswas, Robindra Kumar. *Arthur Hugh Clough: Towards a Reconsideration*. Oxford: Clarendon Press, 1972.
Scholarly examination of Clough's life and works, attempting to establish him as an important figure in Victorian poetry and intellectual life. Demonstrates how Clough's religious scruples affected him not only early in life but throughout his career. Traces his progress as a writer whose failure to live up to early promise haunted him and diminished his accomplishments in the eyes of contemporaries. Sees his marriage as a compromise with conventional Victorian expectations. Includes chapters on the major poetry; lengthy analyses of *Amours de Voyage* and *Dipsychus*.

Chorley, Katharine. *Arthur Hugh Clough: The Uncommitted Mind*. Oxford: Clarendon Press, 1962.
Systematically examines Clough's life to show how biography influences the production of poetry. Begins with the assumption that Clough's career did not fulfill the promise his contemporaries saw in him when he was young; attempts to explain reasons for this apparent failure. Organizes chapters around Clough's Oxford days and around the production of his major poetic works. In a conclusion, discusses the psychological reasons for the poet's inability to reconcile competing desires for commitment and withdrawal; illustrates how his use of imagery suggests the deep, unconscious level of that conflict.

Dawson, Carl. "Dramatic Elegists: Arnold, Clough, and Browning at Mid-Century." In *Victorian Noon: English Literature in 1850*. Baltimore: Johns Hopkins University Press, 1979.
Discusses Clough's relationship with Matthew Arnold; also examines the reaction of contemporary critics, especially the Pre-Raphaelite Brotherhood, to his work. Explores the question of Clough's psychological makeup and the special quality of his artistic temperament. Analyzes *Dipsychus* as an example of Clough's most personal poetry.

Goode, John. "1848 and the Strange Disease of Modern Love." In John
    Lucas, ed. *Literature and Politics in the Nineteenth Century*. London:
    Methuen, 1971.
    Claims Clough is a poet motivated and energized by political concerns;
    his best works spring from his reaction to political events, especially
    the Revolution of 1848. The poet's writings reveal his deep sense that
    "individual being can only be defined in its relationship to the social
    structure it confronts." Extensive examination of Clough's *Bothie* and
    brief commentary on *Dipsychus* to illustrate the poet's preoccupation
    with political and social themes. Compares Clough's attitude toward
    social engagement with that of Matthew Arnold, whose insistence on
    detachment ultimately made the two intellectually incompatible.

Greenberger, Evelyn Barish. *Arthur Hugh Clough: The Growth of a Poet's
    Mind*. Cambridge, Mass.: Harvard University Press, 1970.
    Offers extensive study of Clough's prose writings as a background to
    understanding his poetry. Argues the poet's thought on politics and
    religion, the underpinnings of his creative work, is best exemplified in
    his prose. Demonstrates the growth of Clough's ideology from naïve
    idealism through a period of activity and disappointment to a final stage
    of wisdom grounded in an understanding both of society and of the
    individual's ability to achieve virtue. Examines many works not in-
    cluded in anthologies or collections of Clough's writings.

Hardy, Barbara. "Clough's Self-Consciousness." In Isobel Armstrong, ed.
    The Major Victorian Poets: Reconsiderations. Lincoln: University of
    Nebraska Press, 1969.
    General assessment of Clough's stature as a poet. Argues he is not a
    modern figure but instead very Victorian in his concern over econom-
    ics, religion, and sexual matters. Focuses on the lyrical qualities of the
    poetry, which carry the argument in Clough's works. Though he is
    primarily a narrative poet, his writings are more lyrical than novelistic.
    Believes the apparent "disorder" of Clough's poetry arises because he
    is genuinely unable to develop final answers to personal, social, and
    philosophical problems. Comments on Clough's three major long
    poems to illustrate the poet's method of dealing with his major themes.

Harris, Wendell V. *Arthur Hugh Clough*. New York: Twayne, 1970.
    Argues most of Clough's poetry dramatizes the poet's doubts about
    God and about humankind's relationship with God and with the world.
    Sees the poet eventually accommodating himself to his doubts as his

work progressed. Provides brief biographical sketch. Devotes separate chapters to discussion of Clough's major long poems and one to his important collection of lyrics, *Ambarvalia*. Concludes with a chapter on Clough's relationship with Matthew Arnold and an assessment of his literary merits. Includes a brief chronology and an annotated bibliography of secondary sources.

Houghton, Walter E. *The Poetry of Clough: An Essay in Revaluation.* New Haven, Conn.: Yale University Press, 1963.

Important critical reconsideration of Clough's work, focusing on the artistic and intellectual qualities of his poetry, in most cases divorced from their biographical context. Begins with extensive analysis of the poet's reputation, demonstrating misperceptions and wrongheaded assessments. In separate chapters, discusses the shorter lyrics and the major longer works: *Adam and Eve, The Bothie, Amours de Voyage, Dipsychus,* and *Mari Magno.* Concludes with a brief assessment of Clough's place among Victorian poets.

Johnson, Wendell Stacy. *Sex and Marriage in Victorian Poetry.* Ithaca, N.Y.: Cornell University Press, 1975, pp. 79-86.

Abbreviated discussion of Clough's attitude toward sexual relationships and marriage. Notes how the poet's essentially ironic view of life keeps him from being definitive about the idealized quality of such relationships praised by many of his contemporaries. Briefly analyzes four poems, including *Amours de Voyage* and *Dipsychus*; in the latter works, Clough seems to choose as his heroes men who are consciously unwilling to make the commitment required by marriage. Argues the poet's work reveals the problems Victorians had in dealing with sexual love stripped of its "sacramental quality."

Kenny, Anthony. *God and Two Poets: Arthur Hugh Clough and Gerard Manley Hopkins.* London: Sidgwick & Jackson, 1988.

Focuses primarily on the religious writings of Clough; uses works of Hopkins as points for comparison to illustrate important characteristics of Clough's poetry. Believes these two men were "the two most significant religious poets" of the century, and because they came from similar backgrounds, a study of their work is useful in explaining how one could end up an agnostic, the other a Roman Catholic priest. Follows the chronology of Clough's work; includes a lengthy chapter on *Dipsychus*. Examines the poet's compositions from a philosophical rather than a literary perspective.

McGhee, Richard D. "Arnold and Clough." In *Marriage, Duty, and Desire in Victorian Poetry and Drama.* Lawrence: University Press of Kansas, 1980.

Discusses the influence of Arnold on Clough's poetry and on his life. Believes Clough was always concerned with the conflicting notions of an individual's duty toward the world and the concurrent desire for self-fulfillment. Studies several of the poet's lyrics and his three major works to show how Clough works toward a balance between these polar opposites. Notes the poet is often concerned with distinguishing between true and false duties.

Shaw, W. David. "Clough's Agnostic Imagination: The Uses of Uncertainty." In *The Lucid Veil: Poetic Truth in the Victorian Age.* Madison: University of Wisconsin Press, 1987.

Brief essay exploring the sources of Clough's ideas about the nature of God. Finds him influenced by David Friedrich Strauss, Friedrich Schiller, Thomas Carlyle, and his Oxford tutor W. G. Ward. Examines a minor lyric, "Qui Laborat, Orat," paying careful attention to Clough's choice of words and syntax to show how the poet creates and qualifies his idea of the deity. Concludes with brief comments about the ways Clough's agnosticism shows through in *Amours de Voyage.* In parts of other essays in the volume, examines Clough's debt to John Keble's theological pronouncements and his acknowledged pragmatism.

Thorpe, Michael, ed. *Clough: The Critical Heritage.* New York: Barnes & Noble, 1972.

Collection of excerpts from reviews, letters, and essays, more than forty of which were written by Clough's contemporaries; these focus on individual volumes of Clough's works as they appeared in print. Selections include work by both British and American reviewers. Also contains nineteen later estimates of the poet's accomplishments and his place in English letters.

Timko, Michael. "Arthur Hugh Clough: Palpable Things and Celestial Fact." In Richard A. Levine, ed. *The Victorian Experience: The Poets.* Athens: Ohio University Press, 1982.

General assessment of Clough's poetic achievements; attempts to explain why Clough's works still command critical attention. Argues it is impossible to separate the poet's personal beliefs from his art. Discusses Clough's ongoing dialogue with Matthew Arnold, which helped Clough develop his ideas about the appropriate form and content of his poetry; Clough always subordinates personal feeling to moral statement, because for him "poetry has to be both consolatory and interpretive." Compares Clough's *Amours de Voyage* to Tennyson's *Maud*, observing that in these poems with similar themes, Clough is more successful than the Victorians' laureate in creating a believable and sympathetic hero whose "experiences and comments help bring into sharper focus the meaning of human existence."

_____. *Innocent Victorian: The Satiric Poetry of Arthur Hugh Clough*. Athens: Ohio University Press, 1963.
Believes Clough is a major thinker and significant poet whose natural positivism has been misunderstood. Argues the poet is a realist who believes in humanity's innate goodness; Clough saw poetry's main function as being a commentary on contemporary life. The poet's best work is his satire, which offers insightful commentary into the modern condition. Devotes a chapter to careful exposition of Clough's thought, and a second chapter to his artistry, especially as it is demonstrated in poems such as *Amours de Voyage* and *Dipsychus*.

Amours de Voyage

Biswas, Robindra Kumar. "Rome and *Amours de Voyage*." In *Arthur Hugh Clough: Towards a Reconsideration*. Oxford: Clarendon Press, 1972.
Extensive analysis of Clough's ironic commentary which highlights the "psychology of the radically self-conscious intellectual." Briefly notes previous criticism, especially comparisons between Clough's hero and T. S. Eliot's Prufrock. Presents biographical background, noting its significance; also discusses the importance of Rome as a symbol of eternal truths against which the hero's attitude is contrasted. Careful analysis of structure, imagery, and other poetic techniques, especially Clough's use of hexameters. Ultimately judges this work Clough's best, and one of the finest poems of its time.

Chorley, Katharine. "Rome and *Amours de Voyage*." In *Arthur Hugh Clough: The Uncommitted Mind*. Oxford: Clarendon Press, 1962.
Traces the influence of Clough's visit to Rome during the Italian Republic's revolution of 1848 on the composition of this poem. Suggests the work has significant autobiographical elements; quotes extensively from the poem and from Clough's letters to support this claim. Explains how the poem has both a political and a personal plot line, as the hero finds himself caught up in the revolution and in his

affair with Mary Trevellyn. Briefly comments on criticism of the work
offered to Clough by his friend J. C. Shairp.

Goode, John. "*Amours de Voyage*: The Aqueous Poem." In Isobel Armstrong, ed. *The Major Victorian Poets: Reconsiderations*. Lincoln:
University of Nebraska Press, 1969.
Argues forcefully that this poem is a masterpiece, the most important
work of "high Victorian poetry." The poem's rich verbal texture serves
as a medium for Clough to investigate a problem central to his age: the
"search for continuity." The central issue Clough explores is the place
of the self in society. Within the poem, the hero searches for continuity
in tradition (symbolized by Rome), in love, and finally in himself,
through an analysis of his own growth. Explains how the hexameter
form is particularly appropriate to the kind of inquiry Clough is
making. Concludes the poem is a great experiment, with no precedents
in English.

Harris, Wendell V. "*Amours de Voyage*: An Epistolary Novel in Hexameters." In *Arthur Hugh Clough*. New York: Twayne, 1970.
Extensive analysis, providing brief commentary on the history of
composition and detailed plot summary. Focuses on Clough's development of the central character, whose skepticism and ambivalence
about personal feelings keep him from taking any decisive action or
making any commitments; centers discussion on Claude's relationship
with Mary, an affair which ultimately goes nowhere. Suggests the
poem is Clough's attempt to portray "a mind recoiling from action
because of fear of error." Also discusses the problem of ambiguity
arising from the prologues and epilogues to the various sections of the
work.

Houghton, Walter E. "*Amours de Voyage*." In *The Poetry of Clough: An
Essay in Revaluation*. New Haven, Conn.: Yale University Press, 1963.
Extensive examination of the poem's major concern: Clough's analysis
of the modern intellectual, a figure extremely sensitive about himself
and his place in society. Detailed character study of Claude, whose
ennui and skepticism paralyze him and prevent any form of activity
that might make him a traditional hero; instead, he becomes a kind of
antihero. Lengthy examination of Claude's long-distance love affair
with Mary, showing how the hero vacillates between detachment and
enthusiasm. Comments on the impact of the poem's conclusion, which
upset many of the poet's contemporaries because it is not a traditional
happy ending.

Mermin, Dorothy. *The Audience in the Poem: Five Victorian Poets*. New Brunswick, N.J.: Rutgers University Press, 1983, pp. 109-126.

Claims the poem has many characteristics of the dramatic monologue; Clough is constantly concerned with the power of speech, especially its ability to serve as an agent of "morbidity or self-deception or violence." The poem also shares affinities with the novel. Believes the work is essentially a study of character, and throughout Clough is attempting to promote the virtues of sincerity, a trait held in high esteem by Victorians. Claude, the poem's hero, is struggling to avoid falling into the trap of conventionality, though his behavior is at times farcical. Defends Clough's use of the epistolary form, which was criticized by his contemporaries.

Slinn, E. Warwick. "Fact and the Factitious in *Amours de Voyage*." In *The Discourse of Self in Victorian Poetry*. Charlottesville: University Press of Virginia, 1991.

Reading of the poem that relies heavily on theories of semiotics to establish the notion that Clough's hero is unable to find a center or ground for his experiences. Claude discovers that all of nature participates, as he does, in a process of constant flux; both he and the world he inhabits are part of a dynamic process of change. Explains Claude's vacillations by noting his preference to identify "with the potentially infinite and permanent world within" rather than to limit his potential by committing himself to a person or a course of action.

Thorpe, Michael, ed. *Clough: The Critical Heritage*. New York: Barnes & Noble, 1972, pp. 108-199.

Twelve excerpts from British and American reviews published immediately after the appearance of *Poems by Arthur Hugh Clough* in 1862, a volume which included *Amours de Voyage*. Positive and negative estimates by writers such as Americans Ralph Waldo Emerson and Charles Eliot Norton and British critics David Masson, G. H. Lewes, and Walter Bagehot. Also provides Clough's own estimate of the work, contained in an exchange of letters with his friend J. C. Shairp.

Timko, Michael. *Innocent Victorian: The Satiric Poetry of Arthur Hugh Clough*. Athens: Ohio University Press, 1963, pp. 137-152.

Argues that, far from being autobiographical, this poem is Clough's satire on the Victorian dilettante who, unable to accept the natural world and incapable of finding a balance between the ideal and the real, is paralyzed by his skepticism. Believes the use of hexameter and the epistolary form heighten the comic effect of the work, the first because it suggests mock epic, the second because it allows Clough to reveal the hero's psychological foibles while distancing readers from him. Concludes Clough is satirizing the artificial world of the Victorians, where conventionality has replaced natural standards of behavior.

Dipsychus

Biswas, Robindra Kumar. *"Dipsychus."* In *Arthur Hugh Clough: Towards a Reconsideration*. Oxford: Clarendon Press, 1972.
   Reads this dramatic dialogue as Clough's examination of the conflict between "the question of purity and the problem of action"; Dipsychus is a "romantic idealist" debating the Spirit which represents eighteenth century values. Discusses critical reaction to the poem; examines its structure and its debt to Goethe's *Faust*. Makes extensive use of unpublished materials to show how Clough shaped the poem. Notes the tone of equivocation throughout; argues Clough never resolves the dilemmas he raises. Explains the poem's biographical significance. Judges it less worthy than *Amours de Voyage* to be called Clough's greatest work.

Chorley, Katharine. *"Dipsychus."* In *Arthur Hugh Clough: The Uncommitted Mind*. Oxford: Clarendon Press, 1962.
   Notes Clough's debt to Byron for the tone of the poem and its method of composition; acknowledges several shorter poems by Clough written in the same satiric vein. Argues the theme of the work is the conflict of "engagement *versus* disengagement"; believes Dipsychus stands clearly for Clough himself, who was unable to decide firmly what role he should play in the confusing modern world. Quotes extensively from the text and from letters by Clough and his friends to illustrate both method and theme. Concludes with a note about the date of composition of *Dipsychus Continued*, which is considered an integral part of this poem.

Dawson, Carl. "Dramatic Elegists: Arnold, Clough, and Browning at Mid-Century." In *Victorian Noon: English Literature in 1850*. Baltimore: Johns Hopkins University Press, 1979.
   Examines the complex relationship between the title character and the Spirit with whom he converses in the poem; argues this Spirit is a character separate from Dipsychus, not simply a reflection of the hero's divided self. Points out parallels between Clough's poem and Goethe's *Faust* which is a kind of intellectual forebear of *Dipsychus*.

Greenberger, Evelyn Barish. *Arthur Hugh Clough: The Growth of a Poet's Mind*. Cambridge, Mass.: Harvard University Press, 1970, pp. 174-180.
Brief comments about Clough's treatment of the themes of isolation, alienation, and the presence of evil in the world. Notes the overriding ambiguity which characterizes the work: the reader is never certain if the Spirit which argues with Dipsychus is an external force or an inner voice. Argues the poem reveals "Clough's perception that the nature of morality itself is changing." Observes the highly modern approach to the discussion of sin and evil, and the poet's honesty in dealing with problems of morality and human beings' responsibility for their own fate.

Harris, Wendell V. "Inner Tension as Dialogue: *Dipsychus*." In *Arthur Hugh Clough*. New York: Twayne, 1970.
Briefly assesses the reputation of the poem among nineteenth and twentieth century critics. Analyzes the structure, focusing on ways Clough presents the ongoing debate between Dipsychus and the Spirit who urges him to submit to the ways of the world; notes the difficulties in determining Clough's motive, since the poem remained unfinished at his death. Extensive commentary on the debate between the central characters. Believes Dipsychus, like all of Clough's heroes, chooses inactivity because he is unable to find certainty in any course of action. Discusses Dipsychus' eventual submission to the Spirit and concludes with an abbreviated review of the work's poetic qualities.

Houghton, Walter E. "*Dipsychus*." In *The Poetry of Clough: An Essay in Revaluation*. New Haven, Conn.: Yale University Press, 1963.
Calls the poem Clough's "masterpiece." Acknowledges problems with the incomplete text but argues the series of dialogues displays the poet's mature interest in investigating the individual's struggle "to determine the shape of his own life." Extensive character analysis of Dipsychus and of the Spirit, showing how the latter has a satiric function: to question the intellectual's readiness to retreat from the everyday world. Sees the central struggle between worldliness and asceticism. Carefully examines the development of individual scenes within the two-part structure of the work; notes the heavy religious imagery in the second section. Judges the work a satire in which extreme introspection is seen as damaging to both individuals and society.

Kenny, Anthony. *God and Two Poets: Arthur Hugh Clough and Gerard Manley Hopkins*. London: Sidgwick & Jackson, 1988.
Four chapters offer extensive commentary and interpretation of a poem

Kenny considers Clough's most important statement on religion. Explores problems with the text and the structure of the work; notes its unfinished qualities. Discusses the autobiographical aspects and the ambiguity of the Spirit who debates with the title character throughout. Explores the central religious debate in which the two characters engage and describes the poem's concern with the concept of self and the place of the self in the world. Quotes extensively from the poem to illustrate central points.

Timko, Michael. *Innocent Victorian: The Satiric Poetry of Arthur Hugh Clough*. Athens: Ohio University Press, 1963, pp. 152-168.
Considers the poem Clough's most significant achievement, distinctly modern in its use of meter, allusion, and imagery to convey philosophical ideas. Believes the poet is concerned in the poem with examining "the question of man's role in life." Dipsychus is ultimately a realist, willing to compromise between the two extremes presented by the Spirit. The hero sees the need for flexibility in living within the world. Demonstrates Clough's mastery of poetic techniques in the work.

Chapter 5
GERARD MANLEY HOPKINS

General Studies

Allsopp, Michael E., and Michael W. Sundmeier, eds. *Gerard Manley Hopkins (1844-1889): New Essays on His Life, Writing, and Place in English Literature*. Lewiston, N.Y.: Edward Mellen Press, 1989.
Eleven original essays published to honor the centenary of Hopkins' death. Concentrating on no central theme, the contributors explore the poet's techniques of composition, his religious vocabulary, his use of classical authors and methods, and his relationship to Dante and Milton; also includes an essay on "The Windhover" and one on the later sonnets.

Bergonzi, Bernard. *Gerard Manley Hopkins*. New York: Collier Books, 1977.
Critical biography focusing on the major events of Hopkins' life: his Oxford days, his conversion to Roman Catholicism, his life as a Jesuit priest. Generally includes brief discussions of his poetry in the context of the poet's life, but includes a separate chapter examining in greater detail Hopkins' mature works; analyzes his poetic techniques and offers an assessment of his place in English letters.

Bloom, Harold, ed. *Gerard Manley Hopkins*. Modern Critical Views. New York: Chelsea House, 1986.
Collection of eight essays by distinguished critics of Victorian literature, reprinted from monographs and journals. Provides overview of Hopkins' achievements and offers detailed analysis of several major works, including commentary on "The Windhover" and *The Wreck of the Deutschland*. Essayists claim Hopkins should be considered a Victorian writer allied closely with the Pre-Raphaelites and Pater, rather than regarded as a modern poet.

Bottrall, Margaret, ed. *Gerard Manley Hopkins: Poems—A Casebook*. London: Macmillan, 1975.
Collection of secondary source materials, including selections from Hopkins' notebooks and letters, comments from nineteenth century reviewers and friends of the poet, and reprints or excerpts of seventeen

twentieth century critical essays on the poet and his works. Includes an introductory essay outlining the critical response to Hopkins' writings.

Bump, Jerome. *Gerard Manley Hopkins*. Boston: Twayne, 1982.
Survey of the poet's life and work, offering a general overview of Hopkins' "contribution to our civilization." Provides an assessment of the poet's use of nature in his works and his reliance on typology. Reviews the poetry to illustrate the competing tendencies toward medievalism and modernism which characterize Hopkins' writings. Acknowledges the unspectacular nature of the poet's life. Includes a chronology and brief annotated bibliography of secondary sources.

Cotter, James Finn. *Inscape: The Christology and Poetry of Gerard Manley Hopkins*. Pittsburgh: University of Pittsburgh Press, 1972.
Claims previous studies fail to examine the Christian writers on which Hopkins depended to shape his ideas about the nature of Christ, which in turn influence all his poetic writings. Argues that, in his poetry, Hopkins creates his own myth of Jesus, through which he achieves genuine *gnosis*, an understanding of the Deity. Explores writers Hopkins read; shows how ideas gleaned from them appear in the poet's works and investigates "the acquisition of gnosis as it developed within Hopkins himself." Appendices contain essays Hopkins wrote while a student at Oxford explaining his ideas about myth and metaphysics.

Ellsberg, Margaret R. *Created to Praise: The Language of Gerard Manley Hopkins*. New York: Oxford University Press, 1987.
Examines the perennially controversial question of the influence of the poet's religious vocation on his development as a poet; believes the two professions proved complementary in Hopkins' case. Discusses the poet's use of sacramental language and his exploration of the phenomenon of the particular in nature. Concludes Hopkins' language is intimately tied to the experiences, objects, and ideas about which he writes; his style as well as his "metaphysical attitude" can best be described as "baroque."

Fraser, Hilary. "Epistemology and Perception: Gerard Manley Hopkins." In *Beauty and Belief: Aesthetics and Religion in Victorian Literature*. Cambridge, England: Cambridge University Press, 1986.
Argues there was not as pronounced a split between Hopkins' religious ideology and his devotion to the craft of poetry as other critics have

suggested. Shows how sensualism and aestheticism are subtly present in Hopkins' religious verse. Sees Hopkins' theory of inscape developing from his interest in explaining why some objects in nature and some experiences strike people as particularly significant, and how these objects and experiences lead to an apprehension of the divine.

Fulweiler, Howard D. *Letters from the Darkling Plain: Language and the Grounds of Knowledge in the Poetry of Arnold and Hopkins.* Columbia: University of Missouri Press, 1972.
Extended examination of two poets who shared similar concerns about the efficacy of poetry in the nineteenth century. Devotes approximately half the study to an examination of Hopkins' works, focusing on the poet's exploration of metaphysical and epistemological issues. Discusses how Hopkins uses theology as an analogy for the difficulties of communication people face in an age when language has been divorced from stable meanings.

Harris, Daniel A. *Inspirations Unbidden: The "Terrible Sonnets" of Gerard Manley Hopkins. Berkeley: University of California Press, 1982.*
Extended study of the six sonnets Hopkins wrote in 1885, the last poetry he produced. Careful analysis of the structure and imagery of these works, which Harris sees as distinctly different from Hopkins' earlier poems and not in accord with the theory of poetry Hopkins espoused. Claims they show a shift in the poet's imagination; they "deviate sharply from the patterns of meditation" which Hopkins, following his Jesuit mentor St. Ignatius Loyola, sought to promulgate. Makes frequent connections between these sonnets and earlier works. Includes facsimiles of Hopkins' drafts for these poems.

Johnson, Wendell Stacy. *Gerard Manley Hopkins: The Poet as Victorian.* Ithaca, N.Y.: Cornell University Press, 1968.
Offers a reading of Hopkins focusing on ways he reflects his age through his poetry. Analyzes selected poems to show how the poet answers the question crucial to many Victorian writers: how are people to resolve the problem of their relationship to nature? Begins with a chapter on Hopkins' place in Victorian England's intellectual tradition; devotes individual chapters to four poems, including *The Wreck of the Deutschland* and "The Windhover"; concludes with an assessment of Hopkins' impact on modern literature.

_____. *Sex and Marriage in Victorian Poetry.* Ithaca, N.Y.: Cornell University Press, 1975, pp. 71-74.

Contrasts Hopkins with Matthew Arnold, both Oxford graduates who developed decidedly different attitudes toward life: Arnold became skeptical, Hopkins deeply committed to religious ideology. Hence, it is not surprising to see Hopkins infuse sexual love with a sacramental quality. Notes the presence of sexual imagery in Hopkins' poetry; discusses Hopkins' "Epithalamion" in some detail to show how the poet recognizes both the physical and spiritual qualities of sexual love.

Jones, A. R. "Gerard Manley Hopkins: Victorian." In Isobel Armstrong, ed. *The Major Victorian Poets: Reconsiderations*. Lincoln: University of Nebraska Press, 1969.

Counters argument of many twentieth century critics that Hopkins is essentially a modern poet; demonstrates his great debt to Victorian and Romantic predecessors and discovers the ground of the poet's work in his strong religious sentiments, which are specifically Victorian. Examines several works, including *The Wreck of the Deutschland* and "The Windhover," to demonstrate how the poet explores the possibilities of language and how form is important in Hopkins' best works. Notes the parallels between Hopkins' interests and those of contemporaries who focused on medieval literature and the medieval church.

Kenny, Anthony. *God and Two Poets: Arthur Hugh Clough and Gerard Manley Hopkins*. London: Sidgwick & Jackson, 1988.

In a study aimed primarily at examining Clough's religious writings, Hopkins' works are used for comparison and contrast to show how poets of remarkably similar upbringing and intellectual background could develop in such contrasting ways: one became an agnostic, the other a Roman Catholic priest. Brief discussion of numerous poems, but little extended analysis. Chiefly interested in exploring philosophical implications of both poets' works.

Lichtman, Maria R. *The Contemplative Poetry of Gerard Manley Hopkins*. Princeton, N.J.: Princeton University Press, 1989.

Study of Hopkins' fascination with a particular poetic device: parallelism, a technique adopted from Hebrew poetry and used throughout his career as a poet. Examines Hopkins' essays to show how this theory of poetry emerged from his readings. Discusses *The Wreck of the Deutschland*, several sonnets, and other poems to show how Hopkins uses parallelism both to establish antitheses and to promote an atmosphere of contemplation. Considers Hopkins a contemplative rather than a meditative poet.

Loomis, Jeffrey B. *Dayspring in Darkness: Sacrament in Hopkins*. Lewisburg, Pa.: Bucknell University Press, 1988.

Grounds a study of Hopkins' poetry in theological discussion about the nature of sacramentalism as the poet knew it. Argues Hopkins derives his poetic techniques from principles of early Church fathers who sought inner spiritual meaning beneath the surface of everyday life. Draws heavily on theological arguments about sacramentalism to debunk earlier theories that Hopkins moved from a period of tentative affirmation to a glorious middle period of productivity only to decline in his later years; sees the pattern of the poet's life tied closely to his changing perceptions of the nature of sacrament. Includes an excellent bibliography of secondary sources.

MacKenzie, Norman H. *A Reader's Guide to Gerard Manley Hopkins*. Ithaca, N.Y.: Cornell University Press, 1981.

Analysis of all 159 poems and fragments written by Hopkins in his lifetime. Also includes an excellent, detailed chronology and a reference section providing definitions of key terms the poet uses to describe his work and brief sketches of people important in Hopkins' poetic and religious life. Extensive examination of *The Wreck of the Deutschland*.

Mariani, Paul L. *A Commentary on the Complete Poems of Gerard Manley Hopkins*. Ithaca, N.Y.: Cornell University Press, 1970.

Attempts to offer a prose paraphrase of the argument in every one of Hopkins' poems, providing detailed explications which illuminate the meaning of many difficult and obscure pieces. Organized chronologically to help show Hopkins' development as a poet. Includes a separate chapter on *The Wreck of the Deutschland* and appendices on Hopkins' use of the sonnet form and on his unusual prosody.

Martin, R. B. *Gerard Manley Hopkins: A Very Private Life*. New York: G. P. Putnam's Sons, 1991.

Comprehensive biography based on letters, journals, reminiscences, and critical opinions by Hopkins, his friends, and later scholars. Believes Hopkins is an exceptionally hard figure to know very well. Attempts to draw out of the available documents the "emotional, intellectual, and psychological makeup of a great poet." Pays considerable attention to Hopkins' undergraduate years, arguing that much of the poet's thought and character was formed then, before he converted to Roman Catholicism.

Miller, J. Hillis. *The Linguistic Moment: From Wordsworth to Stevens.* Princeton, N.J.: Princeton University Press, 1985.

In a book designed to explore ways language functions within a poem, Miller traces the intellectual background against which Hopkins' poetry was written. Especially focuses on Hegelian and Nietzschean ideas about the function of language, art, and reality. Argues Hopkins saw the function of poetry to be the creation of a bridge between human beings to communicate what is inherently incommunicable: the sense of the self. Examines *The Wreck of the Deutschland* as a case study of how Hopkins worked out his theory in his poetry.

Milward, Peter, S.J. *Landscape and Inscape: Vision and Inspiration in Hopkins's Poetry.* Grand Rapids, Mich.: William Eerdmans, 1975.

Series of brief analyses of selected sonnets and other lyrics, with accompanying photographs showing the places and objects which inspired Hopkins. Loose chronological and geographical organization suggests how different scenes affected the poet's artistic vision. Includes discussion of most major works, including "Pied Beauty," "God's Grandeur," and "The Windhover."

Motto, Marylou. *"Mined with a Motion" : The Poetry of Gerard Manley Hopkins.* New Brunswick, N.J.: Rutgers University Press, 1984.

Argues Hopkins' poems contain "discernible patterns" which mirror the poet's religious beliefs. Focuses on two characteristics, "assent" and "recurrence"; devotes four chapters to a definition of these terms and an exploration of their appearance in Hopkins' poetry. Believes the poet constantly struggles to separate himself from his Romantic predecessors and from contemporaries, neither of whose worldviews adequately recognizes the presence of God in the universe and humankind's dependence on the Deity. Concludes with an extended reading of *The Wreck of the Deutschland.*

North, John S., and Michael D. Moore, eds. *Vital Candle: Victorian and Modern Bearings on Gerard Manley Hopkins.* Waterloo, Canada: University of Waterloo Press, 1984.

Nine essays addressing several aspects of the poet's work, grouped in three general categories: the relationship of the poet to his age, the parallels between Hopkins and writers whose interests were similar, and the poet's unusual use of language. Includes comments on Hopkins' affinities with fellow Catholic poet Francis Thompson and with the late nineteenth century iconoclastic poet James Thomson. One essayist notes how what appear to be eccentricities in Hopkins' language were also found in works by Tennyson and Swinburne.

Ong, Walter J. *Hopkins, the Self, and God.* Toronto: University of Toronto Press, 1986.
Concerned with the development of self-consciousness in Hopkins and its effect on his perception of God. Notes throughout the poet's intense interest in this subject in his poetry; argues no other Victorian can "quite match Hopkins" in his fascination with the idea "of being different" from other selves. Sees Hopkins' "acute self-consciousness" derived from his training in the classics and his association with the Society of Jesus. Demonstrates that Hopkins was simultaneously a product of his time, a follower of the ascetic tradition, and a precursor of the moderns in his obsession with the notion of self. Includes an excellent bibliography of secondary sources.

Preyer, Robert. "'The Fine Delight that Fathers Thought': Gerard Manley Hopkins and the Romantic Survival." In Malcolm Bradbury and David Palmer, eds. *Victorian Poetry*. Stratford-on-Avon Studies 15. London: Edwin Arnold, 1972.
Argues Hopkins' complex style is a result of his attempt to speak to and about God, who is essentially unknowable. Offers brief analysis of Hopkins' criticism, especially his notions of prosody. Reviews several of the poet's works, noting his intense concern with language and his concurrent lack of interest in social and psychological themes. Instead, Hopkins limited himself to exploring the ways God communicates to men and ways men can use language to express their understanding and appreciation of God's gifts.

Roberts, Gerald, ed. *Gerard Manley Hopkins: The Critical Heritage.* New York: Routledge & Kegan Paul, 1987.
Excerpts from more than one hundred early reviews and notices of Hopkins' work, beginning with references to individual poems which appeared in anthologies shortly after the poet's death and concluding with commentary from critical works published as late as 1940. Because Hopkins did not publish his work during his lifetime, most of these excerpts are selected from reviews of early editions of the poetry. Includes a chronology and a list of principal publishing dates for Hopkins' work up to 1940.

Robinson, John. *In Extremity: A Study of Gerard Manley Hopkins.* Cambridge, England: Cambridge University Press, 1978.

Sophisticated argument asserting that modern criticism is wrong to stress the dichotomy between the religious influence in Hopkins' life and the poet's desire to write poetry. Instead, "Hopkins' verse is at one with his religious commitment," and is "attendant to the same aspirations in the man." Sees Hopkins as a product of his age, which valued self-sacrifice; explicates the poetry to show how it reveals Hopkins' intense desire to achieve excellence in his work as a means to serve God and to celebrate God's grandeur and purpose for the world. Highly technical analysis throughout.

Shaw, W. David. "Hopkins and Scotus: Univocal and Equivocal Signs"; "Hopkins, Plato, and the New Realism." In *The Lucid Veil: Poetic Truth in the Victorian Age*. Madison: University of Wisconsin Press, 1987.
Two brief essays sketching the philosophical and theological basis of Hopkins' thought. The first explores his debts to St. Thomas Aquinas and John Duns Scotus, medieval theologians whose ideas about the human ability to see God in the universe through a process of analogy held great sway with the poet. The second discusses Hopkins' Platonism and his revulsion from the philosophical positions of Hegel and Spinoza. Careful attention given to the poet's developing theory of language and his fear that nineteenth century philosophy was becoming too atomistic, leading people away from an understanding of and appreciation for God.

Sprinker, Michael. *"A Counterpoint of Dissonance": The Aesthetics and Poetry of Gerard Manley Hopkins*. Baltimore: Johns Hopkins University Press, 1980.
Deconstructionist reading of the Hopkins corpus. Argues the central tension in the poet's work arises from the act of writing itself. Analyzes "The Windhover" as an example of the stress produced by the author's confrontation of his text. Examines Hopkins' aesthetic theory, linking it to several modern movements. Also provides an extended reading of *The Wreck of the Deutschland*.

Sulloway, Alison G. *Critical Essays on Gerard Manley Hopkins*. Boston: G. K. Hall, 1990.
Collection of eleven essays, most published previously as articles or chapters of books on Hopkins. Selections attempt to demonstrate the editor's belief that it is possible for critics to "transcend the traditional critical conflict[s]" which earlier scholars saw inherent in Hopkins' life and art. Includes three essays written originally for this volume, one

being a lengthy analysis of the Jesuit community's gradual acceptance of Hopkins and his work.

_____. *Gerard Manley Hopkins and the Victorian Temper*. New York: Columbia University Press, 1972.
Attempts to correct earlier notions of Hopkins as an iconoclastic poet misplaced among his Victorian contemporaries by demonstrating how closely his poetry expresses the concerns of his age. Sees his innovations in poetic technique springing from the literary tradition he inherited and which he knew well. Explores Hopkins' days at Oxford and the impact of religious issues in shaping his life; also discusses the influence of John Ruskin's writings on the poet. Contains a useful selected bibliography.

Tennyson, G. B. *Victorian Devotional Poetry*. Cambridge, Mass.: Harvard University Press, 1981.
Discussion of the influence of Tractarian doctrine on Hopkins' poetry. Claims Hopkins owes much of his poetics to Tractarian ideology; notes how clearly the poet follows earlier Tractarian writers in his concern for "nature, sacramentalism, and incarnationalism." Cites several poems which exhibit similarities to earlier devotional works.

Walhout, Donald. *Send My Roots Rain: A Study of Religious Experience in the Poetry of Gerard Manley Hopkins*. Athens: Ohio University Press, 1981.
Study by a philosopher of the religious experience that informs Hopkins' poetry; throughout, the focus is on the "phenomenology of religion as disclosed in literature" rather than on the literary qualities of the poetry. Examines the stages through which Hopkins passes as he came to understand and accept God; demonstrates how he reflects his progress toward this philosophical position in his writings. Concludes with a chapter discussing Hopkins' philosophical interests.

Warren, Austin. "Instress of Inscape: Gerard Manley Hopkins." In Shiv Kumar, ed. *British Victorian Literature: Recent Revaluations*. New York: New York University Press, 1969.
Focuses on the middle period of Hopkins' career, during which the poet wrote his greatest works. Looks briefly at influences which shaped Hopkins' writings: his Catholicism, his English heritage, his reaction to members of the Pre-Raphaelite movement, and the specific impact of four figures whose works touched him deeply: Walter Pater, John

Ruskin, John Henry Newman, and John Duns Scotus. Examines the poet's use of language, particularly his borrowings from Old English and from various dialects. Argues for the influence of American scholar George P. Marsh and of Anglophiles such as E. A. Freeman and members of the Early English Text Society on Hopkins' ideas about the importance of his native tongue.

Zaniello, Tom. *Hopkins in the Age of Darwin.* Iowa City: University of Iowa Press, 1988.
Analysis of Hopkins' interaction with ideas about science as they were developed during this crucial century. Offers chronological assessment of the poet's career as he encountered the highly charged atmosphere at Oxford where Darwin and his followers began to receive significant attention; devotes two chapters to Hopkins' development as a religious poet at a time when theology was under fire from science; includes a chapter on the poet's own scientific experiments. Concludes with a review of his ability to find "in science a complement to art."

God's Grandeur

Cotter, James Finn. *Inscape: The Christology and Poetry of Gerard Manley Hopkins.* Pittsburgh: University of Pittsburgh Press, 1972, pp. 168-172.
Argues the poem shows how Hopkins sees "nature" and "grace" as complementary forces in the world. God is present in the natural world; humanity's problem is that it is unable to recognize the Creator's presence. Cites several biblical passages, especially ones from the prophet Joel and from Acts of the Apostles, as the sources of the poet's ideas about eschatology which shape the poem. Examines in detail each stanza, explaining how the imagery emerges from biblical roots. Concludes the final lines reinforce the notion that "the day of the Lord is the present morning."

Harris, Daniel A. *Inspirations Unbidden: The "Terrible Sonnets" of Gerard Manley Hopkins.* Berkeley: University of California Press, 1982.
Brief analysis of the poem, showing how it is a good representation of Hopkins' use of the Ignatian pattern within his sonnets. Explains how the speaker in the work, following the method promoted by Jesuit founder St. Ignatius Loyola, brings himself to contemplate the presence of God in the world by exploring the natural setting. The primary

purpose of the poem is to provide a rationale for responding properly to God's creation.

Johnson, Wendell Stacy. *Gerard Manley Hopkins: The Poet as Victorian.* Ithaca, N.Y.: Cornell University Press, 1968, pp. 128-130.
Brief explication focusing on Hopkins' use of imagery. Offers a prose paraphrase of the poet's argument: human beings have turned their back on God and perverted the gifts of the natural world. Alludes to other nineteenth century writers, especially Wordsworth and Ruskin, who express similar sentiments in their works. Claims almost all of Hopkins' images suggest the brightness of the world; concludes, however, that much of the imagery is very vague.

MacKenzie, Norman H. *A Reader's Guide to Gerard Manley Hopkins.* Ithaca, N.Y.: Cornell University Press, 1981, pp. 63-66.
Detailed explication of the images in the poem, explaining how Hopkins intends readers to understand the "foil" and "oil" (which MacKenzie believes is olive oil, not petroleum). Also provides careful analysis of the sextet, pointing out that though the world is seen as spent and polluted, the final image is one of rebirth. Concludes with a paragraph on the rhythm of the poem, suggesting readings for individual phrases and lines.

Mariani, Paul L. *A Commentary on the Complete Poems of Gerard Manley Hopkins.* Ithaca, N.Y.: Cornell University Press, 1970, pp. 93-98.
Detailed explication of the sonnet, providing a prose paraphrase of Hopkins' argument. Sees the poet representing God's grandeur "in terms of light and density"; images of God's brilliance, portrayed in the opening lines, are contrasted with images of darkness which represent men's behavior in the world. Pays careful attention to the poet's choice of words, explaining the multiplicity of meaning several words and phrases carry and noting the "liturgical overtones" which characterize the poem.

Milward, Peter, S.J. "The Dearest Freshness." In *Landscape and Inscape: Vision and Inspiration in Hopkins's Poetry.* Grand Rapids, Mich.: William Eerdmans, 1975.
Detailed explication of what Milward calls the first of Hopkins' "'bright' series of sonnets," ones in which the poet ecstatically celebrates the presence and power of God in the world. Notes the many other places in Hopkins' canon where the poet expresses similar

sentiments about God's magnificence and people's unwillingness to recognize the Creator. Also shows Hopkins' reliance on biblical literature and on other writers such as Keats for his imagery.

Pied Beauty

Bump, Jerome. *Gerard Manley Hopkins.* Boston: Twayne, 1982, pp. 153-155.
Reads the poem as an example of Hopkins' "fairly single-minded quest for unity." The poet focuses on the variety found within individuals, using metaphor to show how different individuals and different species have underlying similarities. The "nature" he sees around him seems in constant flux, but God, who is immanent in this changing world, remains constant.

Cotter, James Finn. *Inscape: The Christology and Poetry of Gerard Manley Hopkins.* Pittsburgh: University of Pittsburgh Press, 1972, pp. 183-185.
Brief analysis, showing how the poem illustrates Hopkins' belief that the world has already been "transfigured through the creating action of the Son." The diversity of nature and the many seeming contrasts he finds in the world around him are joined by their sharing in the Divine Presence which inhabits them all. Cites several biblical passages which offer support for Hopkins' theological stance in the work.

Loomis, Jeffrey B. *Dayspring in Darkness: Sacrament in Hopkins.* Lewisburg, Pa.: Bucknell University Press, 1988, pp. 90-92.
Brief examination of the work as one of several "nature lyrics" Hopkins wrote to celebrate God's presence in the natural world. Notes its possible origin in the Psalms. Claims the poet is willing to accept nature as inherently flawed; the physical dappling of the outer world symbolizes moral decay present in nature, including human nature. Nevertheless, humanity cannot know why nature is flawed, he can only praise God, nature's creator, for providing the beauty which exists along with the "moral darkness."

MacKenzie, Norman H. *A Reader's Guide to Gerard Manley Hopkins.* Ithaca, N.Y.: Cornell University Press, 1981, pp. 84-87.
Remarks on the unconventional approach Hopkins takes in this poem. Believes he was reacting to the common feeling in Victorian England that modern society had imposed a certain uniform quality on life;

variety had come to be denigrated. Hopkins, on the other hand, sees variety as beautiful: "what public opinion condemns as bad or inferior" is "defiantly recognized" in the poem as "equally divine with the unblemished and radiant."

Milward, Peter, S.J. "Dappled Things." In *Landscape and Inscape: Vision and Inspiration in Hopkins's Poetry*. Grand Rapids, Mich.: William Eerdmans, 1975.
Careful analysis of the many images Hopkins uses to suggest the variety of the natural world. Claims Hopkins is always interested in portraying physical objects as a starting point for any contemplation of God's presence in the world. Suggests the sonnet follows the pattern of a school exercise in the Jesuit tradition: all of these begin with the Latin tag *Ad Majorem Dei Gloriam* (for the greater glory of God) and end with *Laus Deo Semper* (praise God always); both phrases are paraphrased in the opening and closing lines of the sonnet. Notes that, unlike "God's Grandeur," this poem acknowledges people's commercial activities as being beautiful.

Sulloway, Alison G. *Gerard Manley Hopkins and the Victorian Temper*. New York: Columbia University Press, 1972, pp. 105-107.
Explains how the poem, a curtal sonnet, exemplifies Ruskin's doctrine that the highest art subordinates the joys of nature to some divine purpose. Describes the poem as "a hymn to Ruskin's 'majesty of motion.'" The poem expresses the beauty of change and the presence of the unchangeable Creator who is responsible for both variety and beauty: the speaker's need for change and his equally strong longing for permanence are resolved in his recognition that God, the source of permanence, is also the source of change.

The Windhover

Bump, Jerome. *Gerard Manley Hopkins*. Boston: Twayne, 1982, pp. 129-145.
Offers a systematic interpretation of the poem, following the four levels of criticism popularized during the Middle Ages: the literal, metaphorical, moral (or tropological), and anagogical. Examines individual words and lines to show how the poem can be read on each of these levels. Believes "The Windhover" is both "the best illustration of Hopkins' poetics" and "the ultimate test of one's ability to explicate a poem."

Cotter, James Finn. *Inscape: The Christology and Poetry of Gerard Manley Hopkins*. Pittsburgh: University of Pittsburgh Press, 1972, pp. 177-183, 278.
Explains how the natural phenomenon of the hawk in flight suggests for Hopkins the unifying presence of Christ in the world. Believes Christ is represented in the poem not by the bird but by the Sun, which touches everything. Cites passages from Clement of Alexandria and from Shakespeare's *Macbeth* as sources and analogues for Hopkins' imagery and intent in the work. Pays special attention to the poet's unusual and enigmatic use of the verb "Buckle" at the opening of the sextet.

Hartman, Geoffrey H. "The Dialectic of Sense-Perception." In Harold Bloom, ed. *Gerard Manley Hopkins*. Modern Critical Views. New York: Chelsea House, 1986.
Uses this poem to illustrate the way Hopkins focuses his attention—and the reader's—on the immediate, sensual qualities of the physical universe. Claims the "sense of pressure or stress" of the senses on the individual demonstrates for the poet the individuality and resilience of the natural world. Extensive focus on Hopkins' use of language and rhythm in the poem. Explains how the poet transforms the windhover into a symbol of Christ.

Johnson, Wendell Stacy. "The Windhover." In *Gerard Manley Hopkins: The Poet as Victorian*. New York: Cornell University Press, 1968.
Detailed explication of Hopkins' most heavily examined lyric; considers it a good example of the poet's contribution to the Victorian tradition of works celebrating the joys of nature. Prefaces his analysis of the poem with brief examinations of other works in which Hopkins celebrates birds, comparing the poet's use of the bird in "The Windhover" with other aviary creatures. Discusses the multiple meanings Hopkins suggests for his windhover: a real bird, a symbol of Christ, and a representative of the poet himself.

Loomis, Jeffrey B. *Dayspring in Darkness: Sacrament in Hopkins*. Lewisburg, Pa.: Bucknell University Press, 1988, pp. 97-104.
Calls the poem Hopkins' "most famous, and perhaps greatest"; notes the enigmatic quality of the bird, which seems to stand at once for Christ and also for those forces of pride in nature which must be made subservient to God's will. Reviews previous critical commentary on the work, noting that the best readings take into account the dualism Hopkins saw in nature. Carefully examines each image in the poem to explain its theological implications.

MacKenzie, Norman H. *A Reader's Guide to Gerard Manley Hopkins*. Ithaca, N.Y.: Cornell University Press, 1981, pp. 76-84.
Careful explication of the sonnet, prefaced by a description of the windhover's characteristics in flight. Suggests Hopkins is faithful to the literal aspects of the bird's behavior as he compares him to Christ. Reviews the many interpretations of the enigmatic word "Buckle!"; suggests it may be associated with an electric charge, an image Hopkins uses in other poems to describe God's effect in the world. Also provides glosses for terms used to describe the humble act of ploughing in the concluding lines of the work.

Mariani, Paul L. *A Commentary on the Complete Poems of Gerard Manley Hopkins*. Ithaca, N.Y.: Cornell University Press, 1970, pp. 109-113.
Notes how numerous critical readings overlook the literal level of the poem. Offers a detailed analysis of the flight of the kestrel hawk which inspired Hopkins, explaining how the images in the work are suggested by the bird's coloration and behavior. Believes the central religious meaning of the poem is "the earthly beauty of the God-man Christ." Offers a symbolic interpretation of the work, equating the bird's behavior with Christ's sacrifice of Himself for humankind.

Milward, Peter, S.J. "Dapple-Dawn-Drawn Falcon." In *Landscape and Inscape: Vision and Inspiration in Hopkins's Poetry*. Grand Rapids, Mich.: William Eerdmans, 1975.
Considers this poem the best example of Hopkins' use of inscape and instress to inspire a work. Sees the poet concentrating on a single moment in the flight of the bird as the starting point for his intense speculation on the suggestiveness of this natural phenomenon. Discusses in detail Hopkins' use of the image of horse and rider in the octave. Describes how the poet shifts his focus from the outside world, the subject of the octave, to an examination of his inner self in the sextet.

Robinson, John. *In Extremity: A Study of Gerard Manley Hopkins*. Cambridge, England: Cambridge University Press, 1978, pp. 42-52.
Detailed analysis of the language of the poem to show how Hopkins captured the essence of the falcon, which stands as a symbol of Christ and as an example of God's presence in the natural world. Focuses attention to the poet's use of the word "caught"; examines passages from Hopkins' notebooks and letters which help illuminate the specific meaning the poet attached to this word, one he used to suggest an individual's ability to grasp the essence of something.

Sprinker, Michael. *"A Counterpoint of Dissonance" : The Aesthetics and Poetry of Gerard Manley Hopkins.* Baltimore: Johns Hopkins University Press, 1980, pp. 3-15.
Extended deconstructionist reading of the poem, arguing it can be read as "an allegory of the writing of poetry." Sees Hopkins trying to establish an identity for the poetic self through his description of the reaction of the "lyrical I" to the flight of the bird. Looks carefully at a number of the images in the work to show how the poet can sustain multiple meanings simultaneously. Also notes how the poem functions as "a figurative response to the figures of Romanticism" who precede Hopkins in the poetic tradition.

Sulloway, Alison G. *Gerard Manley Hopkins and the Victorian Temper.* New York: Columbia University Press, 1972, pp. 107-114.
Argues this poem may be Hopkins' best lyric statement of the Ruskinian doctrine that great art always serves a higher purpose: the glorification of God. Demonstrates how the action of the poem—both the flight of the windhover and the work of the ploughman—models the principles Ruskin set forth in his works on the nature and purpose of art. Claims the bird in flight is not a symbol of Christ, but rather it represents those natural forces which must be seen as subservient to God and his plan for the world.

Ward, Dennis. "The Windhover." In Margaret Bottrall, ed. *Gerard Manley Hopkins: Poems. A Casebook.* London: Macmillan, 1975.
Detailed analysis of the language and structure of the poem to determine what the work meant to Hopkins himself. Explores Hopkins' religious readings and his other poems to construct a consistent reading. Believes the poet saw the falcon as a Christian knight and drew parallels between the bird's mastery of the skies and his own attempts to master life's trials. Concludes the work is "a triumphant confirmation of the poet's personal faith."

The Wreck of the Deutschland

Bergonzi, Bernard. *Gerard Manley Hopkins.* New York: Collier Books, 1977, pp. 157-167.
Acknowledges the extreme obscurity of the poem, noting that readers have always had exceptional difficulty deciphering its meaning. Describes the two-part structure and points out how the poem displays

Hopkins' familiarity with medieval scholastic logic. Notes the highly personal elements in the poem but argues the poet is not simply concerned with autobiographical exploration. Briefly discusses Hopkins' use of sprung rhythm in the work.

Bump, Jerome. *Gerard Manley Hopkins.* Boston: Twayne, 1982, pp. 93-128.
Briefly examines the circumstances of the poem's genesis. Surveys the poet's development of rhythm and meter in the work; discusses his use of typology to enrich the poem's meaning. Extensive analysis of the work as Hopkins' response to the sublime; argues that, when read in this light, the poem appears unified. Also discusses Hopkins' notion of Providence as it appears in the *Wreck*; reviews the poet's focus on his personal awareness of God and his idea of the notion of "sacrament," the immanent presence of God in nature.

Cotter, James Finn. "Inscaping *The Wreck of the Deutschland.*" In *Inscape: The Christology and Poetry of Gerard Manley Hopkins.* Pittsburgh: University of Pittsburgh Press, 1972.
Examines the poem carefully to determine its "inscape," the "dynamic and unifying force" behind the work. Argues the poem is Hopkins' most comprehensive statement of *gnosis*, the knowledge of Christ as a living presence. Throughout the work the poet keeps his attention on Christ as immanent in the world, even at this moment of crisis. The poem is "a dramatic bodying forth of the theology of death" as that concept has been examined by twentieth century theologians. Hopkins uses the catastrophe of the shipwreck as a metaphor to highlight human beings' immediate confrontation with God at moments of crisis.

Fulweiler, Howard D. *Letters from the Darkling Plain: Language and the Grounds of Knowledge in the Poetry of Arnold and Hopkins.* Columbia: University of Missouri Press, 1972, pp. 110-122.
Identifies the central paradox which Hopkins explores in this poem: God's ability to manifest Himself externally (through the power He demonstrates in the storm which causes the wreck), while simultaneously manifesting Himself internally through the saving power of grace. This poem explores the effects of God's presence in people's lives and His effect on people's hearts. Extensive examination of the imagery, especially sea imagery, used by Hopkins to show how God is made present in the world.

Johnson, Wendell Stacy. "The Wreck of the Deutschland." In *Gerard Manley Hopkins: The Poet as Victorian*. New York: Cornell University Press, 1968.

Pays particular attention to ways Hopkins' poem is similar to other Victorian and Romantic narrative and dramatic works. Like many poems by contemporaries, Hopkins' *Wreck of the Deutschland* "is largely a personal revelation," tracing the poet's struggle to understand something about the nature of the self in its relationship with God. Reviews other Victorian poems in which sea imagery is used and discusses Hopkins' use of such imagery. For Hopkins, the sea is a terrible reality whose power can destroy lives, but through such destruction his heroines come to glorify God. Carefully examines individual stanzas to show how Hopkins moves from the literal to the symbolic level.

Loomis, Jeffrey B. *Dayspring in Darkness: Sacrament in Hopkins*. Lewisburg, Pa.: Bucknell University Press, 1988, pp. 72-77.

Highly theoretical assessment of the theological basis of the work. Calls the poem "a double-structured Jesuit meditation" in which the poet also argues for the efficacy of poetry to have spiritual impact upon readers. Claims the nun who speaks out in the work symbolizes the power of those imbued with the spirit of Christ to bring His message of salvation into the contemporary world. Believes Hopkins is affirming the power of words and the power of poetry to bring salvation to humankind; the poet modified his rather strident belief in the power of language in his later works.

MacKenzie, Norman H. *A Reader's Guide to Gerard Manley Hopkins*. Ithaca, N.Y.: Cornell University Press, 1981, pp. 28-59.

Brief sketch of the situation in Germany which drove the nuns to emigrate on the *Deutschland*, followed by a description of the ship's voyage that ended in disaster. Stanza-by-stanza explication, carefully explaining Hopkins' meaning as he builds his theological argument out of his analysis of the significance of the nuns' drowning. Concludes with an analysis of the poem's structural strengths and weaknesses, especially Stanzas 28-30, which have been criticized as failing to represent adequately the idea Hopkins had for the tall nun.

Mariani, Paul L. "*The Wreck of the Deutschland*: 1875-1876." In *A Commentary on the Complete Poems of Gerard Manley Hopkins*. Ithaca, N.Y.: Cornell University Press, 1970.

Believes this poem is uncharacteristic of the age in which it was written, even though it shares affinities with works by Tennyson, Robert Browning, and others. Unlike his contemporaries, Hopkins never doubts the existence of God or His plan for humankind; further, the work is intensely emotional and difficult to understand. Notes the movement of the poem from personal reflection through a description of the larger society (the shipwreck scenes) to a final prayer that all of England will finally accept God. Offers a stanza-by-stanza explication of the work, paraphrasing both the action and the argument in great detail.

Martin, R. B. "Deutschland: A Double Desperate Name." In *Gerard Manley Hopkins: A Very Private Life*. New York: G. P. Putnam's Sons, 1991.

Deals chiefly with the genesis of the poem, explaining how the nuns' exile from Germany because of their faith paralleled the poet's own story; Hopkins felt himself in exile because of his conversion. Describes the poet's efforts to publish the work, which was misunderstood by his contemporaries and ultimately rejected. Notes the highly autobiographical elements in the poem, describing how Hopkins revised the work to shift primary attention from the nuns' story to his own "spiritual desolation."

Miller, J. Hillis. *The Linguistic Moment: From Wordsworth to Stevens*. Princeton, N.J.: Princeton University Press, 1985, pp. 245-265.

Complex analysis of the poem as a web of signs and symbols displaying Hopkins' intense concern with the nature and function of language, especially as it is used by the poet. Examines the rhythmic qualities of the poem and Hopkins' reliance on repetition and variation as techniques to highlight his belief in the efficacy of language. Links Hopkins' use of language to his theological ideas, focusing on his belief in the idea of God as the Word.

Milward, Peter, S.J., ed. *Readings of The Wreck: Essays in Commemoration of Gerard Manley Hopkins's 'The Wreck of the Deutschland.'* Chicago: Loyola University Press, 1976.

Fourteen essays by distinguished Hopkins scholars focusing on the historical background of the poem; the poet's personal reaction to the tragedy which inspired the work; the religious dimensions of his argument; Hopkins' use of classical sources; and techniques developed by Hopkins in composing his masterpiece. Also includes essays on the impact of Hopkins' poems on some of his critics; provides a complete text of the poem.

Ong, Walter J., S.J. *Hopkins, the Self, and God.* Toronto: University of Toronto Press, 1986, pp. 46-53.

Places the poem in the larger context of Hopkins' development of self-consciousness through his poetry. Argues this poem exhibits "significant social and technological connections" between Hopkins and his subject. Compares the work to Milton's *Lycidas* to show how much more intimately Hopkins enters into the emotions of the drowning victims than Milton does in his elegy for his friend Edward King. Claims Hopkins makes the tall nun an elegiac heroine, but because he knows so much more about the circumstances of her drowning—a result of nineteenth century technology, through telegraph and newspaper—he is able to present a more realistic portrait of her.

Schneider, Elisabeth W. "The Dragon in the Gate." In Harold Bloom, ed. *Gerard Manley Hopkins.* Modern Critical Views. New York: Chelsea House, 1986.

Outlines how this work, now being acknowledged as one of the century's greatest, not only represents a major accomplishment for Hopkins but also introduces a new form and meter into English poetry. Reviews the two-part structure which gives the poem unity, noting how the poet's personal conversion to Catholicism (the subject of Part I) serves as prelude to the hoped-for conversion of England (the focus of Part II). Provides detailed explication of individual stanzas, explaining the theological premises on which Hopkins' poetry is constructed.

Sprinker, Michael. "The Elegiac Sublime and the Birth of the Poet: 'The Wreck of the Deutschland.'" In *"A Counterpoint of Dissonance": The Aesthetics and Poetry of Gerard Manley Hopkins.* Baltimore: Johns Hopkins University Press, 1980.

Detailed analysis of the language and rhetoric of the poem by a deconstructionist critic who argues that the central concern of the work is with the nature and limitations of the act of writing. Through this poem Hopkins gave birth to his poetic self, establishing his distinctive style. Sees the semiotic difficulties Hopkins struggles with in trying to express his ideas about the significance of the event as paralleling the central theological question which is his stated subject: an explanation of the significance of sacrifice.

Sulloway, Alison G. "'The Horror and the Havoc and the Glory of It': *The Wreck of the Deutschland* and the Calamitarian Mood." In *Gerard Manley Hopkins and the Victorian Temper.* New York: Columbia University Press, 1972.

Explains how the story of the wreck provided Hopkins with a vehicle for constructing an apocalyptic poem modeled closely on the pattern of catastrophe followed by joy found in St. John's Revelation. Provides extensive background on Hopkins' familiarity with apocalyptic literature and the attitudes of his Victorian contemporaries regarding the subject. Demonstrates how pervasive interest in apocalypse and calamity was throughout the period. Reads the poem as an expression of Hopkins' belief that an impending new age would follow the heretical period in which he lived in England. Examines the character of the nun in the poem as a type of prophet, similar to St. John in Revelation, as well as a prefigurement of Christ.

Chapter 6
GEORGE MEREDITH

General Studies

Beer, Gillian. *Meredith: A Change of Masks*. London: Athlone Press, 1970.
Study focusing primarily on the novels, with scattered references to *Modern Love*; nevertheless, offers significant assessment of Meredith's artistry, examining in detail six novels that are representative of the writer's achievement. Offers readers of Meredith's poetry insight into the writer's interests and his imagination.

Bernstein, Carol. *Precarious Enchantment: A Reading of Meredith's Poetry*. Washington, D.C.: Catholic University Press, 1979.
Systematic examination of all of Meredith's poetical works. Attempts to trace a pattern through the individual lyrics, explaining how Meredith's principal aim in his poetry is to uncover a "plot in nature"—a design and purpose in the world. Concentrates on works published originally in three volumes during the 1880's. Discusses in detail Meredith's unusual, complex style.

Harris, Wendell. "Sifting and Sorting Meredith's Poetry." In Richard A. Levine, ed. *The Victorian Experience: The Poets*. Athens: Ohio University Press, 1982.
Brief general assessment of Meredith's poetic talent. Believes he has been devalued by critics and much of his work is both technically sound and artistically pleasing. Reviews previous critical commentary; examines Meredith's "poems of earth," those which praise nature, and the sonnets in *Modern Love*. Argues these sonnets are particularly modern and exceptionally complex in exploring human feelings.

Johnson, Wendell Stacy. *Sex and Marriage in Victorian Poetry*. Ithaca, N.Y.: Cornell University Press, 1975, pp. 45-53.
Examines Meredith's poetry to show his intense concern with matters of sexuality, love, and marriage. Believes the poet deals directly and explicitly with these subjects, much more so than most of his contemporaries. Analyzes "Love in the Valley" and "A Ballad of Fair

Ladies in Revolt" in some detail; also comments on *Modern Love.* Believes Meredith is "fascinated by the intense power of sexuality" but claims he is not blind to the limitations that marriage as a legal contract can place on people who no longer share a relationship based on love.

Lucas, John. "Meredith as Poet." In Ian Fletcher, ed. *Meredith Now: Some Critical Essays.* New York: Barnes & Noble, 1971.
General assessment of Meredith's poetic corpus. Frankly acknowledges the poet's shortcomings, especially his clumsy handling of rhyme and his tendency toward didacticism. Argues that despite his faults, Meredith is often a fine poet, especially in his ballads and other narrative works. Discusses several short poems and *Modern Love* in some detail to illustrate what is best in Meredith's work.

McGhee, Richard D. "Rossetti and Meredith." In *Marriage, Duty, and Desire in Victorian Poetry and Drama.* Lawrence: University Press of Kansas, 1980.
Compares Meredith's works to those of Dante Gabriel Rossetti, claiming both poets were concerned with the problem of egoism and the need for people to escape from the prison of selfhood. Discusses *Modern Love,* citing the many ways Meredith uses irony to dramatize the futility of a marriage relationship gone bad. Also discusses several later poems in which the conflict of duty and desire is presented; notes how Meredith again uses marriage as a metaphor for suggesting the potential union of these opposites.

Muendel, Renate. *George Meredith.* Boston: Twayne, 1986.
General assessment of the writer's work, focusing on Meredith's "radically new concept of realism," which rejected familiar linear concepts in favor of a view that was "complex, shifting and paradoxical." Introductory chapter sketches Meredith's life. Succeeding chapters discuss his poetry and major fiction. Includes annotated selected bibliography of secondary sources and a chronology of significant events in the writer's life. Chapter on poetry discusses the philosophical basis of Meredith's verse and explicates several poems written both early and later in the author's career.

Stone, J. S. *George Meredith's Politics.* Port Credit, Ontario: P. D. Meany, 1986.
Study of Meredith's political ideas as they are revealed in his fiction and poetry. Argues that, like most Victorians, Meredith was intensely

interested in political issues, especially in their moral implications. The writer believed progress in politics, as in other areas, could best be achieved by slow, evolutionary processes, not radical change; he used his art to expose weaknesses of politicians and to take a stand on various political issues. Throughout the study, cites examples from the poetry to illustrate Meredith's political concerns.

Williams, Ioan. *Meredith: The Critical Heritage*. New York: Barnes & Noble, 1971.
One hundred twenty-six reviews, notices, and excerpts from publications by Meredith's contemporaries on his novels and poems. Includes four entries on *Modern Love and Other Poems* and nineteen on other volumes of Meredith's poetry. Also includes assessments of Meredith's career by Robert Louis Stevenson and George Gissing, two writers whose works may be said to have been influenced by Meredith.

Modern Love

Ball, Patricia M. "If I Be Dear to Someone Else." In *The Heart's Events: The Victorian Poetry of Relationships*. London: Athlone Press, 1976.
Discusses this sonnet sequence as an example of the Victorians' ability to turn cliché experiences (in this case, the jilted lover) into art. Claims Meredith, unlike some earlier sonneteers, sees no value to the concept of love in the abstract, but rather finds meaningful love only in individual relationships; these in turn help people establish meaning in their lives. Hence, when a relationship goes bad, the life of the jilted lover is shattered. Argues the sonnet sequence is particularly appropriate for portraying the growing dissolution of the love affairs; provides a close reading of the individual sonnets to show how Meredith works out the complex feelings the jilted lover experiences and the growing realization that there is no reason to live after love is gone.

Bernstein, Carol. *Precarious Enchantment: A Reading of Meredith's Poetry*. Washington, D.C.: Catholic University Press, 1979, pp. 9-17.
Notes the poem's special appeal to modern readers. Briefly summarizes the story told by the sequence of lyrics and analyzes narrative structure, placing the sequence in the context of similar nineteenth century long poems made up of shorter pieces. Discusses some of the major symbols. Examines in detail Meredith's exploration of the concept of self within the work; argues the poet's complex view is built

on Victorian notions that the self is often divided and difficult to comprehend.

McGhee, Richard D. In *Marriage, Duty, and Desire in Victorian Poetry and Drama*. Lawrence: University Press of Kansas, 1980, pp. 160-168.
Points out similarities between Meredith's sonnet sequence and that of Dante Gabriel Rossetti, *The House of Life*: in both, the poets deal with love and marriage. Meredith's treatment is ironic, because the poet examines the consequences of a failed marriage; Meredith's hero discovers how desires to escape the prison of selfhood are thwarted when marriage fails. Discusses the poet's persistent use of the image of the ocean; the speaker feels adrift, symbolizing his inability to find stability in his life.

Mermin, Dorothy. *The Audience in the Poem: Five Victorian Poets*. New Brunswick, N.J.: Rutgers University Press, 1983, pp. 126-144.
Discusses autobiographical genesis of the poem. Examines major images used by the poet to depict a marriage gone bad, especially the images of acting and game-playing; sees the main character moving toward self-discovery. Discusses the poet's treatment of the "fatal woman" in this and other works. Frequently compares the poetry to Meredith's novels. Discusses the function of the narrator, who helps give the work a broader perspective than the central characters provide.

Muendel, Renate. "Meredith's Poetry." In *George Meredith*. Boston: Twayne, 1986.
Extended analysis of structure and technique. Provides a brief summary of major action in the sequence, noting parallels and dissimilarities to Meredith's life. Sees Meredith dealing simultaneously with repressed feelings and "denial of change." A central concern in the sequence is the husband's gradual realization that even in love relationships, change is inevitable. Briefly discusses the function of dual narrative perspective and comments on patterns of imagery used to highlight the themes. Judges the work one of the great sonnet sequences in the English language.

Williams, Ioan. *Meredith: The Critical Heritage*. New York: Barnes & Noble, 1971.
Excerpts from four reviews which appeared in British periodicals shortly after the first edition of *Modern Love and Other Poems* was published. R. H. Hutton's and J. W. Marston's harsh commentaries are

included, as is A. C. Swinburne's response to Hutton's accusation that Meredith's poem is a series of "clever, meretricious, turgid pictures" and that the author "does not bring either original imaginative power or true sentiment to the task" of writing poetry; Swinburne believes Meredith is bold in venturing to explore subjects which make conventional Victorians uncomfortable.

Chapter 7
WILLIAM MORRIS

General Studies

Aho, Gary L. *William Morris: A Reference Guide*. Boston: G. K. Hall, 1985.
Comprehensive annotated bibliography of criticism about Morris and his works, covering the period 1897 through 1982. Organized chronologically. Includes published and unpublished works. Contains a brief introduction on the status of criticism about Morris, and a chronology.

Boos, Florence S. *The Design of William Morris's The Earthly Paradise*. Lewiston, N.Y.: Edwin Mellen Press, 1990.
Exhaustive analysis of the work Boos calls one of the longest unified poems in the language. Examines in detail dozens of the individual lyrics and narratives which make up the four-volume story. Contains appendices surveying twentieth century criticism and texts of two works not published in Morris' lifetime. Includes numerous illustrations.

Calhoun, Blue. *The Pastoral Vision of William Morris: The Earthly Paradise*. Athens: University of Georgia Press, 1975.
Extensive analysis of one of Morris' major long poems, intended as a general introduction to the study of his poetry. Explains how the poet's choice of subject, his narrative stance, and his use of the past "contribute to a unified social vision." Discusses the work in light of the pastoral tradition to which the work belongs. Also provides glosses to several other poems, including "The Defence of Guenevere."

Ellison, R. C. "'The Undying Glory of Dreams': William Morris and the 'Northland of Old.'" In Malcolm Bradbury and David Palmer, eds. *Victorian Poetry*. Stratford-on-Avon Studies 15. London: Edwin Arnold, 1972.
Examines Morris' lifelong fascination with Icelandic materials. Notes how his style as a poet, given to elaboration and exploration of characterization, influenced his ability to render the spare Norse stories into English. Nevertheless, concludes that his translations from the Icelandic and his original works based on these tales are his most significant contributions to nineteenth century letters. Includes an

extensive commentary on "The Lovers of Gudrun" and "Sigurd the Volsung."

Faulkner, Peter. *Against the Age: An Introduction to William Morris*. London: George Allen & Unwin, 1980.
Overview of Morris' life and career; organized biographically with individual chapters devoted to analysis of his poetry, prose, design work, and socialist activities. Intended for the general reader. Brief comments on dozens of Morris' poems scattered throughout the text.

_____, ed. *William Morris: The Critical Heritage*. Boston: Routledge & Kegan Paul, 1973.
Eighty-four excerpts from reviews and articles by Morris' contemporaries commenting on each of the writer's major volumes of poetry, prose, and translations. Includes assessments by distinguished men of letters such as John Ruskin, Tennyson, Robert Browning, Dante Gabriel Rossetti, Swinburne, Hopkins, Henry James, and Oscar Wilde; also contains commentary by critics such as Walter Pater, Sidney Colvin, Theodore Watts, and A. T. Quiller-Couch.

Fletcher, Pauline. "Morris: The Field Full of Folk." In *Gardens and Grim Ravines: The Language of Landscape in Victorian Poetry*. Princeton, N.J.: Princeton University Press, 1983.
Sees Morris using landscapes in his poetry not merely to further a seemingly escapist philosophy; even in poems set in medieval times, Morris employs natural setting to highlight social issues. Discusses in some detail the poet's use of the enclosed garden as a setting for several of his more important works. Finds that such gardens have ambiguous value for Morris; they are not merely places of innocence. Brief commentary on almost twenty of Morris' poems, including *Sigurd the Volsung*, to demonstrate his particular use of idyllic landscape and his aversion for the untamed character of many natural settings.

Gent, Margaret. "'To Flinch from Modern Varnish': The Appeal of the Past to the Victorian Imagination." In Malcolm Bradbury and David Palmer, eds. *Victorian Poetry*. Stratford-on-Avon Studies 15. London: Edwin Arnold, 1972.
Uses the works of Morris to illustrate ways Victorian writers of imaginative literature made use of the past as subjects for their works and as a means of commenting on both contemporary and universal issues. Extensive analysis of *The Earthly Paradise* and of poems in *The Defence of Guenevere* volume; special attention given to "The

Haystack in the Floods" and "Concerning Geoffrey Teste Noire." Compares Morris' treatment of death and immortality with that of contemporaries such as Dickens, Robert Browning, and the Pre-Raphaelites.

Hodgson, Amanda. *The Romances of William Morris.* Cambridge, England: Cambridge University Press, 1987.
Extended analysis of Morris' romances, offering a serious and systematic assessment of their literary value. An introductory chapter provides a definition of romance, outlines the Victorians' fascination with the form, and describes Morris' gradual acceptance of this genre; notes the tension the poet felt between "the concept of art as escapist and the belief in art as an incentive to practical commitment." Separate chapters investigate the early romances, *The Earthly Paradise*, *Sigurd the Volsung*, the political poems, and Morris' later works.

Latham, David, and Sheila Latham. *An Annotated Critical Bibliography of William Morris.* New York: St. Martin's Press, 1991.
Brief annotations provided for both primary and secondary materials by and about Morris and his works. Covers the period 1854 through 1990. Includes entries for all of Morris' volumes of poetry and prose works. Entries for secondary sources are selective; commentaries on twentieth century works are predominant. Also includes information about Morris' wife.

Lindsay, Jack. *William Morris: His Life and Work.* New York: Taplinger, 1975.
Comprehensive biography that tries to do justice to a man who excelled as a poet and prose writer, socialist reformer, artisan, and patron of the arts. Examines Morris' formative years and his many friendships, as well as his unusual relationship with his wife and the wife of Edward Burne-Jones. Includes extensive notes and bibliography.

Marshall, Roderick. *William Morris and His Earthly Paradise.* Tisbury, England: Compton Press, 1979.
Biography written by a scholar steeped in Jungian psychology; focuses on the development of Morris' personality. Relies heavily on Morris' creative writings as well as his critical works to form an estimate of the man. Argues the guiding principle behind all of Morris' endeavors was to create an "earthly paradise," a place of happiness on earth; producing works of art allowed Morris to escape the miseries of life he found continually surrounding him.

Oberg, Charlotte H. *A Pagan Prophet: William Morris.* Charlottesville: University Press of Virginia, 1978.
Looks for the elements which unify Morris' poetry and prose writings. Three chapters examine *The Earthly Paradise*; two discuss Morris' attempts at the epic, focusing on *The Life and Death of Jason* and *Sigurd the Volsung*; three provide an assessment of his prose and later works. Contains numerous illustrations of painting, furniture, tapestry, and other furnishings by Morris and others associated with the Pre-Raphaelite Brotherhood.

Silver, Carole, ed. *The Golden Chain: Essays on William Morris and Pre-Raphaelitism.* New York: William Morris Society, 1982.
Collection of five essays examining Morris' relationship with his contemporaries among the Pre-Raphaelites, his sources, his influence on succeeding writers, and his psychological and aesthetic development. Two essayists look carefully at the poet's early romances; one discusses similarities between Morris' work and the philosophy of Søren Kierkegaard; a fourth reviews his relationship with Dante Gabriel Rossetti; the final essayist explores the Pre-Raphaelites' understanding of dream theory and their use of dreams in literary works.

_____. *The Romance of William Morris.* Athens: Ohio University Press, 1982.
Traces Morris' intellectual development as it is exhibited in the literary works he produced; argues these are the best source for understanding his progress from a Romantic to an epic or heroic conception of life. Throughout, explains how Morris integrated romance and realism in his writings. Generally biographical in approaching the works; comments on numerous poems included in the discussion of Morris' ideas and attitudes. Exceptionally useful bibliography.

Stevenson, Lionel. "William Morris." In *The Pre-Raphaelite Poets.* Chapel Hill: University of North Carolina Press, 1972.
Outlines Morris' life and his relationships with members of the Pre-Raphaelite Brotherhood, especially Edward Burne-Jones. Notes how Morris' financial stability allowed him to engage in various schemes for social improvement. Traces the influence of medieval literature, especially the work of Sir Thomas Malory, on all of Morris' works. Discusses individual poems in Morris' *The Defence of Guenevere* volume, his long poem on the classical hero Jason, those in the collection he titled *The Earthly Paradise*, his medieval imitation *Love*

Is Enough, and his saga *Sigurd the Volsung*. Offers a concluding assessment of the value of his poetry.

Thesing, William B. "Noel and Morris: From Observation to Revolution." In *The London Muse: Victorian Poetic Responses to the City*. Athens: University of Georgia Press, 1982.
Compares works by Morris with those of Roden Noel, a contemporary who, like Morris, was born an aristocrat but whose sympathies lay with the working classes. Traces Morris' growing belief that the only hope for society was the overthrow of the present system and its replacement with a worker-controlled political and economic system. Demonstrates how much of his poetry promotes these political themes. Extensive analysis of *The Pilgrim of Hope*, which is "unique in Morris's poetic canon for its realistic descriptions of city employment, city crowds, and early socialist meetings."

Thompson, E. P. *William Morris: Romantic to Revolutionary*. Rev. ed. New York: Pantheon Books, 1977.
Comprehensive study of Morris' life and works, focusing on his attempts to introduce radical reform into later Victorian society. Concentrates on his writings as a source for understanding the background to his position and for forming a judgment on the effectiveness of his programs. Sees Morris as an inheritor of Romantic idealism. Relies heavily on unpublished sources and on Morris' contributions to the periodical *Commonweal*.

Thompson, Paul. *The Work of William Morris*. New York: Viking Press, 1977.
Study intended to provide an extensive introduction to Morris' principal achievements and to reconsider his status as an artist of the Victorian period. Begins with a chapter summarizing major biographical information; follows with individual chapters on Morris' contributions in architecture, furniture and furnishings, textiles, stained glass, and book design. Devotes a chapter to assessing his accomplishments as a writer and another to reviewing his contributions to British politics. Includes numerous illustrations of Morris' works.

Tompkins, J. M. S. *William Morris: An Approach to the Poetry*. London: Cecil Woolf, 1988.
Major study of Morris' poetic works by a critic who spent twenty years compiling data on the background to these writings. Offers highly biographical interpretation of the poetry, arguing that it "grows com-

pulsively" from Morris' "private imaginative life." Aims to fill in gaps
for contemporary readers who may fail to understand the value of these
poems to Morris himself. Devotes individual chapters to analysis of
the major volumes of Morris' poetry; also examines several of his
unpublished works.

The Defence of Guenevere

Boos, Florence. "Justice and Vindication in William Morris's 'The Defence of Guenevere.'" In Valerie M. Lagorio and Mildred Leake Day,
eds. *King Arthur Through the Ages*. Vol. 2. New York: Garland, 1990.
Argues forcefully that Morris' heroine is essentially guiltless in her
relationship with Lancelot; through her the poet is exploring the consequences of repression in the female psyche. Reviews earlier criticism
to extract important commentary which has shaped opinion about the
work. Provides careful textual analysis to support the argument that
Morris intends to show Guenevere not as deceptive or disingenuous
but rather as a strong spokesperson for her own moral point of view.

Calhoun, Blue. *The Pastoral Vision of William Morris: The Earthly
Paradise*. Athens: University of Georgia Press, 1975, pp. 41-47.
Sees the poem as one of several in which Morris examines the "destructive disparity" of "innocence and experience." Guenevere is thrust
into the role of victim, defending herself and her values against a hostile
society. In the process of presenting her defense, she wins over the
reader's sympathy. Discusses Morris' use of natural imagery as a
means of associating Guenevere with Edenic innocence.

Mermin, Dorothy. *The Audience in the Poem: Five Victorian Poets*. New
Brunswick, N.J.: Rutgers University Press, 1983, pp. 152-154.
Links this work to a tradition among Victorian poets: poems with
auditors present in the text and influencing both the action in the work
and the reader's perception and judgment of the main character. Claims
Guenevere, an example of the Pre-Raphaelite's version of the fatal
woman, is constantly aware of her immediate audience, and attempts
to hold them at bay by presenting herself as an object for admiration.
She lacks sincerity and perverts language until it cannot be trusted to
represent truth.

Silver, Carole. *The Romance of William Morris*. Athens: Ohio University
Press, 1982, pp. 18-25.

Discusses in some detail the moral complexity of the poem. Focuses on the character of Guenevere, whose speech both reveals her guilt and provides a strong justification for her illicit affair with Launcelot. From the first lines, the poem is morally ambiguous. Morris sees the Queen as both an image of beauty and a "fatal woman," loved by all but destined to "destroy herself and those who adore her." Suggests the poet intends this poem to be paired with "King Arthur's Tomb"; together they offer a fully developed portrait of Guenevere.

Tompkins, J. M. S. *William Morris: An Approach to the Poetry.* London: Cecil Woolf, 1988, pp. 52-55.
Detailed analysis of the chief source for Morris' conception of both character and situation in the poem: Sir Thomas Malory's *Le Morte D'Arthur.* Explains how incidents in Malory serve to give depth to phrases Morris places in the mouth of his queen. Notes this is the first dramatic poem Morris wrote; points out his debt to Robert Browning, citing parallels between this work and Browning's "The Statue and the Bust."

The Story of Sigurd the Volsung

Faulkner, Peter. *Against the Age: An Introduction to William Morris.* London: George Allen & Unwin, 1980, pp. 78-83.
Praises this work as Morris' greatest among his many translations and adaptations of Icelandic texts. Mentions some of the modifications Morris undertook to make the poem more acceptable to Victorian readers. Provides lengthy summary, quoting liberally from the text. Acknowledges the diffuseness of the work, but claims it is effective when read aloud. Cites Morris' reaction to the lukewarm reception of the poem by his contemporaries.

Goode, John. "William Morris and the Dream of Revolution." In John Lucas, ed. *Literature and Politics in the Nineteenth Century.* London: Methuen, 1971, pp. 239-246.
Discusses the work as one of several examples of Morris' political writings in which he asserts the importance of dreams and visions in shaping social action. Claims that, beneath the archaic and sometimes inept language of the work, Morris is exploring the implications of the individual's alienation from society. Carefully reviews the action of the poem to show how Sigurd is gradually isolated from the various groups with whom he is initially identified.

Hodgson, Amanda. "'The dawn that waketh the dead': *Sigurd the Volsung*." In *The Romances of William Morris*. Cambridge, England: Cambridge University Press, 1987.

Extensive review of the Victorians' knowledge of Icelandic stories and of new developments in philology which caused Morris to become excited about this tale. Sees the work as the first in which the poet is optimistic about humankind's fate: Sigurd's death is not an ending but a promise of hope, since he has acted heroically. Discusses the poet's use of repeated imagery (especially wolves and gold) to depict the unending battle between the forces of good and evil in the world.

Oberg, Charlotte H. *A Pagan Prophet: William Morris*. Charlottesville, Va: University Press of Virginia, 1978, pp. 86-93.

Briefly compares the poem to Morris' other epic, *The Life and Death of Jason*. Points out the poet's fascination with the Norse story because of its depiction of a fallen world; the poem has apocalyptic qualities. Analyzes the character of Sigurd as a hero fated to die; discusses his acceptance of destiny. Calls Sigurd a "prophet" and a "great leveler" who has concern for the downtrodden and who serves as a model for those living in difficult times.

Silver, Carole. *The Romance of William Morris*. Athens: Ohio University Press, 1982, pp. 111-119.

Claims the poem "transcends its sources" to become an original work. Carefully delineates Morris' alterations of the Norse saga, pointing out emendations to plot, structure, characterization, and theme; argues he makes moral distinctions more clear than they are in the original. Stresses the poet's "unification and repatterning" of materials from the source. Notes the influence on the work of philologists, especially Max Müller. Shows how Sigurd is an admirable hero who faces his destiny calmly; the work shows the poet's own growing acceptance of death and a growing sense that heroism consists of doing well while on earth.

Thompson, E. P. *William Morris: Romantic to Revolutionary*. Rev. ed. New York: Pantheon Books, 1977, pp. 188-192.

Brief discussion of Morris' introduction of Icelandic literature to the British reading public. Discusses the freedoms he took in translating the legend of Sigurd into English verse. Comments on ways Morris makes the Icelandic poem a modern Romantic work; though Morris does not finally succeed in giving the poem the feel of an epic, he does imbue it with heroic qualities admired by his contemporaries.

Thompson, Paul. *The Work of William Morris*. New York: Viking Press, 1977.

Considers the poem the greatest of Morris' poetic accomplishments. Discusses his poetic techniques in rendering this Norse folk legend into a Victorian epic poem. Acknowledges the work's deficiencies, including the weak concluding section. Quotes liberally from the text to illustrate points about poetic style and to show how Morris extends the narrative of the original saga.

Tompkins, J. M. S. "*Sigurd the Volsung*." In *William Morris: An Approach to the Poetry*. London: Cecil Woolf, 1988.

Chapter exploring the genesis of this long poem, detailing Morris' fascination with the Icelandic saga and concentrating on his reshaping of the original story to emphasize its mythic qualities. Also examines the character of Odin in the poem and the function of the creation myth. Focuses attention on Morris' development of his hero, who becomes for the poet "the herald of a better world on earth"; notes Christian imagery and biblical allusions used throughout. Explains the loose-knit construction of the poem, offering a thematic explanation for the introduction of the opening and closing books, which extend the legend beyond the specific tales of Sigurd's adventures.

Chapter 8
COVENTRY PATMORE

General Studies

Johnson, Wendell Stacy. *Sex and Marriage in Victorian Poetry*. Ithaca, N.Y.: Cornell University Press, 1975, pp. 74-79.

Briefly discusses Patmore's view of love and marriage. Argues the poet believed marriage was essentially sacramental in nature, and its physical component, which he did not deny, was subordinate to its spiritual quality. Reviews *The Angel in the House* and other works in which Patmore dramatizes his beliefs. Notes how thoroughly conventional Patmore was in his conviction that women should be subservient to men in marriage.

Oliver, E. J. *Coventry Patmore*. New York: Sheed & Ward, 1956.

A sympathetic treatment of the poet's life and character, aimed at explaining the many apparent contradictions earlier critics had noted in Patmore's life. Discusses the poet's relationship with the three women who were, successively, his wives; notes how each influenced certain poems. Includes a chapter on *The Angel in the House*.

Shaw, W. David. *The Lucid Veil: Poetic Truth in the Victorian Age*. Madison: University of Wisconsin Press, 1987, pp. 71-73, 179-180.

Commentary in two separate essays using Patmore's works to illustrate points about Victorian poets' ways of vivifying systems of knowledge. In the first, Patmore's lyric "Departure" is used to show how John Keble's theological ideas which "subordinate art to doctrine" are adopted by poets. In the second, Patmore is cited as a writer whose works illustrate the contemplative imagination. Several of the poet's lyrics are mentioned as examples of works offering reflections on religious subjects.

The Angel in the House

Hughes, Linda K., and Michael Lund. *The Victorian Serial*. Charlottesville: University Press of Virginia, 1991, pp. 18-29.

Focuses on the way serial publication affected the production and reception of the first edition of this poem, as Patmore brought it out over six years. Cites several contemporary reviews to show how favorably the first sections of Patmore's love story were received by the British reading public. Claims the theme of the work is the growth of true love over time; the serial publication reinforced this theme to the poem's first readers. Also discusses Patmore's unusual attitude toward love; the poet promotes the idea that as married couples grow older, their love grows stronger.

Oliver, E. J. "Verse at Home." In *Coventry Patmore*. New York: Sheed & Ward, 1956.
General discussion of the merits of the poem, with an honest assessment of its weaknesses, especially the verse form. Compares Patmore with several other poets, especially Byron, Tennyson, and Swinburne. Examines the poet's view of marriage and amorous relationships. Points out ways the poem is a tribute to Patmore's first wife.

Praz, Mario. "The Epic of the Everyday: 'The Angel in the House.'" In Harold Bloom, ed. *Pre-Raphaelite Poets*. Modern Critical Views. New York: Chelsea House, 1986.
Argues critics have not fully understood Patmore's debt to the Metaphysical poets in his development of the story and imagery in the poem. Discusses his reliance on Wordsworth and his conscious decision to appeal to the popular audience with a subject well received by readers in the nineteenth century: domestic, married love. Examines the influence of seventeenth century poets, both Cavalier and religious, on Patmore's work. Also points out parallels between Patmore's approach to his subject and that of numerous Victorian contemporaries.

Schulz, Max F. "Mid-Victorian London and the Angel in the House." In *Paradise Preserved: Recreations of Eden in Eighteenth- and Nineteenth-Century England*. Cambridge, England: Cambridge University Press, 1985.
Discusses Patmore's poem in the context of mid-Victorian works written to idealize women. Compares it with Tennyson's *The Princess*; judges the latter more directly concerned with feminist issues. Examines Pater's idealization of married love, noting the heavy religious overtones of his presentation; concludes that the poet defines human love as "an unlost part of paradise available to every man and woman." Pater sees a wife as a "ministering angel" who helps a man survive the rigors of the working world.

Chapter 9
CHRISTINA ROSSETTI

General Studies

Battiscombe, Georgina. *Christina Rossetti: A Divided Life*. New York: Holt, Rinehart and Winston, 1981.
Biography centering on the personal crises in Rossetti's life. Traces the development of her poetry, especially her religious work, to its roots in these crises and in a constant internal struggle she felt between competing psychological and cultural forces impinging on her personality. Details her relationships with her brothers and with other members of the Pre-Raphaelite Brotherhood. Includes a chapter on her *Goblin Market* volume, a selected bibliography, and numerous illustrations.

Buckley, Jerome H. "Pre-Raphaelite Past and Present: The Poetry of the Rossettis." In Malcolm Bradbury and David Palmer, eds. *Victorian Poetry*. Stratford-on-Avon Studies 15. London: Edwin Arnold, 1972.
Claims the Pre-Raphaelites are often described as introducing the passion for medieval subjects in Victorian society. Finds the three Rossettis most greatly affected by the Brotherhood's efforts to contrast the past with the present. Does not see Christina using medieval materials explicitly in her poetry, but does note that she "eschewed almost completely current events and contemporary allusions" in favor of more timeless subjects and references.

Charles, Edna Kotin. *Christina Rossetti: Critical Perspectives, 1862-1982*. Cranbury, N.J.: Associated University Presses, 1985.
Bibliographical essay summarizing the critical reception of Rossetti's work by her contemporaries and the continuing examination of her poetry by scholars of the twentieth century. Divides the study into three major phases: the first, covering the years 1862-1899, focuses on contemporary reaction to the poet's volumes as they appeared before the Victorian reading public; the second discusses scholarship published between 1900 and 1930, when Rossetti, like Elizabeth Barrett Browning, was praised as a fine woman poet; the final section, covering 1940-1982, summarizes works heavily influenced by psychological criticism and feminist ideology. Also includes a brief biographical sketch in the introduction.

Harrison, Antony. *Christina Rossetti in Context*. Chapel Hill: University of North Carolina Press, 1988.
Extended analysis of Rossetti's work, focusing on the poet's constant struggle to express the tension she felt between the aesthetic and ascetic impulses that dominated not only her own life but the consciousness of most Victorians as well. Examines the reception of Rossetti's poetry by her contemporaries, connections between her work and the writings by the Tractarians and by John Ruskin, and her reliance on the Neoplatonic tradition exemplified most vividly in the work of Petrarch and Dante. Concludes Rossetti turns her back on the everyday world not because she found it sordid but because the real world could not satisfy the higher desires Rossetti felt.

Hickok, Kathleen. "Christina Rossetti." In *Representations of Women: Nineteenth-Century British Women's Poetry*. Westport, Conn.: Greenwood Press, 1984.
Discusses ways Rossetti depicts women in her poetry. Notes how she frequently focuses on their relationships with other women, rather than with men. Explicates numerous poems to show how Rossetti portrayed women in various conventional roles: sister, wife, daughter, mother. Most are seen as happy with the status assigned to them by a male-dominated society. Believes Rossetti did on occasion dare to deal frankly with subjects that displayed the oppression inflicted on women by society.

McGann, Jerome. "The Poetry of Christina Rossetti." In Harold Bloom, ed. *Pre-Raphaelite Poets*. Modern Critical Views. New York: Chelsea House, 1986.
Two-part essay examining the religious background and the social and symbolic dimensions of Rossetti's work. Explains how the poet's belief in the Adventist Theory of Soul Sleep provides a key to understanding many of her lyrics, even some not considered overtly religious. Describes her enduring concern for the single woman, especially one spurned in love. Examines in detail several poems, including "Goblin Market," to illustrate ways Rossetti gives her work a moral dimension.

Packer, Lona Mosk. *Christina Rossetti*. Berkeley: University of California Press, 1963.
Extensive, detailed biography, examining Rossetti's life and relationships with her artistic family, members of the Pre-Raphaelite Brotherhood, and the men who courted her or with whom she was deeply in

love. Suggests the poet's strong religious convictions and reclusive lifestyle were reactions to these interpersonal relationships. Speculates about Rossetti's relationship with William Bell Scott, an artist and married man, whom Packer believes influenced much of the poet's amorous composition. Integrates discussion of the poetry into the life study. Illustrated.

Rosenblum, Dolores. "Christina Rossetti: The Inward Pose." In Sandra M. Gilbert and Susan Gubar, eds. *Shakespeare's Sisters: Feminist Essays on Women Poets*. Bloomington: Indiana University Press, 1979. Discusses Rossetti's lifelong concern with the problem of inner reality versus outward appearance in people. Explains how both structure and imagery in her poetry reveal that obsession. Examines her fascination with the various ways people mask their inner selves from the world. Looks at more than a dozen poems as illustrations of the poet's preoccupation with the issue. Believes Rossetti found it better for the woman artist to stifle impulses to express her desires openly in favor of working subversively through her art to achieve personal ends. Only through "vigilance and stoic endurance" could women gain self-possession and realize individual fulfillment.

_____.. *Christina Rossetti: The Poetry of Endurance*. Carbondale: Southern Illinois University Press, 1986. Reclaims Rossetti from traditional judgments which consider her a minor poet; close textual reading of several poems shows how Rossetti uses "stylized gestures or renunciation" as a means of protesting her status as an object in a man's world. Individual chapters provide biographical background, analyze *Goblin Market* and some of Rossetti's devotional poetry, examine the poet's central metaphors, and review her portrayal of women in various roles. Compares her work to that of her male contemporaries, especially Algernon Charles Swinburne.

Shaw, W. David. *The Lucid Veil: Poetic Truth in the Victorian Age*. Madison: University of Wisconsin Press, 1987, pp. 196-198, 253-255. Two brief discussions of Rossetti's poetry interwoven into larger essays within a collection focusing on Victorian poets' attitudes toward language and knowledge. Both excerpts focus on Rossetti's religious poetry and trace her debt to theologians John Keble and E. S. Dallas. Explains how Rossetti's poetry displays great empathy with the natural world, through contemplation of which she is able to see types of the divine.

Stevenson, Lionel. "Christina Rossetti." In *The Pre-Raphaelite Poets.*
Chapel Hill: University of North Carolina Press, 1972.
Largely biographical examination of Rossetti's development as a poet.
Looks briefly at numerous works, providing commentary on their
technical qualities. Debunks earlier theories that suggest almost all of
Rossetti's poetry was inspired by her illicit love for William Bell Scott.
Notes her borrowings from literary sources; also examines the devo-
tional qualities of much of her output. Considers her the most lyrical
but least intellectual of Victorian poets. Believes she is deserving of
greater recognition than she has received.

Goblin Market

Battiscombe, Georgina. *"Goblin Market."* In *Christina Rossetti: A Divided Life.* New York: Holt, Rinehart and Winston, 1981.
Sees a close relationship between this poem and others in the volume
in which it first appeared. Acknowledges the sexual overtones of the
work and reviews the interpretations of other critics who emphasize
this reading. Suggests the poem can also be read as a further example
of Rossetti's concern for religious issues. Laura, like Eve in the Garden
of Eden, falls victim to temptation but is saved by the self-sacrificing
actions of her sister Lizzie.

Charles, Edna Kotin. *Christina Rossetti: Critical Perspectives, 1862-
1982.* Cranbury, N.J.: Associated University Presses, 1985.
Includes numerous references to the poem in a volume assessing the
critical reception of Rossetti's works by both nineteenth and twentieth
century readers. Offers abbreviated summaries by Victorian reviewers
responding to the poem upon its appearance at mid-century. Cites
judgments of several early twentieth century critics. Devotes more
attention to the analyses by scholars of the 1960's through the 1980's,
including work by Lona Mosk Packer and C. M. Bowra and feminist
critics such as Cora Kaplan, Sandra Gilbert, and Susan Gubar.

Gilbert, Sandra M., and Susan Gubar. *The Mad Woman in the Attic: The
Woman Writer and the Nineteenth Century Literary Imagination.* New
Haven, Conn.: Yale University Press, 1979, pp. 564-575.
Argues Rossetti places high value on renunciation as a noble virtue for
women. Acknowledges the overtly sexual implications of this poem,
but suggests it has other levels of meaning "about and for women in
particular." Embedded in the work is an element of female sensuality

which patriarchal society finds unnatural and disturbing. The imagery of the poem also suggests that Rossetti intends the work to symbolize the quest of the female artist to speak out plainly about women's sexuality, but ultimately the quest is abandoned, even renounced, in favor of more conventional roles for women.

Hickok, Kathleen. *Representations of Women: Nineteenth-Century British Women's Poetry*. Westport, Conn.: Greenwood Press, 1984, pp. 207-210.
Close reading of the poem to reveal how Rossetti portrays the three women who represent types common to Victorian literature. Discusses the overtly sexual nature of the work, in which the imagery of the fruits has sexual overtones. Argues the unselfish and courageous actions of one sister who faces up to the goblins (symbols of masculinity) provides a way for the fallen sister to be saved. Notes that, although Rossetti does not usually treat feminist issues in her work, in this poem she is able "both to sympathize and to identify with her fallen sisters."

Moers, Ellen. *Literary Women*. Garden City, N.Y.: Doubleday, 1976, pp. 100-107.
Discusses the poem in the context of other Gothic works by women writers, especially Emily Brontë's *Wuthering Heights*. Recites the plot, highlighting ways Rossetti plays up the horrific aspects of the work. Notes the importance of brother-sister relationships in the poem; suggests that, beneath the surface, the poet is dealing with fantasies which emerge from the Victorian nursery, where many young women, including Rossetti, came in contact with members of the opposite sex—who often treated them roughly.

Packer, Lona Mosk. *Christina Rossetti*. Berkeley: University of California Press, 1963, pp. 140-151.
Offers a biographical reading of the poem. Outlines the plot and explains the significance of central images such as the fruit, the goblins, and the fire. Acknowledges the poem is about temptation and its effects; in it, Rossetti clearly delineates two kinds of love, one acceptable, one destructive. Argues the work springs from the poet's broken love affair with William Bell Scott, a married man; speculates from evidence in Rossetti's work and comments by Scott and others that their affair, never made public, caused the poet to transform her feelings for Scott into this fairy story.

Rosenblum, Dolores. "*Goblin Market*: Dearth and Sufficiency." In *Christina Rossetti: The Poetry of Endurance*. Carbondale: Southern Illinois University Press, 1986.
Considers the poem a "subversive fantasy"; beneath the fairy-tale story of the surface narrative, Rossetti explores the problem of woman's ability to fulfill her desires in a patriarchal society. The poem offers insight into "what constitutes a female community." Provides careful textual explication and analysis to illustrate how Rossetti uses language, especially imagery, to create the mythic quality of her tale. Relates the work to several others in the poet's canon, especially her devotional poetry.

Chapter 10
DANTE GABRIEL ROSSETTI

General Studies

Buckley, Jerome H. "Pre-Raphaelite Past and Present: The Poetry of the Rossettis." In Malcolm Bradbury and David Palmer, eds. *Victorian Poetry*. Stratford-on-Avon Studies 15. London: Edwin Arnold, 1972. Claims all three Rossettis struggled in their artistic lives to resolve tensions between past and present. Surveys Dante Gabriel Rossetti's works to show how little attention he paid to contemporary issues; even in topical works like "Jenny" he widens his focus to include more timeless concerns. His most constant aim is to "distance the subjective emotion" so he can explore his real subjects without the confusion generated by contemporary trappings.

Cooper, Robert M. *Lost on Both Sides: Dante Gabriel Rossetti, Critic and Poet*. Athens: Ohio University Press, 1970. Examines Rossetti's writings to show the development of his critical theory. While acknowledging the paucity of evidence in the writer's nonpoetical works, Cooper reconstructs Rossetti's attitude toward poetry and shows how his own poems exhibit qualities Rossetti valued and how his theory shaped the creation of his oeuvre. Claims that, despite the brilliance of many of his individual poems, Rossetti failed to live up to his potential as a poet.

Doughty, Oswald. "Rossetti's Conception of the 'Poetic' in Poetry and Painting." In James Sambrook, ed. *Pre-Raphaelitism: A Collection of Critical Essays*. Chicago: University of Chicago Press, 1974. Discusses Rossetti's tendency to view the world as a poet rather than as a painter, translating visual imagery into words rather than into pictures on canvas. Examines the principal motivations for the poet's genius, finding Rossetti intensely interested in beautiful impressions which strike the senses. Sees his attraction to sensual love as an outgrowth of his interest in Platonism.

Fennell, Francis L. *Dante Gabriel Rossetti: An Annotated Bibliography*. New York: Garland, 1982. Contains nearly twelve hundred entries, almost all annotated; includes notation on bibliographies, editions of the writer's work, letters, biographical studies, and criticism of Rossetti's writings and paintings. Also provides a list of dissertations on Rossetti, a brief chronology, and a topical index.

Fletcher, Pauline. "Rossetti: The Embowered Consciousness." In *Gardens and Grim Ravines: The Language of Landscape in Victorian Poetry*. Princeton, N.J.: Princeton University Press, 1983.
Claims that in his best work Rossetti is a "subjective poet" for whom the best landscapes are places of "refuge and retreat." Provides brief analysis of the Pre-Raphaelites' use of landscape in painting and explains how, especially in poems written as companion pieces to his paintings, Rossetti uses landscape imagery to create moods and reflect character traits. Argues the use of "bleak, open spaces to convey loss or alienation" is peculiar to Rossetti's poetry and is absent from his painting.

Gelpi, Barbara Charlesworth. "The Feminization of Dante Gabriel Rossetti." In Richard A. Levine, ed. *The Victorian Experience: The Poets*. Athens: Ohio University Press, 1982.
Discusses ways Rossetti was heavily influenced by women in his life, beginning with the strong influence of his mother. Believes his close association with women allowed him to enter into the feminine consciousness in his writings; it also caused a psychological tension which informs all of his art, because he recognized his dependence on women while simultaneously resenting the power they had over him.

Hollander, John. "Human Music." In Harold Bloom, ed. *Pre-Raphaelite Poets*. Modern Critical Views. New York: Chelsea House, 1986.
Brief but insightful analysis of Rossetti's imagery, attempting to show how the poet has been underrated by twentieth century critics. Discusses his attachment to great art and its impact on his poetry. Shows how natural scenes had significant influence on him as well, especially the sounds he heard in natural settings. Notes Rossetti's close affinities to Romantic poets, whose imagery he clearly parallels.

Howard, Ronnalie Roper. *The Dark Glass: Vision and Technique in the Poetry of Dante Gabriel Rossetti*. Athens: Ohio University Press, 1972.
Systematic chronological study of selected poems, attempting to arrive inductively at the source of Rossetti's strengths as a poet; consciously promotes this approach as a corrective to earlier biographical studies. Pays special attention to the themes and techniques of individual

poems and the relationship of poems written during the various stages of Rossetti's life. Includes a useful annotated bibliography of earlier criticism.

Johnson, Wendell Stacy. "Dante Gabriel Rossetti as Painter and Poet." In James Sambrook, ed. *Pre-Raphaelitism: A Collection of Critical Essays*. Chicago: University of Chicago Press, 1974.
Traces the many similarities in subject matter and technique between Rossetti's poems and paintings. Explores his fascination for women as subjects, especially the extremes of virgin and prostitute; also discusses patterns of imagery common to productions in both genres. Careful analysis of several paintings and poems with similar subjects to illustrate the close relationship of these arts for Rossetti and his contemporaries.

_____. *Sex and Marriage in Victorian Poetry*. Ithaca, N.Y.: Cornell University Press, 1975, pp. 86-90.
Brief assessment of Rossetti's attitude toward sexual love and marriage. Believes Rossetti is one of the most extreme of all Victorian poets, alternatively presenting sexual relationships as wholly spiritual or completely sensual. Such portraits make conventional marriages impossible. In much of his poetry, sexual love and "true marriages" can be realized "only in death, only in heaven." His treatment of women and sexual relationships is reminiscent of the courtly love tradition.

Johnston, Robert D. *Dante Gabriel Rossetti*. New York: Twayne, 1969.
General study of Rossetti's poetry and his art, attempting to fill in gaps of previous biographical and literary studies which gave short shrift to the writer's thematic development. Offers chronological survey of his growth as a poet and theorist, concentrating attention on *The House of Life* in two central chapters. Includes chronology and annotated bibliography of selected criticism.

McGann, Jerome. "Rossetti's Significant Details." In James Sambrook, ed. *Pre-Raphaelitism: A Collection of Critical Essays*. Chicago: University of Chicago Press, 1974.
Takes issue with critics who claim Rossetti's poetry is muddled and vague. Traces the poet's use of imagery in several important poems, including "My Sister's Sleep" and "The Blessed Damozel," to show how Rossetti uses Christian images in a new way, demythologizing them so they become emblematic of sensual rather than religious love. Argues the poet is clear in his celebration of Eros; even if critics find

his position on sensual love uncomfortable, he cannot be accused of writing vaguely about his topic.

McGhee, Richard D. "Rossetti and Meredith." In *Marriage, Duty, and Desire in Victorian Poetry and Drama.* Lawrence: University Press of Kansas, 1980.
Brief comparison of Rossetti with George Meredith, both of whom dealt with the problem of egoism in their works; believes Rossetti's poetry shows his constant struggle to fulfill his public duties by reconciling them with his private desire to "escape from the prison of his own self-consciousness." Briefly sketches the poet's life as a member of a family in exile and the effect of that situation on his work. Examines more than a dozen poems to illustrate the central theme. Concludes with an analysis of *The House of Life.*

Richardson, James. *Vanishing Lives: Style and Self in Tennyson, Dante Gabriel Rossetti, Swinburne, and Yeats.* Charlottesville: University Press of Virginia, 1988.
Careful analysis of syntax, imagery, sentence structure, and rhyme schemes in several of Rossetti's lyrics, focusing on sonnets in *The House of Life* sequence. Demonstrates how the poet's attention to the details of his writing is his way of constructing works of intense, momentary experience which mirror "the shadowiness of life." Explains many of Rossetti's idiosyncrasies as efforts to portray an intensity of experience.

Riede, David G. *Dante Gabriel Rossetti and the Limits of Victorian Vision.* Ithaca, N.Y.: Cornell University Press, 1983.
Study of Rossetti's development as a poet and painter; aims at debunking the idea that Rossetti had fully developed his ideology and artistic powers at an early age. Examines the poet's work chronologically to show how he moved progressively through periods of religious symbolism and skepticism to his final belief in the ennobling value of sexual love. Also discusses his attempts to unify the sister arts of painting and poetry.

Sonstroem, David. *Rossetti and the Fair Lady.* Middletown, Conn.: Wesleyan University Press, 1970.
Assessment of a single theme running through all of Rossetti's work: the poet's fascination with "the fair lady" as she appears in various guises in his poetry. Systematically categorizes poems according to four major recurring images: the blessed damsel or virgin (the Lady as

savior); the femme fatale; the fallen woman; and the woman wronged. Sonstroem describes his study as "a biography of a fantasy" and focuses throughout on ways Rossetti's fascination with the figure of woman influenced all of his artistic endeavors.

Stein, Richard L. "Dante Gabriel Rossetti." In *The Ritual of Interpreta-tion: The Fine Arts as Literature in Ruskin, Rossetti, and Pater.* Cambridge, Mass.: Harvard University Press, 1975.
Two chapters examine Rossetti's continuing concern for the relation-ship between literature and the visual arts. Discusses his debt to Blake and to Ruskin; shows how he subverts the latter's ideas about medieval art. Discusses the development of Rossetti's aesthetic in his essays for *The Germ*; analyzes several of his poems, especially the sonnets and "The Blessed Damozel," focusing on both theme and structure and noting the special difficulties posed by juxtaposition of form and content in his work. Includes lengthy discussion of Pre-Raphaelite painting to show its links with the literature produced by Rossetti and others in the movement. Concludes with remarks on Rossetti as a modern writer.

Stevenson, Lionel. "Rossetti as Poet." In *The Pre-Raphaelite Poets.* Chapel Hill: University of North Carolina Press, 1972.
Essay concentrating first on the poet's life, tracing his family history and exploring his relationship with fellow poets and painters; also discusses his affairs with various women in the circle. Comments on the biographical background of several works. Remarks how little attention Rossetti gave to his poetry in early years. Follows this life study with a summary of critical commentary on the poet's merits and an examination of his poetic techniques, discussing both his narrative and lyric verse. Concludes his strength lay in the sonnet form; exam-ines in some detail the poet's sonnet sequence published as *The House of Life*.

The Blessed Damozel

Harrison, Antony. *Victorian Poets and Romantic Poems: Intertextuality and Ideology.* Charlottesville: University Press of Virginia, 1990, pp. 94-99.
Discusses the many unconventional aspects of Rossetti's poem, which is modeled on the traditional elegy. Notes the reversal at the center of the work: the lover already in heaven is mourning because she is not

able to be united with her earthbound beloved. Argues the poem contains many elements of parody; Rossetti uses the elements of the elegy in a parodic way to question the traditional values normally associated with that genre.

Howard, Ronnalie Roper. *The Dark Glass: Vision and Technique in the Poetry of Dante Gabriel Rossetti.* Athens: Ohio University Press, 1972, pp. 40-49.
Reviews previous criticism of the poem, much of which faults Rossetti for his inability to handle the cosmology he creates. Carefully explicates individual stanzas to show that, far from being merely decorative, the juxtaposition of heaven and hell has a thematic purpose, emphasizing the central irony of the work: even heaven is hell for lovers who are separated from each other. Carefully demonstrates how the two lovers move from feeling hopeful for some reunion to resigning themselves to the grief they feel at being separated.

Johnston, Robert D. *Dante Gabriel Rossetti.* New York: Twayne, 1969, pp. 54-57.
Claims that, though the poem owes something to Dante Alighieri's vision of Beatrice in *Vita Nuova*, Rossetti gives the work an atmosphere uniquely its own. Points out the influence of Edgar Allan Poe on Rossetti's conception of the situation for his work. Notes how the poet creates the atmosphere of tension between ideal and erotic love, but claims Rossetti offers no real sense of belief in a heavenly world. Rather, the Damozel is "a sublimated metamorphosis of unfulfilled lover experience," more a psychological than a religious portrait of the mortal lover's desires.

Riede, David G. *Dante Gabriel Rossetti and the Limits of Victorian Vision.* Ithaca, N.Y.: Cornell University Press, 1983, pp. 82-85.
Focuses on changes Rossetti made to the poem for its inclusion in his 1870 volume. Notes how the poet carefully excised specifically Christian overtones, replacing "faith with skepticism" and "optimism with pessimism." Argues Rossetti made changes in order to have this poem appear compatible with others in the volume.

Sonstroem, David. *Rossetti and the Fair Lady.* Middletown, Conn.: Wesleyan University Press, 1970, pp. 20-30.
Extended comparison of Rossetti's Damozel with Dante's Beatrice from *Vita Nuova*. Though both women are portrayed as saviors of men, Rossetti's Damozel is considerably more human and earthly. Rossetti's

heaven is also much more sensual than Dante's; the nineteenth century poet fills his heaven with "earthly beings, feelings, and activities." Believes Rossetti's conception of heaven as a kind of Earthly Paradise stems from his youth, his reaction against traditional Christianity, his egoism, and the temper of the age.

Stein, Richard L. *The Ritual of Interpretation: The Fine Arts as Literature in Ruskin, Rossetti, and Pater.* Cambridge, Mass.: Harvard University Press, 1975, pp. 147-153.

Reads the poem as an illustration of Rossetti's concern with the relationship between "real and imagined worlds"; the division between the Damozel's speculations in heaven and her lover's daydreams on earth mirrors the complexity of experience and an ultimate inability to reconcile these realms. Suggests the style in which the lovers' story is presented may indicate the entire episode is simply an ironic fiction, a dream fabricated in the mind of the male lover who has lost his lady but still finds a way to be united with her through imagination.

Sussman, Herbert L. *Fact into Figure: Typology in Carlyle, Ruskin, and the Pre-Raphaelite Brotherhood.* Columbus: Ohio State University Press, 1979, pp. 130-136.

Examines the version of the poem printed in *The Germ* in 1849 to show how Rossetti originally intended the work to exhibit the conflict between a longing for spiritualized love and the attraction of "earthly eroticism." Demonstrates how changes made for Rossetti's 1870 volume and for subsequent editions in which this work appeared no longer contain the "transcendental context" the poet gave to his original composition. In the earliest version Rossetti was concerned with giving tangible expression to the visionary experience, following the model of Italian poet Dante Alighieri. His original Damozel is "presexual"; by the 1870's Rossetti had changed her into an erotic lover. Includes in the volume the text of the 1849 version of the poem.

Trail, George Y. "Time in 'The Blessed Damozel.'" In Harold Bloom, ed. *Pre-Raphaelite Poets.* Modern Critical Views. New York: Chelsea House, 1986.

Makes a strong case that Rossetti presents a "rigorously conceptual" view of heaven in the poem, and his central concern is to demonstrate the "mutual exclusiveness" of traditional concepts of heaven and earth. The poem is an ironic look at the impossibility of the lovers' reunion on terms outlined by the Damozel. Offers a careful, systematic reading of the text, focusing on the poet's choice of words and imagery.

The House of Life

Howard, Ronnalie Roper. "The House of Life." In *The Dark Glass: Vision and Technique in the Poetry of Dante Gabriel Rossetti*. Athens: Ohio University Press, 1972.
General review of the sequence, illustrating Rossetti's concern for important, recurring themes and examining the poet's technique in composing within the sonnet form. Cites numerous examples to support the claim that Rossetti was adept at handling the complexities of the Italian sonnet. Notes the differences between individual sonnets composed at various periods in Rossetti's life, but sees him constantly interested in "the yearning for union," expressed alternately as happiness in shared moments and as "a sense of incompleteness in being alone."

Johnston, Robert D. "*The House of Life*: Youth and Change"; "*The House of Life*: Change and Fate." In *Dante Gabriel Rossetti*. New York: Twayne, 1969.
Notes previous critical responses to the work that is generally considered Rossetti's masterpiece. Careful analysis of the poet's style. Extensive discussion of selected sonnets, including "Bridal Birth" and "Love's Last Gift," to show Rossetti's mastery of the form and his use of traditional materials, especially as these were used by medieval and Renaissance forebears. Also examines the sensuous qualities of the work and explores the intensely personal nature of individual sonnets. Attempts to account for the note of despair which overshadows the hope for fulfillment in love professed at the end of the sequence.

McGhee, Richard D. *Marriage, Duty, and Desire in Victorian Poetry and Drama*. Lawrence: University Press of Kansas, 1980, pp. 154-160.
Describes the way Rossetti deals with the close relationship between death and desire throughout this work. Notes the poet's heavy reliance on Dante and classical sources for his imagery; sees the central character in the sequence as a kind of Orpheus figure, yearning to be united with the object of his love. Explicates several sonnets to show how the poet expresses his constant desire for "spiritual and fleshly fulfillment." Sees Rossetti using marriage as a symbol of completeness.

Riede, David G. *Dante Gabriel Rossetti and the Limits of Victorian Vision*. Ithaca, N.Y.: Cornell University Press, 1983, pp. 187-201.
Studies composition of the sonnets in the sequence, especially ones added late, as evidence of the poet's growing concern for artifice and

his need to polish his works so they might stand alone as small gems, monuments to the power of the artist to create beauty which could be enjoyed for its own sake. Examines the highly artificial qualities of many of the sonnets; argues Rossetti was intensely interested in surface qualities because he saw them as expressing deeper psychological insights into love and life.

Sonstroem, David. *Rossetti and the Fair Lady*. Middletown, Conn.: Wesleyan University Press, 1970, pp. 140-153.
Considers this sequence "Rossetti's finest and most representative work." Claims it is inspired by his love for Jane Burden Morris, whom the poet transforms into the figure of the Lady as Savior. The sonnets in the sequence celebrate not only earthly love but also a vision of love as a means of salvation. Examines Rossetti's use of the word "soul," which carries not only emotional but also metaphysical overtones. Quotes extensively from a number of the sonnets to illustrate Rossetti's continuing fascination with the figure of the fair lady and the metaphysical substructure of the sequence.

Stein, Richard L. "Dante Gabriel Rossetti." In *The Ritual of Interpretation: The Fine Arts as Literature in Ruskin, Rossetti, and Pater*. Cambridge, Mass.: Harvard University Press, 1975.
Throughout an essay on Rossetti's continuing concern for the relationship between literature and the visual arts, Stein uses individual sonnets from the sequence to illustrate key recurrent themes and common structural patterns in the poet's work. Notes how the sequence, organized in 1870, demonstrates the progress of its central character from physical love to spiritual love. Claims the poems "alternate between two modes of being," "physical existence and metaphysical self-awareness." Argues against a purely autobiographical interpretation of the sonnets.

Jenny

Howard, Ronnalie Roper. *The Dark Glass: Vision and Technique in the Poetry of Dante Gabriel Rossetti*. Athens: Ohio University Press, 1972, pp. 100-111.
Reviews previous scholarship on the work to highlight the central critical problem: "the question of tone and treatment." Carefully examines the text to illustrate the ambiguous responses of the male speaker who views Jenny alternately as a typical prostitute and as an individual

wronged by society. Notes the ironic and paradoxical tone interjected by Rossetti's skillful use of imagery. Concludes the poem is a "moral drama" because the speaker becomes aware of the "realities of human character and the human condition"; nevertheless, Rossetti is not didactic in demanding certain actions should follow from that awareness.

Rodgers, Lise. "The Book and the Flower: Rationality and Sensuality in *Jenny.*" In Harold Bloom, ed. *Pre-Raphaelite Poets.* Modern Critical Views. New York: Chelsea House, 1986.
Claims "Jenny" is the "most radical" of Rossetti's poems because it is his most openly and unabashedly sensual: "fleshly sensuality" is presented as good. Criticism which has focused on the narrator's ambivalence has largely failed to acknowledge this fact. The narrator and Jenny symbolize opposite poles within the work: the rational and sensual. Rossetti's sympathetic portrait of his heroine makes it clear which side he takes in the debate; however, he found the poem haunting him for years after its publication because of its open support of sensuality.

My Sister's Sleep

Howard, Ronnalie Roper. *The Dark Glass: Vision and Technique in the Poetry of Dante Gabriel Rossetti.* Athens: Ohio University Press, 1972, pp. 2-5.
Argues earlier criticism describing the work as an artistic failure is wrongheaded. Sketches the action of the poem, noting the central irony created by the death of the young girl juxtaposed with the joy of the Christmas season. Believes the poem does not necessarily represent Rossetti's personal beliefs about religion, but instead ends with the mother in the poem affirming the importance of belief. The work is "an objective portrayal of human grief and of a faith in the supernatural which transcends that grief."

Riede, David G. *Dante Gabriel Rossetti and the Limits of Victorian Vision.* Ithaca, N.Y.: Cornell University Press, 1983, pp. 80-83.
Focuses on revisions Rossetti made to the poem after its initial appearance in 1850 to remove religious overtones. Cites lines and stanzas dropped or altered, noting how the effect is to move the poem away from its original status as a devotional work to one which explores the psychological dimensions of the speaker's plight. The work becomes one which touts skepticism, not faith.

Sister Helen

Howard, Ronnalie Roper. *The Dark Glass: Vision and Technique in the Poetry of Dante Gabriel Rossetti.* Athens: Ohio University Press, 1972, pp. 68-80.
Extended examination of this work as an example of Rossetti's use of medieval materials and forms. Discusses his adaptation of the ballad stanza for more literary uses. Sees the refrain functioning in ways similar to that of the Greek chorus in classical drama. Extensive recapitulation of the narrative, focusing on the reaction of the central character to other figures in the poem. Concludes Helen is a truly tragic heroine who arouses the reader's sympathy because of her alienation from society.

Johnston, Robert D. *Dante Gabriel Rossetti.* New York: Twayne, 1969, pp. 114-116.
Classifies the poem as one of several in which Rossetti attempts to portray the mental state of his protagonist. Notes the changes made to the text after its original composition in 1851. By 1870, Helen is less the demon who delights in destroying her love and more the genuinely tragic heroine who sees that by destroying the one she loves she is also destroying herself. Discusses techniques the poet uses to achieve his success, notably juxtaposition of points of view and repetition of key phrases.

Chapter 11
ALGERNON CHARLES SWINBURNE

General Studies

Beetz, Kirk H. *Algernon Charles Swinburne: A Bibliography of Secondary Works, 1861-1980.* Metuchen, N.J.: Scarecrow Press, 1982.
Comprehensive listing of secondary works dealing with Swinburne's poetry, fiction, and nonfiction; also contains entries providing biographical information and estimates of the writer's character and reputation. Organized chronologically. Most entries are not annotated. Brief introduction and headnotes to various sections provide information about the status of Swinburne scholarship. Cross-indexed by author, title, and subject.

Brisman, Leslie. "Of Lips Divine and Calm: Swinburne and the Language of Shelleyan Love." In Harold Bloom, ed. *Pre-Raphaelite Poets.* Modern Critical Views. New York: Chelsea House, 1986.
Extensive analysis of Ruskin's concept of the distinction between "imagination penetrative" and "imagination contemplative," using Swinburne's poems, especially *Anactoria*, as examples of works in which the contemplative process is paramount. Compares Swinburne's work with that of both Shelley (of whom he is a disciple) and Shakespeare, whose imagination tends to penetrate to the heart of the human condition; Swinburne, on the other hand, opts to contemplate the possibilities of experience and revel in those possibilities.

Buckler, William E. "The Poetry of Swinburne: An Essay in Critical Reenforcement." In *The Victorian Imagination: Essays in Aesthetic Exploration.* New York: New York University Press, 1980.
Makes the case for Swinburne as a major poetic voice, bridging the gap between the major Victorian poets of the early years of the century and those of the modern period. Argues that, far from being unconcerned with form or overly intent on pure expression, Swinburne was intensely interested in the varieties of poetic genres and experimented frequently with many standard forms. Believes Swinburne aims to modify his readers' consciousness about themselves through his poetry; his techniques point to an intensifying of experience within individual poems to heighten readers' self-awareness. Briefly explicates "Hertha," "Thalassius," "To the Cliffs," "A Nympholet," and "The Lake of Gaube."

Cassidy, John A. *Algernon Charles Swinburne*. New York: Twayne, 1964.
Modest critical survey of the Swinburne canon, noting throughout the
close relationship between the writer's life and his art. Devotes chapters to the major publications. Deals frankly with Swinburne's tendencies toward sadomasochism. Concludes he was an important influence
on his age because he refused to be limited by Victorian conventions.
Includes detailed chronology.

Cochran, Rebecca. "An Assessment of Swinburne's Arthuriana." In
Valerie M. Lagorio and Mildred Leake Day, eds. *King Arthur Through
the Ages*. Vol. 2. New York: Garland, 1990.
Argues that Swinburne, unlike Tennyson, turned to medieval sources
for poetic inspiration because in them he found characters of strength
and interest. Finds the poet faithful to the medieval spirit. Briefly
surveys several of Swinburne's early Arthurian works, stressing the
importance of the medieval sources to which Swinburne turned for
inspiration in all of his Arthurian poems. Provides lengthy analysis of
Tristram of Lyonesse and more abbreviated discussion of *The Tale of
Balen*.

Eliot, T. S. "Swinburne as Poet." In Shiv Kumar, ed. *British Victorian
Literature: Recent Revaluations*. New York: New York University
Press, 1969.
Reprint of the influential critic's assessment of Swinburne's poetic
qualities. Claims "Atalanta in Calydon," "The Triumph of Time," "The
Leper," and "Laus Veneris" are Swinburne's most representative works;
believes that few readers would want to read the poet's corpus. Sees
Swinburne's diffuseness as his special strength; few of his poems could
be condensed without changing their artistic merits. Believes Swin-
burne, more than many poets, appreciates language for its own sake.

Fletcher, Ian. *Swinburne*. London: Longmans, 1973.
Brief monograph intended to provide the general reader an overview of
Swinburne's works and his contributions to English literature. Separate
sections sketch out each of the major volumes of poetry, the prose
fiction, and the criticism. Includes an excellent bibliography of Swinburne's publications, as well as a listing of selected secondary sources.

Fletcher, Pauline. "Swinburne: The Sublime Recovered." In *Gardens and
Grim Ravines: The Language of Landscape in Victorian Poetry*.
Princeton, N.J.: Princeton University Press, 1983.
Believes Swinburne's landscapes reflect clearly his "rejection of soci-

ety" while revealing his passionate longing for an escape from life's social demands. Focuses on the poet's use of garden imagery but also explores his use of the sea. Pays some attention to his use of untamed natural settings, noting his strong attraction to these surroundings; considers Swinburne the most antisocial of Victorian poets.

Fuller, Jean Overton. *Swinburne: A Critical Biography.* London: Chatto & Windus, 1968.
Comprehensive life study of the poet, interspersing assessments of the major works amid the details of Swinburne's career. Relies heavily on previously published reminiscences by Swinburne's family and friends, as well as manuscript collections of letters. Stresses the significance of French literature on Swinburne's development as a writer. Includes an appendix listing primary materials available in the British Library.

Harrison, Antony. *Swinburne's Medievalism: A Study in Victorian Love Poetry.* Baton Rouge: Louisiana State University Press, 1988.
Comprehensive examination of Swinburne's use of medieval subjects and his attitude toward the Middle Ages. Believes he is "a relentless iconoclast" who does not share his contemporaries' unadulterated love of the medieval period; though he admires much of the literature of that age, he resents writers who bowed to the hegemony of the Catholic Church. A thorough introduction outlines Swinburne's critical stance toward this material. Separate chapters examine major poems, including *Queen Yseult, Rosamond, Chastelard, The Tale of Balen*, and *Tristram of Lyonesse*, which Harrison considers Swinburne's greatest poem. Includes an appendix listing the poet's works on medieval subjects.

Henderson, Philip. *Swinburne: The Portrait of a Poet.* London: Routledge & Kegan Paul, 1974.
Comprehensive biography based on the Lang edition of Swinburne's letters, on previous published biographical studies, and on reminiscences by Swinburne's friends and relations. Carefully integrates commentary on the poetry into the narrative of Swinburne's life. Deals sympathetically with the writer's works, judging him one of the major figures of the Victorian era.

Hyder, Clyde K. *Swinburne: The Critical Heritage.* New York: Barnes & Noble, 1970.
Collection of critical commentaries by Swinburne's contemporaries. Includes reviews of several collections of poems published during Swinburne's lifetime and several retrospective analyses of the poet's

career. Also includes an introductory essay outlining the critical reception of Swinburne's work.

Johnson, Wendell Stacy. *Sex and Marriage in Victorian Poetry*. Ithaca, N.Y.: Cornell University Press, 1975, pp. 90-107.
Discussion of Swinburne's attitude toward sexual relationships and marriage; believes the poet was opposed to conventional marriage not only because of his life experiences but also because the real-life institution did not foster the idealized union Swinburne believed should exist between men and women. In his poetry, Swinburne considered marriage "the quintessential social lie" because it was an easy, conventional response to the complex problem of the earnest human desire to achieve oneness with another individual. Extensive discussion of "Atalanta in Calydon" and brief analyses of other poems.

Louis, Margot. *Swinburne and His Gods*. Montreal: McGill-Queens University Press, 1990.
Traces the progress of Swinburne's changing attitudes toward traditional and nontraditional views of religion. Outlines his exceptional training in conventional theology at Oxford; shows how his reaction against these ideas leads him gradually through a celebration of classical gods, to a position close to the Romantics (for whom the perfectibility of humankind was possible without appeal to traditional deities), to a final stance in which agnosticism holds sway. Examines poems in each of his major volumes to illustrate the growth of his ideology.

McGann, Jerome. *Swinburne: An Experiment in Criticism*. Chicago: University of Chicago Press, 1972.
Unusual critical analysis of Swinburne's oeuvre, cast in the form of a dialogue among various fictional critics who take opposing or complementary positions on the poet's work. Examines the major poems and dozens of minor ones; explores Swinburne's relationship with numerous contemporary figures such as Tennyson, Arnold, Robert Browning, Mallarmé, and Baudelaire, as well as the influence on his poetry of writers such as Shelley and Blake. An appendix discusses Swinburne's merits as an elegiac poet.

McGhee, Richard D. "Swinburne and Hopkins." In *Marriage, Duty, and Desire in Victorian Poetry and Drama*. Lawrence: University Press of Kansas, 1980.
Discusses the expansive quality of Swinburne's poetry, noting its dissimilarities from modern verse, which tends to be terse and depen-

dent on concentrated imagery. Examines several poems and dramas to illustrate a central tension in Swinburne's work: the conflict "between love and death, between pleasure and pain." Includes extensive analysis of "Atalanta in Calydon," "The Triumph of Time," *Erechtheus*, and the writer's trilogy of plays about Mary Stuart; also contains brief discussion of *Tristram of Lyonesse*.

McSweeney, Kerry. *Tennyson and Swinburne as Romantic Naturalists*. Toronto: University of Toronto Press, 1981.
Study intended to "call attention to the central importance of naturalistic vision," a distinctly Romantic concept, in Swinburne and Tennyson. Two chapters compare the strengths and weaknesses of these writers; two others are devoted to an exploration of what McSweeney considers Swinburne's major early and later works. Believes Swinburne is consistent in displaying the naturalistic vision which places him in the Romantic tradition.

Paglia, Camille. "Nature, Sex, and Decadence." In Harold Bloom, ed. *Pre-Raphaelite Poets*. Modern Critical Views. New York: Chelsea House, 1986.
Claims Swinburne "invented English Late Romanticism" by combining Shelley's style with an interest in sexual matters borrowed from nineteenth century French writers. Argues he was premier among British poets at celebrating the matriarchy; shows how his poetry returns to the ritualistic roots of the art. Examines "Dolores," "Faustina," and "Laus Veneris" as examples of Swinburne's innovative style and treatment of sensual themes. Extensive analysis of *Anactoria*, which Paglia considers Swinburne's greatest work.

Peters, Robert L. *The Crowns of Apollo: Swinburne's Principles of Literature and Art*. Detroit, Mich.: Wayne State University Press, 1965.
Extensive analysis of Swinburne's criticism, documenting his "contributions to the aesthetics of his time." Sketches a framework for examining the writer's works; explores Swinburne's reaction to the dominant moral tone of criticism in his time and looks carefully at his attempts to define beauty (especially his effort to draw "distinctions between the varieties of *passion*"). Comments on specific poems are scattered throughout the study.

_____. "Swinburne: A Personal Essay and a Polemic." In Richard A. Levine, ed. *The Victorian Experience: The Poets*. Athens: Ohio University Press, 1982.

Personal essay explaining why Swinburne has special appeal and why
he is simultaneously difficult for many readers to appreciate. Claims the
poet rapidly developed his mature style and his entire oeuvre is remarkably consistent in technical merit. Believes Swinburne's poetry deserves
serious study because the poet is one of the premier artists of the
Victorian period. Provides a systematic analysis of Swinburne's techniques of subordinating details to a single effect in his works; examines
his use of synaesthesia and discusses his impressionistic style.

Richardson, James. *Vanishing Lives: Style and Self in Tennyson, Dante
    Gabriel Rossetti, Swinburne, and Yeats.* Charlottesville: University
    Press of Virginia, 1988.
    Detailed analysis of Swinburne's style, focusing on the poet's use of
    imagery, metaphor, syntax, and sentence structure. Sees the poet torn
    between two competing passions: a desire to pursue passionate expe-
    riences, even when these experiences bring pain, and a need to establish
    distance from and mastery over life's experiences by achieving clarity
    and restraint in his work. Reviews comments by several earlier critics
    who offer insight into Swinburne's style.

Riede, David G. *Swinburne: A Study of Romantic Mythmaking.* Char-
    lottesville: University Press of Virginia, 1978.
    Analysis of Swinburne's work as a continuation of the Romantic
    tradition, focusing on his relationship to and use of ideas and writings
    of Blake, Coleridge, Shelley, and Wordsworth. Introduction provides
    an overview of the tradition of which Swinburne is an inheritor.
    Separate chapters examine his two collections of *Poems and Ballads*,
    his writings modeled on Greek subjects, and the works of his later life.
    Concludes that, while an iconoclast among Victorian poets, Swinburne
    is in the mainstream of the Romantic tradition, forming a link between
    Shelley and Thomas Hardy.

Snodgrass, Chris. "Swinburne's Circle of Desire: A Decadent Theme." In
    Ian Fletcher, ed. *Decadence and the 1890s.* Stratford-on-Avon Studies
    17. London: Edward Arnold, 1979.
    Reads the body of Swinburne's work as an attempt by the poet to display
    humanity's heroic quest for self-fulfillment; notes how Swinburne uses
    erotic desire as a metaphor for all human impulses toward that goal.
    Examines numerous poems in the poet's canon to illustrate this thesis.
    Notes the influence of Blake on Swinburne's concept of humankind's
    relationship with the deity; believes Swinburne, following Blake, saw
    the traditional concept of God as inhibiting the ability of human beings

to liberate themselves and achieve self-fulfillment. Includes useful bibliographical notes on primary and secondary source materials.

Stevenson, Lionel. "Algernon Charles Swinburne." In *The Pre-Raphaelite Poets*. Chapel Hill: University of North Carolina Press, 1972.
Biographical sketch of the poet's contributions to literature and his development as a poet and leader of the Pre-Raphaelite movement. Surveys his formative years and his growing belief in his vocation as a man of letters. Systematically reviews publication and reception of his literary output, including *Atalanta in Calydon*, the first of the *Poems and Ballads* series (which provoked hostile reaction from Victorian critics), and later volumes of poetry and drama. Traces the reaction against Swinburne's promotion of sensuality. Examines the influence of the poet Dante Gabriel Rossetti and the politician Giuseppe Mazzini on his writings. Comments throughout on the technical qualities of the poet's work, especially his innovations in meter and his mastery of prosodic techniques that give speed, rhythm, and sensuousness to all his verse.

Thomas, Donald. *Swinburne: The Poet in the World*. New York: Oxford University Press, 1979.
Biography focusing on Swinburne's relationship to Victorian society. Points out ways the poet exemplified the rebellious spirit which characterized his youth; describes his relationship with Theodore Watts-Dunton, who saved Swinburne from alcoholism and sexual debauchery, extending his life by three decades.

Atalanta in Calydon

Cassidy, John A. *Algernon Charles Swinburne*. New York: Twayne, 1964, pp. 85-92.
Discusses the autobiographical elements in the work. Provides succinct plot summary. Points out differences between Swinburne's version of the story and that found in his source, Ovid's *Metamorphoses*. Concludes the work is one of the finest English adaptations of classical literature, noting how Swinburne uses verse forms masterfully.

Fuller, Jean Overton. *Swinburne: A Critical Biography*. London: Chatto & Windus, 1968, pp. 94-103.
Briefly discusses the history of composition, citing Swinburne's sources both in classical literature and among the British Romantics. Provides a plot summary and explication, noting occasions where the

poet's own experiences provide images for his description of setting and character. Posits the poet stresses the importance of his characters' responsibility for the tragedy: choice, not fate, leads to the disaster at the close of the poem.

Johnson, Wendell Stacy. *Sex and Marriage in Victorian Poetry.* Ithaca, N.Y.: Cornell University Press, 1975, pp. 92-100.
Discussion of the poem as a dramatization of "sexual attraction and response." In it, Swinburne portrays his belief that humanity is plagued by the problems of division and isolation; everyone strives (often unsuccessfully) to achieve a oneness with other individuals. Both the action and the imagery of the poem support this notion. Notes the many ironies of both characterization and action. Love becomes important as a way of overcoming division, but Swinburne does not favor marriage because, as an institution, marriage "insists upon the individuality" of each partner.

Louis, Margot. *Swinburne and His Gods.* Montreal: McGill-Queens University Press, 1990, pp. 24-35.
Calls the work "the most explicit in its use of language" in all of Swinburne's poems. Discusses ways Swinburne reverses traditional Christianity by having the gods in this work serve as forces of destruction. Examines words used by the poet to stress the divisiveness of language itself. Relies heavily on an earlier analysis of the structure of the poem by Richard Mathews.

McGann, Jerome. *Swinburne: An Experiment in Criticism.* Chicago: University of Chicago Press, 1972, pp. 95-107.
Extended discussion of the tragic qualities of the work, cast in the form of a dialogue among fictional critics. Focuses on the character of Althaea, acknowledged to be the central tragic figure; discusses her relationship with her son Meleager, who also possesses tragic attributes. Points out how the drama depends heavily on poetic qualities, even its lyrical dimension, for its overall effect on readers.

McGhee, Richard D. *Marriage, Duty, and Desire in Victorian Poetry and Drama.* Lawrence: University Press of Kansas, 1980, pp. 170-183.
Cites the poem as an example of Swinburne's belief in the power of language as a means of communicating both the best and the most dangerous aspects of culture. Discusses ways the poet anticipates Freud in his understanding that language is a means through which human beings sublimate sexual energy. The poem's major characters

play out a sexual drama in which the lovers attempt to express their energy, while Meleager's mother strives to control her son's passion.

Riede, David G. "The Greek Plays: *Atalanta in Calydon* and *Erechtheus*." In *Swinburne: A Study of Romantic Mythmaking*. Charlottesville: University Press of Virginia, 1978.
Briefly discusses Swinburne's use of Greek mythology as a source for his writings. Detailed reading of the poem, quoting liberally from the text to demonstrate how the major characters present key ideas through dialogue and how imagery supports the poet's vision of the world. Refutes earlier readings which see the poem as an exploration of the conflict between the old and new orders. Argues the central vision of the poem is a bleak one: Swinburne laments "the cosmic law" under which all people must live.

Thomas, Donald. *Swinburne: The Poet in the World*. New York: Oxford University Press, 1979, pp. 82-86.
Describes the critical reaction to the poem by Swinburne's contemporaries. Explains the impact it had on a reading public already accustomed to works based on Greek mythology. Suggests some of the work's immediate popularity was due to its ability to generate excitement in readers tired of Tennyson and others among Swinburne's older contemporaries. Points out affinities to many modern poets, especially W. H. Auden.

Dolores

Riede, David G. *Swinburne: A Study of Romantic Mythmaking*. Charlottesville: University Press of Virginia, 1978.
Discusses Swinburne's reliance on the philosophy of the Marquis de Sade in creating a series of poems, including "Dolores," in which pain and sexual gratification are glorified; points out differences between the two men as well. Argues the main theme of "Dolores" is the glorification of the senses; Swinburne adopts this posture as a reaction to Victorian repression of all sexual matters. Extensive citations from other critical works on the poem.

Hertha

Buckler, William E. *The Victorian Imagination: Essays in Aesthetic Exploration*. New York: New York University Press, 1980, pp. 235-238.

Considers this poem crucial to appreciating both Swinburne's methodology and his aesthetic stance. Notes the concentration of powerful metaphysical and epistemological ideas in the form of the dramatic lyric. Acknowledges Swinburne's debt to various Eastern and Western mythological traditions in formulating the ideas which inform the poem. Reads the work as a statement about the poet's concept of the nature of reality and of people's ability to determine their "place in the universe of time and space." Like Hertha, the goddess who speaks in the poem, readers are asked to contemplate the possibilities of existence as a means of liberating themselves from conventional ways of apprehending the world.

Louis, Margot. *Swinburne and His Gods*. Montreal: McGill-Queens University Press, 1990, pp. 110-118.
Discusses the poem as Swinburne's attempt "to harmonize myth with didactic allegory." Outlines the three-part structure of the work. Notes the poet's reliance on ideas gleaned from Eastern religions, specifically those found in the *Bhagavad Gita*, as well as ones from primitive Western mythology, for his development of the poem's title character. Suggests ways the poet counters conventional religious thought in the work.

McGann, Jerome. *Swinburne: An Experiment in Criticism*. Chicago: University of Chicago Press, 1972, pp. 249-253.
Uses fictional critics to present a dialogue outlining the central criticism leveled against the poem—its apparent lack of structure—and to provide an explanation of the poet's methods of composition. Describes the composition process. Argues the poet's aim is to suggest a "perception of a universe of continuous, vital transformations." Explains the function of the long section on the Tree of Life; concludes the structure is intentionally nonlinear, suggesting the cyclic nature of the life force in the world.

Riede, David G. *Swinburne: A Study of Romantic Mythmaking*. Charlottesville: University Press of Virginia, 1978, pp. 110-113.
Sees the poem as one of the best illustrations of the "philosophical core of Swinburne's republicanism," emblematic of all his later work. Compares Hertha to the other female characters who dominate Swinburne's work, describing her as a life force to which all must submit. Believes this earth-mother figure represents inevitable change, but not necessarily progress toward "an eternal republic."

The Lake of Gaube

McGann, Jerome. *Swinburne: An Experiment in Criticism*. Chicago: University of Chicago Press, 1972, pp. 183-185.

Brief assessment of the poem as one of Swinburne's "homilies upon fear"; discusses the poet's use of the swimmer's dive as a means of transcending normal boundaries of experience so that, once fear is conquered, new realms of experience are opened up. Discusses the function of the many contrasts Swinburne uses to dramatize the process of transformation which the swimmer must undergo to pass beyond fear to "rapture."

McSweeney, Kerry. *Tennyson and Swinburne as Romantic Naturalists*. Toronto: University of Toronto Press, 1981, pp. 183-186.

Brief review of the poem's major theme and the place of the work in Swinburne's canon. Discusses the metaphoric dimensions of the speaker's plunge into the deep waters of the lake, equating it to a descent toward death and a simultaneous movement toward freedom. Explains how the initial feeling of fear is transformed into a sense of freedom; the speaker comes to accept death not as "longed-for oblivion" but rather as a "culmination" of human life and as "something intimately a part of man's relation to nature."

Laus Veneris

McGann, Jerome. *Swinburne: An Experiment in Criticism*. Chicago: University of Chicago Press, 1972, pp. 254-258.

Analysis of the central theme, presented in the form of a dialogue among fictional critics. Focuses on the character of Tannhaüser, whose dramatic monologue reveals more than the speaker realizes. Claims the work is an attack on traditional Christian values; Tannhaüser lives in a sexual hell of his own making because he believes his passion for his Venus condemns him.

McSweeney, Kerry. *Tennyson and Swinburne as Romantic Naturalists*. Toronto: University of Toronto Press, 1981, pp. 130-133.

Believes many of Swinburne's continuing concerns are addressed in this poem: a "preoccupation with death and change" and questions about the relationship of human beings with "natural process." Notes parallels to Tennyson's "Tithonus" but sees Swinburne's hero in "Laus Veneris" as more positive in accepting his fate with greater affirmation of life;

the natural world may be sufficient to sustain him if he cannot pass on to what is thought to be eternal rest. Argues Swinburne was being ironic when he described the poem as promoting Christian values.

Tristram of Lyonesse

Cassidy, John A. *Algernon Charles Swinburne*. New York: Twayne, 1964, pp. 157-160.
Believes the poem is one of Swinburne's finest. Focuses on the sensual language the poet uses to describe the passion felt by his central characters; suggests, however, the work is flawed because Swinburne allows their relationship to remain purely sensual. Briefly mentions the influence of Theodore Watts-Dunton on the composition.

Henderson, Philip. *Swinburne: The Portrait of a Poet*. London: Routledge & Kegan Paul, 1974, pp. 204-207.
Review of Swinburne's use of description in the poem, praising him for his extended presentations of natural landscapes to mirror the psychological drama in the work; acknowledges, however, that some passages may be overdone. Explains why Edmund Gosse, a longtime friend of the poet, may have devalued the work: Swinburne had moved away from Gosse and was taking advice from Theodore Watts-Dunton when the poem was being written.

McGhee, Richard D. *Marriage, Duty, and Desire in Victorian Poetry and Drama*. Lawrence: University Press of Kansas, 1980, pp. 201-203.
Brief analysis showing Swinburne's use of the Tristram legend to explore various themes important to him, including the nature of passion, the development of the artist, and the role of marriage. Notes the poet's heavy reliance on images of sun and sea, highlighting the sexual overtones of many passages. In Swinburne's hands, the story becomes a way of dramatizing "the failure of formalized marriage." Argues Swinburne's Tristram is a stronger character than his namesake in poems by Tennyson and Arnold, because he is "capable of responding to duty."

McSweeney, Kerry. *Tennyson and Swinburne as Romantic Naturalists*. Toronto: University of Toronto Press, 1981.
Describes the poem as Swinburne's attempt to write an epic; the poem is not flawless, but it is a powerful statement of the poet's belief in "the dignity and grandeur of a wholly naturalistic vision of human existence."

Sees Love and Fate as two forces dominating the action. Extensive analysis of the three main characters, particularly Iseult of the White Hands, who is neither sentimentalized nor made the wronged woman of melodrama. Believes neither medieval Christian ethics nor Victorian moral values provide adequate standards by which to judge the lovers.

The Triumph of Time

Louis, Margot. *Swinburne and His Gods*. Montreal: McGill-Queens University Press, 1990, pp. 53-63.
Close textual analysis of a poem in which Swinburne uses erotic and religious imagery to suggest the sacramental nature of physical love. Briefly touches on the impact of the poem's form, the dramatic monologue; greater attention paid to the use of specific images, especially those evoking ideas about the eucharistic nature of the lovers' union. Points out the irony in the speaker's beloved being unaware of his strong passion and his suffering.

McGann, Jerome. *Swinburne: An Experiment in Criticism*. Chicago: University of Chicago Press, 1972, pp. 211-226.
In a dialogue among fictional critics, McGann offers extensive details about the biographical genesis of the work, citing Swinburne's love for his cousin Mary Gordon as a primary inspiration. Reviews available information about the process of composition. Discusses ways the poet's relationship with and feelings for his cousin are transformed and idealized in this poem and others.

McGhee, Richard D. *Marriage, Duty, and Desire in Victorian Poetry and Drama*. Lawrence: University Press of Kansas, 1980, pp. 184-188.
Highlights the conflict between the pleasures and pains of erotic desire. Compares the poem to other works in the tradition of the *Bildungsroman*, but argues that Swinburne has no illusions about the capability of his hero to transform society. Also discusses the poet's existential notion of time, which has meaning only insofar as individuals invest it with significance. Analyzes Swinburne's ideas about love and death as equally compelling areas of unexplored experience for his hero.

Chapter 12
ALFRED, LORD TENNYSON

General Studies

Albright, Daniel. *Tennyson: The Muses' Tug of War*. Charlottesville: University Press of Virginia, 1986.

Believes Tennyson's aesthetic goals were in continuous conflict: on one hand, he strove toward the sublime, while on the other he felt the need to celebrate the particular and the everyday aspects of life. Examines several works as they exhibit the poet's attitude toward art and display his development of fictional personae. Separate chapters on *Maud, In Memoriam,* and *The Princess*.

Bloom, Harold, ed. *Alfred, Lord Tennyson*. Modern Critical Views. New York: Chelsea House, 1985.

Eleven excerpts by distinguished critics whose works have shaped readers' opinion of Tennyson during the twentieth century. Bloom's introductory note and his discussion of the poet's affinity for Keats's work place Tennyson within the Romantic tradition. The volume includes at least one selection on each of the poet's major works. Also contains a brief chronology and a bibliography of major secondary sources.

Buckley, Jerome H. *Tennyson: The Growth of a Poet*. Cambridge, Mass.: Harvard University Press, 1961.

Influential, sympathetic assessment of Tennyson's career and achievements. Restores the poet's reputation after decades of generally negative criticism. Organized chronologically, integrating discussion of the poems in a general survey of Tennyson's career. Discusses each of the poet's volumes, with chapters devoted to extended analysis of *In Memoriam* and *Idylls of the King*. Establishes Tennyson's position as a major figure in English literature and demonstrates his mastery of prosody and general technical excellence.

Colley, Ann C. *Tennyson and Madness*. Athens: University of Georgia Press, 1983.

Examines Tennyson's life for instances of his bouts with impending madness and illustrates how the poet turned his study of mental instability into poetry. Demonstrates the pervasiveness of Tennyson's interest in the subject by showing its frequent occurrence in his works; argues Tennyson remained an acute observer of madness and used it frequently as a metaphor for many social ills. Includes a chapter on the history of madness and its prevalence in Victorian society and literature as a way of demonstrating Tennyson's debt to a particular tradition of thinking and writing about mental illness.

Culler, A. Dwight. *The Poetry of Tennyson.* New Haven, Conn.: Yale University Press, 1977.
Systematic study of the Tennyson corpus, explaining the poet's fascination with language, specifically poetic language, a powerful instrument which allows the writer to rise above ordinary use to shape reality and convey one's deepest experiences. Calls Tennyson a "Victorian Alexandrian," highly successful in writing short poems in an age when long, epic poetry was impossible. Reviews the poet's development chronologically, devoting individual chapters to the major works. Provides explications of dozens of Tennyson's minor gems.

Danzig, Allan. "The Contraries: A Central Concept in Tennyson's Poetry." In Shiv Kumar, ed. *British Victorian Literature: Recent Revaluations.* New York: New York University Press, 1969.
Claims most of Tennyson's work involves the poet's attempt to represent the notion that life consists of contrary states of experience or feeling which never admit to any resolution or synthesis. These contrary states, which cannot always be explained logically, are the root of much of the tension in people's lives. Extended analysis of "Lucretius" to show how Tennyson views the pervasiveness of this philosophical notion; briefer examination of *Maud* provides additional evidence of this thesis.

Dodsworth, Martin. "Patterns of Morbidity: Repetition in Tennyson's Poetry." In Isobel Armstrong, ed. *The Major Victorian Poets: Reconsiderations.* Lincoln: University of Nebraska Press, 1969.
Argues Tennyson is not morbid, though solemn events are often the impetus for his works. Counters the charge by the poet's contemporary Walter Bagehot that Tennyson's works are needlessly ornate; examines several poems, especially "St. Simeon Stylites," "Œnone," and "Enoch Arden," to prove the poet uses repetition with great effect and calculated purpose. Claims the best of Tennyson's work is not aimed primarily at presenting an argument but rather at dramatizing the frame of mind of the poem's speaker.

Fletcher, Pauline. "Tennyson: The Primal Wilderness"; "Tennyson: From Escapist Paradise to Social Landscape." In *Gardens and Grim Ravines: The Language of Landscape in Victorian Poetry*. Princeton, N.J.: Princeton University Press, 1983.
Two chapters examining Tennyson's concept of the sublime and the picturesque. Discusses the poet's use of landscape imagery in more than three dozen works. Argues Tennyson originally adopted a Romantic attitude toward nature, celebrating the wilds over man-made structures, but eventually rejected that view in favor of one which praises landscapes reflecting the influence of society. Focuses on the poet's use of mountains, valleys, and the sea in the first chapter, and on his use of gardens, contrasted with the wilderness, in the second.

Francis, Elizabeth A., ed. *Tennyson: A Collection of Critical Essays*. Englewood Cliffs, N.J.: Prentice-Hall, 1980.
Twelve essays by distinguished Tennyson critics, covering all of the major long poems and a number of the shorter works. Most are excerpts from monographs, but the collection offers readers a good overview of the important issues which have intrigued twentieth century scholars. Includes a chronology and a brief bibliography of secondary sources.

Goslee, David. *Tennyson's Characters: "Strange Faces, Other Minds."* Iowa City: University of Iowa Press, 1989.
Develops a theory of Tennyson's composition process based on psychology but incorporating elements of formalism and literary history. Describes the poet as continually working to mediate his reaction to an "Other," some outside presence which threatens to invade and overpower his personality. Offers readings of dozens of works to show how this process manifests itself in individual poems.

Hair, Donald S. *Domestic and Heroic in Tennyson's Poetry*. Toronto: University of Toronto Press, 1981.
Concentrates on Tennyson's recurrent use of domestic scenes and themes throughout his career. Shows how he modifies various literary traditions, especially the pastoral and romance, to take full advantage of his readers' familiarity with and sympathy for family values. Devotes individual chapters to studies of *In Memoriam*, *The Princess*, and *Idylls of the King*; also discusses the poet's reliance on domestic images and themes in his use of the idyll and epyllion.

_____. *Tennyson's Language*. Toronto: University of Toronto Press, 1991.

Systematic examination of Tennyson's fascination with language and the influence on his poetry of theories of language prevalent in the nineteenth century. Pays special attention to theories espoused by John Locke, those of the Germano-Coleridgean tradition, ideas of his friends among the Cambridge Apostles, and philological discoveries made on the Continent. Tennyson seems especially influenced by the notion that language is an expression of God's plan for humankind, an idea he echoes in his major poetry. Includes extended study of *In Memoriam* and *Idylls of the King*.

Hellstrom, Ward. *On the Poems of Tennyson*. Gainesville: University Presses of Florida, 1972.

Focuses attention on the major poems, consciously avoiding bio-graphical or psychological interpretations in an attempt to rescue much of the poet's work from charges by early twentieth century critics who valued only the lyric poems which exhibit Tennyson's Romantic qualities. Devotes a chapter to *Maud* and two chapters each to *In Memoriam* and *Idylls of the King*.

Hughes, Linda K. *The Manyfacéd Glass: Tennyson's Dramatic Mono-logues*. Athens: Ohio University Press, 1987.

Explores Tennyson's fascination with dramatic monologue, a form he used for nearly one-fifth of his work. An introductory chapter offers a careful review of the history of the genre and establishes a working definition for examining works classified as dramatic monologues. In four chapters, Hughes analyzes monologues written during each phase of the poet's career, comparing them to lyrical works as a means of highlighting their dramatic qualities. Judges Tennyson a master of the form, equal to Robert Browning in many ways.

Johnson, Wendell Stacy. "Marriage and Divorce in Tennyson." In *Sex and Marriage in Victorian Poetry*. Ithaca, N.Y.: Cornell University Press, 1975.

Examines Tennyson's changing attitudes toward the idea of woman: shows how, in early poetry, women are portrayed as representations of the highest ideals, while in later works, especially *Idylls of the King*, they symbolize sensual desires. Sees parallel changes occurring in Tennyson's view of marriage: at first it seems a holy union, but in later works he finds this ideal more troublesome. Examines several poems in detail, especially *Idylls*, to illustrate this thesis.

Joseph, Gerhard. *Tennyson and the Text: The Weaver's Shuttle*. Cambridge, England: Cambridge University Press, 1992.

Collection of essays that focuses on Tennyson's reputation and on several of his works. Heavily influenced by literary theory; offers insightful analysis of the shifting critical perspectives on the poet's oeuvre. Challenges the portrait of the poet created by nineteenth century writers and supported by twentieth century critics such as Christopher Ricks, editor of Tennyson's poetry. Includes a very useful bibliography.

Jump, John D., ed. *Tennyson: The Critical Heritage*. London: Routledge & Kegan Paul, 1967.

Thirty-five excerpts from reviews and essays by Tennyson's contemporaries. Provides a sound sense of the reaction the poet's works inspired as they appeared throughout the century. Includes Arthur Henry Hallam's early assessment of Tennyson's promise, numerous selections on the major volumes, and several retrospective analyses published shortly after the poet's death.

Kincaid, James R. *Tennyson's Major Poems: The Comic and Ironic Patterns*. New Haven, Conn.: Yale University Press, 1975.

Examines Tennyson's poetry to show the special strength of his best verse arises from the tension between comic and ironic elements. The poet was aware of the absence of meaning in modern life, but he strove to write poetry that will provide meaning, often deriving his sense of hope from the literature of the past. Devotes separate chapters to examination of the early poetry, poems of the 1842 volume, the four major long poems, and the late work. Detailed analysis of all important works. Includes a good bibliography of secondary sources.

Kissane, James D. *Alfred Tennyson*. Boston: Twayne, 1970.

Overview of the poet's achievements. Introductory and concluding chapters offer assessments of Tennyson's reputation and judgments about his overall merits. Three central chapters examine his works by genre, with one chapter each devoted to the poet's lyrics, narratives, and dramatic poems. Includes a useful chronology and a modest annotated bibliography of secondary sources.

Kozicki, Henry. *Tennyson and Clio: History in the Major Poems*. Baltimore: Johns Hopkins University Press, 1979.

Systematic examination of Tennyson's philosophy of history; argues the intellectual unity of the poet's major works derives from his sense of history. Sees Tennyson's ideas about the historical process evolving over time; explores this development chronologically in nine chapters which show how the poet's ideas about history are exhibited in his works. Includes commentary on all the major poems, devoting two chapters to *Idylls of the King*.

McGhee, Richard D. "Tennyson." In *Marriage, Duty, and Desire in Victorian Poetry and Drama*. Lawrence: University Press of Kansas, 1980.
Examines the corpus of Tennyson's work to demonstrate the poet's lifelong concern with the conflict between duty and desire; believes Tennyson felt the "dialectic of love and duty" had metaphysical as well as moral implications. Reviews each volume published by the poet to highlight individual works which illustrate this theme. Includes a detailed analysis of *Maud*, *The Princess*, and *Idylls of the King*; argues for the artistic integrity of *Maud* as a poem in which the hero, like many of Tennyson's characters, undergoes a conversion from misplaced personal desire to acceptance of public duty. Also includes an examination of Tennyson's play *Becket*.

McSweeney, Kerry. *Tennyson and Swinburne as Romantic Naturalists*. Toronto: University of Toronto Press, 1981.
Examines the work of both writers to illustrate "the central importance of naturalistic vision" in each. Argues the Romantic tendencies in Tennyson were often at odds with strong Victorian sentiments; believes the poet's canon contains numerous inferior works but a number of gems. Explores the poems to show qualitative differences among them. Devotes chapters to the early poems, to *In Memoriam*, and to *Idylls of the King*. Two chapters compare the achievements of Swinburne and Tennyson.

Marshall, George O., Jr. *A Tennyson Handbook*. New York: Twayne, 1963.
Useful reference book providing bibliographic, biographic, and critical information on every poem Tennyson published. Organized by date of publication; offers brief analyses of the more important works, with minimal commentary on the poet's less distinguished writings. Includes a selected bibliography of secondary sources from the earlier decades of the twentieth century.

Martin, R. B. *Tennyson: The Unquiet Heart*. New York: Oxford University Press, 1980.
Comprehensive life study of the poet, offering exceptional psychological insight into Tennyson's relationship with his relatives, especially sensitive analysis of his troubled childhood in an family afflicted by

abuse and insanity. Shows how many works of the poet's mature years
bear the marks of early traumas and exhibit Tennyson's continuing fear
that he would go mad. Explains how the poet's wife and son sought to
represent Tennyson to posterity.

Mermin, Dorothy. "Tennyson." In *The Audience in the Poem: Five Victo-
rian Poets*. New Brunswick, N.J.: Rutgers University Press, 1983.
In a book examining poems which include an identifiable auditor,
Mermin analyzes several of Tennyson's works that fall in this subgenre.
Provides interesting discussion of the poet's reasons for creating this
form of poetry. Extended analysis of "St. Simeon Stylites," "Tiresias,"
"Ulysses," *Maud*, and "The Holy Grail" from *Idylls of the King*. Notes
the extensive presence of irony in each of these works.

Millgate, Michael. *Testamentary Acts: Browning, Tennyson, James,
Hardy*. Oxford: Clarendon Press, 1992.
Describes the immense influence Hallam Tennyson, the poet's son, had
in shaping the literary and personal reputation of his father. Discusses
the composition of the famous *Memoir* of Tennyson's life, in which so
many details of the poet's career and so many anecdotes about the
composition of individual poems are preserved. Also relates accounts
of the transmission of Tennyson's manuscripts within the family and
to various collections, and details the creation of the poet's image in
succeeding generations.

Millhauser, Milton. "Tennyson: Artifice and Image." In Shiv Kumar, ed.
British Victorian Literature: Recent Revaluations. New York: New
York University Press, 1969.
Harsh criticism of the poet's style, pointing out several ways Tennyson
limited himself by choosing forms uncongenial to his temperament or
by pressing to make clear the theme of his works through direct
statement rather than through his imagery. Compares his poetry with
several modern works, especially T. S. Eliot's *The Waste Land*, to show
Tennyson's failings. Argues the poet was too quick to compromise his
genius in an attempt to reach his contemporary audience.

Palmer, J. D., ed. *Tennyson*. Writers and Their Background. Athens: Ohio
University Press, 1973.
Nine essays providing a useful introduction to the social, cultural, and
intellectual background of Tennyson's poetry, showing the interaction
of the poet with important figures and movements of his age. Writers
deal with Tennyson's Romantic heritage; his relationship to his reading

public; his ongoing struggles over issues of religious faith; his support for Victorian social values; his work with the dramatic monologue and as a dramatist for the stage; and his tenure as Britain's poet laureate. The introductory chapter is a highly valuable guide to criticism of the poet's work; also contains a useful chronology of the major events of the poet's life and career in the context of important events of the century.

Pattison, Robert. *Tennyson and Tradition.* Cambridge, Mass.: Harvard University Press, 1979.
Extensive analysis of the poet's use of the literary tradition; displays Tennyson's superior craftsmanship in manipulating the works of others for his own special purposes. Explains how he uses borrowings not simply for stylistic purposes but to give resonance to the themes of his works. Chapters on Tennyson's sources for the development of the idyll form, which became a primary genre for him; on his English idylls; and on the major poems.

Pinion, F. B. *A Tennyson Companion: Life and Works.* New York: St. Martin's Press, 1984.
Study designed to introduce general readers to principal themes of Tennyson's work; to explain his wide-ranging interests and his use of various poetic techniques; and to explore his use of literary tradition in producing his art. Organized chronologically; includes a section on the poet's life and provides brief commentary on most of his works. Separate chapters examine the major poems and Tennyson's dramas. Appendices provide a family tree, a glossary of unusual words used by the poet, and a prose summary of *The Princess.*

Pitt, Valerie. *Tennyson Laureate.* London: Barrie & Rockliff, 1962.
Life study of the poet intended to expose as wrongheaded the traditional view of Tennyson as a Romantic poet who put aside his natural temperament to serve as a spokesperson for Victorian values. Demonstrates how the poet's life work is consistent in its revelation of "the sense of order in chaos" which he experienced in life, especially as a result of the death of Arthur Hallam. Includes a chapter on the poet's reputation in the first half of the twentieth century. Balanced study examining both early and late works.

Richardson, James. *Vanishing Lives: Style and Self in Tennyson, Dante Gabriel Rossetti, Swinburne, and Yeats.* Charlottesville: University Press of Virginia, 1988.
Study of Tennyson's style, demonstrating a link between "the motions

of poetry" and the poet's "sense of the self and its movement through time." Focuses on the preponderance of images suggesting dimness or a blurring of senses; also shows how the sensation of loss is conveyed through syntax and rhythm. Believes these poetic techniques reflect a deep psychological concern of the poet, who sensed that the cataclysmic changes in society created in himself and his readers a sense of loss; hence, much of his work takes on an elegiac tone.

Richardson, Joanna. *The Pre-Eminent Victorian: A Study of Tennyson.* London: Jonathan Cape, 1962.
Examines the poet's life within the context of his times. Demonstrates how Tennyson exemplifies what is most characteristic of the Victorian age. Traces his relationship with his family and with the many friends he influenced and who in turn influenced his work. Discusses how his attitude toward his vocation as a poet was shaped by the circumstances of his era. Deals briefly with biographical and intellectual background of major works and cites their impact on the Victorian reading public.

Ricks, Christopher. *Tennyson.* New York: Macmillan, 1972.
Critical overview of the poet's life and major accomplishments by the twentieth century editor of Tennyson's poetry. Focuses on the relationship of the poems to available biographical information. Tries to give a sense of Tennyson's private life, especially his early years. Places greater emphasis on discussion of works generally considered the poet's most important; devotes separate chapters to the major long poems.

Schur, Owen. *Victorian Pastoral: Tennyson, Hardy, and the Subversion of Forms.* Columbus: Ohio State University Press, 1989.
Examines Tennyson's work along with that of Thomas Hardy to show how both use the pastoral tradition to serve their own special purposes. Demonstrates ways Tennyson subverts this tradition to relieve himself from the boundaries and restrictions such a well-established genre imposes on those who choose to write pastorals. Explains how both poets stand as transitional figures between the established tradition and modern pastoral poetry.

Shaw, W. David. *Tennyson's Style.* Ithaca, N.Y.: Cornell University Press, 1976.
Careful analysis of stylistic devices which set Tennyson apart from contemporaries and others in the literary tradition. Devotes chapters to the major works; offers close textual readings of dozens of other poems. Praises the poet throughout for his brilliant handling of lan-

guage, his mastery of the poetic tradition and its conventions, and his ability to manipulate and conflate various literary genres. Includes an excellent bibliographic essay outlining principal critical commentary on the poet's style and about his major works.

_____. "Tyndall on Pictorial Analogy"; "God Knowable and Unknowable: Tennyson and the Boundaries of Consciousness"; "Hegel on Self-Making: Swinburne and Tennyson." In *The Lucid Veil: Poetic Truth in the Victorian Age*. Madison: University of Wisconsin Press, 1987.
Three brief essays and parts of others in this volume discuss Tennyson's understanding of science and philosophy and his use of both in his verse. The first examines the poet's debt to the writings of scientist John Tyndall, whose ideas about the imagination were familiar to Tennyson. The second focuses on the poet's understanding of the boundaries of consciousness, an idea derived from Kant; explains how Tennyson's appreciation of the limits of human understanding influenced his composition of *In Memoriam*. The final essay charts the influence of Hegel on both Tennyson and Swinburne, as these poets sought to express ideas about the ability of human beings to remake themselves.

Tennyson, Charles, and Christine Fall. *Alfred Tennyson: An Annotated Bibliography*. Athens: University of Georgia Press, 1967.
Useful annotations summarizing critical articles and longer studies written by Tennyson's contemporaries and by twentieth century scholars on a great number of the poet's works. Includes citations of writings dealing with the poet's life and with his dramatic works, as well as ones on topical issues such as religion, philosophy, and science. Also contains a section on the critical reception of the poet's works.

Thesing, William B. "Tennyson's Urban Vision: Historical Tremors and Hysterical Tremblings." In *The London Muse: Victorian Poetic Responses to the City*. Athens: University of Georgia Press, 1982.
Brief overview of Tennyson's uses of the city in various poems throughout his career. Sees "four distinct stages" in the poet's treatment of the city. The first is characterized by "ideal or visionary conceptions," seen in early poems such as "Babylon" and "Timbuctoo." In the second stage, exhibited by poems such as *In Memoriam* and *Maud*, the poet makes use of contemporary London. The third stage, one showing tensions between ideal and real, is best exemplified by *Idylls of the King*; the final stage, including poems such as "Locksley Hall Sixty Years After," is characterized by hysterical rantings about the evils of city life.

Turner, Paul. *Tennyson*. London: Routledge & Kegan Paul, 1976.
Study intended for general readers, surveying Tennyson's life and accomplishments. Focuses on the historical, social, political, and cultural background of the poems. Introductory chapters look at the chief characteristics of the Victorian period and sketch highlights of the poet's life. Succeeding chapters examine Tennyson's major volumes; includes assessments of the volumes of 1833 and 1842, *The Princess, In Memoriam, Maud*, and *Idylls of the King*. Concludes with a brief commentary on the poet's reputation.

Crossing the Bar

Kissane, James D. *Alfred Tennyson*. Boston: Twayne, 1970, pp. 159-161.
Brief assessment of a work Kissane considers "a splendid and characteristic lyric." Reviews previous published criticism, which has devalued the work because the poet seems to offer contradictory views about death. Argues the careful balance of images, often repeated in the four stanzas, suggests Tennyson intended to convey both the mystery of death and the sense of familiarity and comfort one should feel when it at last becomes possible to meet the Creator.

Shaw, W. David. *Tennyson's Style*. Ithaca, N.Y.: Cornell University Press, 1976, pp. 268-271.
Brief sympathetic analysis of the poem's language and structure, showing how Tennyson refuses to be led into maudlin thoughts about death. Explains the poet's use of the image of the Pilot, noting how Tennyson understood God was always "the guide as well as the goal" of his journey through life and into the realm beyond death. Points out structural parallels to *In Memoriam*. Also suggests Tennyson's repeated use of the optative allows the poet to withhold his commitment to an afterlife while stressing hope about it.

Enoch Arden

Buckley, Jerome H. *Tennyson: The Growth of a Poet*. Cambridge, Mass.: Harvard University Press, 1961, pp. 156-160.
Brief assessment pointing out the poem's strengths and weaknesses. Claims Tennyson's goal is to engage readers sentimentally in the story, and the narrative is merely a link between several brilliant rustic, domestic, and exotic scenes. Tennyson shifts his style radically, at times

using flat language to achieve a sense of realism, at other times becoming ornate to elevate scenes of working people to epic proportions.

Goslee, David. *Tennyson's Characters: "Strange Faces, Other Minds."* Iowa City: University of Iowa Press, 1989, pp. 189-195.
Brief review of other critics' reading of the work. Commentary on the development of Philip and Annie; more extensive analysis of Enoch, whom Goslee sees as a modern hero. Like several Romantic figures, he seems to be made to suffer for some unknown transgression; his suffering, especially his exile, makes him become acutely aware of the human condition in the cosmos. Believes the poem has decidedly Victorian overtones in the treatment of Annie's unintentional bigamy.

Hair, Donald S. *Domestic and Heroic in Tennyson's Poetry.* Toronto: University of Toronto Press, 1981, pp. 94-98.
Calls the poem "a skilful and effective combination of some of the recurring features of the idyls" which Tennyson wrote with regularity. Sees the poet glorifying domestic ideals by creating Enoch as a heroic figure who upholds those ideals in the face of great personal hardship. Notes frequent instances of irony in the poem, such as Enoch's personal tragedy resulting from his devotion to his family, and the use of an Edenic island setting as the site of Enoch's isolation. Also discusses Tennyson's use of Annie as an earth-mother figure.

Killham, John. "Tennyson and Victorian Social Values." In J. D. Palmer, ed. *Tennyson.* Writers and Their Background. Athens: Ohio University Press, 1973.
Discusses Tennyson's attempts to cater to popular Victorian notions of heroism and self-sacrifice. Shows how the poet reduces complex social, legal, and moral issues to simplistic choices which most of his readers would understand and appreciate. Compares Tennyson's treatment of the story to similar incidents in Byron's *Beppo* and Hardy's *Two on a Tower.*

Kincaid, James R. *Tennyson's Major Poems: The Comic and Ironic Patterns.* New Haven, Conn.: Yale University Press, 1975, pp. 228-230.
Brief comments about reasons the poem appears to be a failure. Notes the many ironic strands in the work which point toward a criticism of contemporary social values; argues Tennyson blunts the force of the poem at every point possible, turning the potentially ironic commentary into mere sentimentalism. Believes the poet stretches the limits of probability in his characterization and plotting.

Pinion, F. B. *A Tennyson Companion: Life and Works.* New York: St. Martin's Press, 1984, pp. 165-169.

Briefly summarizes the plot. Points out ways both Enoch and Philip are at times outsiders to the idyllic domestic society which is clearly presented in a favorable light. Discusses the significance of Tennyson's scene-painting in the work. Defends the poet's style, objecting to early criticism of its ornate qualities; has special opprobrium for Walter Bagehot's remarks about the poem.

Ricks, Christopher. "'Enoch Arden' and 'Aylmer's Field.'" In *Tennyson.* New York: Macmillan, 1972.

Explores the personal overtones of the work. Suggests Tennyson was always interested in the consequences of forced exile and the possibility of absence causing one to lose a spouse. Notes how Providence seems to play an unusual, almost malevolent role in the poem. Discusses the function of the landscape and the ending which has evoked hostile response from Tennyson's contemporaries and twentieth century critics.

Turner, Paul. *Tennyson.* London: Routledge & Kegan Paul, 1976, pp. 179-182.

Despite its poor reputation, Turner considers the work one of Tennyson's "great artistic achievements." Describes the genesis of the poem in a story told to Tennyson by Thomas Woolner. Points out parallels with he *Odyssey*, Shakespeare's works, and the Bible. Briefly outlines the Victorians' fascination with unintentional bigamy. Defends the conclusion, which has been consistently attacked by other critics.

Idylls of the King

Buckler, William E. *Man and His Myths: Tennyson's Idylls in Critical Context.* New York: New York University Press, 1984.

A casebook on the poem, consisting of a brief essay describing the work's chief themes and concerns; an extended critical analysis; selections from several dozen books and essays published between 1953 and 1981, offering a variety of viewpoints from which the poem as a whole and individual idylls may be viewed; and five short essays focusing on more limited subjects such as the poet's use of sources, his treatment of ethics and science in the poem, and his handling of the hero.

Buckley, Jerome H. "The City Built to Music." In *Tennyson: The Growth of a Poet.* Cambridge, Mass.: Harvard University Press, 1961.

Strongly defends the poem as fine art. Describes Tennyson's transformation of Arthurian sources to suit his purposes; provides a history of the composition process. Focuses on the character of Arthur, whose idealism conflicts with the sensual desires of most other figures in the work. Explains how imagery (especially musical imagery), themes, and atmosphere serve as unifying devices in the work. Also discusses Tennyson's use of animal imagery, color imagery, and the wasteland throughout the poem. Briefly notes the reaction to the poem by some of the poet's contemporaries.

Colley, Ann C. "Madness as Metaphor in the *Idylls of the King*." In *Tennyson and Madness*. Athens: University of Georgia Press, 1983.
Extensive examination of Tennyson's use of madness as a metaphor for the evils which bring down the perfect society King Arthur creates in Camelot. Shows how the poet uses the poem to highlight contemporary social problems. Argues Tennyson uses his knowledge of madness and its way of attacking an individual's mind as "a paradigm for analyzing the collapse of the nation's health." Especially good analysis of "The Marriage of Geraint," "Geraint and Enid," "Lancelot and Elaine," and "The Holy Grail." Points out how, in this last idyll, Tennyson explores his country's growing hysteria over religious issues.

Culler, A. Dwight. "*Idylls of the King*." In *The Poetry of Tennyson*. New Haven, Conn.: Yale University Press, 1977.
Penetrating analysis of a poem whose central theme involves the quest to determine the appropriate "spiritual authority" for governing society. Believes the poem is a somber judgment of modern society, where people are unable to uphold high ideals. Points out how most action in the ten internal idylls occurs late in Arthur's reign. Discusses several major characters, including the King, Guinevere, Merlin, and Vivien. Believes the work also mirrors Tennyson's realization that he was incapable of writing heroic poetry.

Eggers, J. Philip. *King Arthur's Laureate: A Study of Tennyson's Idylls of the King*. New York: New York University Press, 1971.
Develops a detailed interpretation of the poem by focusing on its "social meaning." Treats it from various perspectives, examining its place in the literary tradition and its effect on Tennyson's contemporaries. Shows the poem's relationship to its Arthurian sources and to competing nineteenth century versions of the legend; discusses its serial publication and its structure as a completed work.

Gray, J. M. *Thro' the Vision of the Night: A Study of Source, Evolution, and Structure in Tennyson's "Idylls of the King."* Montreal: McGill-Queens University Press, 1980.

Argues *Idylls of the King* is a highly structured work in which Tennyson solves the problem of composing a modern long poem. Reviews the poet's exceptional knowledge of his sources and his ability to modify them to achieve exceptional narrative and thematic unity. Discusses the evolution of the work over more than half a century. Devotes chapters to analyses of allusions, setting, language, characterization, and the use of songs and dreams.

Hair, Donald S. *"Idylls of the King."* In *Domestic and Heroic in Tennyson's Poetry.* Toronto: University of Toronto Press, 1981.

Lengthy analysis of the poem, focusing on Tennyson's methods for transforming the medieval legend into a work palatable to his Victorian readers. Suggests the poet provides a realistic note to the improbable Arthurian romance by centering on domestic issues, specifically marriage and personal commitment to ideals; the central interest for readers is in characters who undergo "the battle within the self" to uphold ideals. Believes Tennyson intended Arthur to be larger than life, representing the ideal toward which his knights would aspire.

_____. "'Man's word is God in man': *Idylls of the King.*" In *Tennyson's Language.* Toronto: University of Toronto Press, 1991.

Shows how contemporary ideas about philology influenced Tennyson's development of the poem and helped him focus on one important theme: the idea that language is "the expression of national character." Pays careful attention to the importance of language within the context of the poem, especially the use of vows, and the use of lies and gossip by those bent on destroying Arthur's kingdom. Also claims the "babble" of individuals who treat words lightly is equally destructive. Describes the value Arthur places on speech; argues the poet uses speech as a reflection of character.

Hellstrom, Ward. *"Idylls of the King*: A Prelude"; "*Idylls of the King*: The Poem."* In *On the Poems of Tennyson.* Gainesville: University Presses of Florida, 1972.

Devotes a chapter to exploring several questions about the poet's composition of his various idylls, the intellectual background of the work, and the structure of the final poem. Discusses Tennyson's adherence to the Liberal Anglican view of history and his inclusion of several devices to give structure to the disparate Arthurian stories. A second chapter focuses on an important theme which runs throughout the work: the proper role of women in society, and the relationship between the sexes. Concludes Tennyson's insistence on women's being merely complementary to men has made this poem unacceptable to many in the twentieth century.

Hughes, Linda K. "Tennyson's Urban Arthurians: Victorian Audiences and the 'City Built to Music.'" In Valerie M. Lagorio and Mildred Leake Day, eds. *King Arthur Through the Ages*. Vol. 2. New York: Garland, 1990.
Explains differences between nineteenth and twentieth century attitudes toward the *Idylls* by reviewing the impact serial publication had on Victorian readers' perceptions of the sequence. Shows how early idylls stressed the human qualities of Arthur and his knights and focused on the women whose roles were equally important in the kingdom. Notes the shift in tone introduced by the 1869 volume of new idylls, in which Tennyson's vision begins to darken and the pattern for the sequence begins to take shape. Because the poem appeared over a long period, Victorian readers were forced to reshape their attitudes about the *Idylls* as the poet added new themes and highlighted others latent in earlier parts of the work.

Hughes, Linda K., and Michael Lund. *The Victorian Serial*. Charlottesville: University Press of Virginia, 1991, pp. 125-154.
Examines the growth of the poem over more than forty years, and its effect on the British who read it serially. Discusses its theme of leadership and its close link to the growth of the poet himself. Quotes extensively from contemporary reviews to show how readers' perception of both subject and poet changed as Tennyson added idylls to his sequence. Notes the central position of King Arthur for Victorian readers, a view not shared by many twentieth century critics. Brief analyses of each idyll, focusing on ways individual idylls help develop the portrait of the king and his ideal society.

Hunt, John Dixon. "The Poetry of Distance: Tennyson's *Idylls of the King*." In Malcolm Bradbury and David Palmer, eds. *Victorian Poetry*. Stratford-on-Avon Studies 15. London: Edwin Arnold, 1972.
Claims Tennyson was always interested in writing about the past as a way of finding in the permanence of art an antidote for the constant flux of modern life. Believes that, in *Idylls of the King*, the poet continues the themes of earlier poetry which focused on the past, but manages to impart universal significance to the action of the work.

Argues Tennyson owes much to the Pre-Raphaelites for his decision to use women to represent psychological types. Discusses the poet's methods for infusing medieval materials with contemporary significance, a decision he made in response to popular demands for contemporary relevance in poetry.

Johnson, Wendell Stacy. *Sex and Marriage in Victorian Poetry*. Ithaca, N.Y.: Cornell University Press, 1975, pp 146-181.
Discusses the important theme of marriage in the poem; notes virtually every one of the twelve idylls focuses on a relationship between lovers, many of whom are married or who are hopeful of marrying. Carefully examines each idyll to show how every relationship contains an element of tension and discontent; most end in failure. Arthur's failure to achieve a good marriage is emblematic of his larger failure to establish a lasting good society. Notes how, as the story progresses, there is a growing sense of sensuality about male-female relationships, putting other characters at odds with Arthur's spiritual ideals.

Jump, John D., ed. *Tennyson: The Critical Heritage*. London: Routledge & Kegan Paul, 1967.
Five extensive excerpts from reviews and essays by Tennyson's contemporaries, offering a good assessment of the impact the poem had as it appeared in serial form over almost four decades. Includes laudatory analyses by Walter Bagehot and William E. Gladstone. Scattered comments on the poem appear in several other reviews and selections in the volume.

Kincaid, James R. "*Idylls of the King*." In *Tennyson's Major Poems: The Comic and Ironic Patterns*. New Haven, Conn.: Yale University Press, 1975.
Lengthy analysis of a work Kincaid calls "one of the two or three most important poems of the century." Considers *Idylls* a masterpiece of ironic art, in which Tennyson undermines the traditions of romance, tragedy, and comedy. The King's attempt to establish a perfect society cannot stand against its greatest enemies: time and internal forces. Others are unable to live up to Arthur's high ideals. Detailed explication of each of the twelve idylls to show how the perfect society Arthur creates is destroyed from within, denying the King even the dignity of a tragic passing.

Kissane, James D. *Alfred Tennyson*. Boston: Twayne, 1970, pp. 99-119.
Sympathetic assessment of the poem often denigrated by twentieth

century critics. Justifies Tennyson's transformation of Arthurian materials into a nineteenth century analysis of moral and social relationships. Briefly reviews each of the twelve idylls to explain how they are unified in their presentation of Tennyson's major themes: the conflicts between spiritual idealism and naturalism, traditional values and individual inclination, and moral absolutism and relativism. Provides balanced view of the hero; argues that, as the standard of moral excellence, Arthur is by nature not as complex as those whose flaws may make them initially more intriguing for readers.

Kozicki, Henry. "The Rise of Camelot"; "The Decline and Fall of Camelot." In *Tennyson and Clio: History in the Major Poems*. Baltimore: Johns Hopkins University Press, 1979.
Two chapters examining the intellectual background of the poem. Explores Tennyson's reading during the 1850's, especially his contact with Hegel's *Philosophy of History*, which provides an explanation for the cyclic theory of civilizations which suited Tennyson's purposes. Also discusses the poet's interest in allegory, which influenced his conception of the story. Explains how the action of the poem follows Hegel's theory of dialectic.

McSweeney, Kerry. "Sexuality and Vision in *Idylls of the King*." *Tennyson and Swinburne as Romantic Naturalists*. Toronto: University of Toronto Press, 1981.
Focuses attention on two groups of idylls: the Holy Grail Group ("The Coming of Arthur," "The Holy Grail," and "The Passing of Arthur") and the Tristram Group ("Balin and Balan," "Pelleas and Ettarre," and "The Last Tournament"). In the former, Tennyson explores several "epistemological and spiritual issues central" to his age. In the latter, he examines the psychological tensions involving conflicts over sexual passion. Provides detailed analyses of the six idylls, especially "Balin and Balan" and "The Last Tournament." Concludes the latter is one of the poet's finest works, but *Idylls of the King* as a whole lacks artistic unity and has been overvalued by critics.

Pattison, Robert. *Tennyson and Tradition*. Cambridge, Mass.: Harvard University Press, 1979, pp. 134-151.
Sensitive and sensible analysis of Tennyson's use of various poetic genres in the work. Believes a central problem for those wishing to comprehend the work is to develop a thorough understanding of this mixture of traditional genres. Examines ways the poet incorporates elements of the idyll, epic, lyric, allegory, and romance into his story

of Arthur. Acknowledges the poet's interest in the "moments of divided mentality" so many characters experience, as they are challenged to rise above the material world toward one more ideal.

Pinion, F. B. *"Idylls of the King."* In *A Tennyson Companion: Life and Works.* New York: St. Martin's Press, 1984.
Describes Tennyson's fascination with the Arthurian story; cites the importance of Arthur Hallam as an inspiration for the poet's hero. Calls King Arthur a creation of the poet, who manipulates sources for his own purposes. Discusses each idyll in order of composition and publication; includes plot summaries and analyses of the various characters' reactions to Arthur's stringent requirements for moral perfection. Concludes with a brief commentary on the significance of the poem and on the uneven qualities of its narrative.

Reed, John R. *Perception and Design in Tennyson's Idylls of the King.* Athens: Ohio University Press, 1969.
Believes the poem contains a carefully crafted moral design, showing the conflicts between faith and doubt and the struggle between humility and pride. In a lengthy chapter, examines each of the twelve narratives which make up the complete poem, showing how, though self-contained stories, each advances the central idea Tennyson portrays: sacrifice of self to higher ideals is essential for moral perfection. Includes a separate chapter exploring the work's major themes.

Ricks, Christopher. *"Idylls of the King 1859-1885."* In *Tennyson.* New York: Macmillan, 1972.
Finds Tennyson's performance uneven. Believes the completed sequence lacks unity. Faults the poet for numerous stylistic infelicities, cataloging several by quoting liberally from the text. Cites commentary from Tennyson's contemporaries who were troubled by the work. Acknowledges the strengths of individual lines and similes, but concludes Tennyson's ability to create narrative fails him in the poem.

Rosenberg, John D. *The Fall of Camelot: A Study of Tennyson's "Idylls of the King."* Cambridge, Mass.: Belknap Press, 1973.
Monograph assessing a work Rosenberg considers one of the greatest long poems in English. Dispels ideas that Tennyson is not a great narrative poet. Displays the poet's genius for creating an illuminating study of the conflict between illusion and reality. Separate chapters examine Tennyson's use of landscape to reveal character and his manipulation of time; explains how the poet coalesces Christian and

pagan myths in his presentation of the cycle of Arthur's coming and passing. Two chapters review the poet's development of character through the use of symbol and story.

Ryals, Clyde de L. *From the Great Deep: Essays on "Idylls of the King."* Athens: Ohio University Press, 1967.

Claims the poem is Tennyson's *magnum opus*, a work in which he displays keen philosophical insight into the human condition. Describes how Arthur is both hero and villain in the work, as his efforts to create the ideal society cause him to impose his will on others and inhibit their freedom. Argues Tennyson saw hope for spiritual redemption through selfless love. Concludes the poet takes a stance as a Christian existentialist in the work.

Shaw, W. David. "Terror and Innocence: *Idylls of the King.*" In *Tennyson's Style*. Ithaca, N.Y.: Cornell University Press, 1976.

Laudatory assessment of a poem Shaw considers a fine assessment of complex forces inside every individual. Points out Tennyson's repeated use of doublings to highlight the duality of human nature. Considers Arthur an idealist who understands the price he must pay for being an authority figure. Explains how each idyll illustrates and advances the poet's central concerns. Extensive analysis of "The Holy Grail," which Shaw calls Tennyson's "most dazzling achievement in visionary writing." Argues the downfall of Camelot results from people's inability to sustain their pursuit of ideals; figures like Guinevere and Lancelot are attractive because readers see themselves in such characters.

Staines, David. *Tennyson's Camelot: The Idylls of the King and Its Medieval Sources*. Waterloo, Canada: Wilfrid Laurier University Press, 1982.

Examines in great detail Tennyson's transformation of medieval Arthurian works into his nineteenth century story of the rise and fall of Camelot. Discusses the poem in the order of composition of individual idylls, describing the poet's changing attitude toward his sources. Concludes with a chapter assessing the significance of the work as a completed poem; evaluates Tennyson as an Arthurian scholar. Several appendices provide additional material on Tennyson's use of source materials, as well as comments from the poet's notebooks on the legend and his plans for constructing a poem from Arthurian materials.

Turner, Paul. "*Idylls of the King.*" In *Tennyson*. London: Routledge & Kegan Paul, 1976.

Focuses on the background of the poem. Reviews Tennyson's first proposals for an allegory based on the story of Arthur, and the changes he made to combine the romance with a study of contemporary social issues. Discusses the influence of evolutionary writings on the poet's ideas about the progress of civilizations. Also investigates transformations of medieval sources, especially Malory; notes how Tennyson idealizes Arthur and Merlin while devaluing Gawaine and Tristram. Reviews the use of epic models and of Theocritus. Concludes with examination of poetic devices used to unify the work, especially imagery.

In Memoriam

Albright, Daniel. "The Muses' Tug of War in *In Memoriam*." In *Tennyson: The Muses' Tug of War*. Charlottesville: University Press of Virginia, 1986.

Sees the poet struggling throughout with two conflicting tendencies, personified by the muses Urania (inspiration for high art) and Melpomene (inspiration for personal grief). Believes the work is full of imaginative excesses which keep it from being successful as a formal elegy; Tennyson is too close to his subject, and he transforms everything he sees around him into a symbol of his feelings for Hallam, making it hard for him to create a grand work of universal significance. Looks carefully at stanzas in this work and at other Tennyson poems to provide examples of the competing tendencies.

Ball, Patricia M. "Till All My Widowed Race Be Run." In *The Heart's Events: The Victorian Poetry of Relationships*. London: Athlone Press, 1976.

Posits the central theme of the poem to be the poet's attempt at dealing with the process of bereavement. Sees Tennyson's decision to link the lyrics into a long poem as wise, because the long poem is an apt vehicle for conveying the theme: the speaker's lengthy investigations of the many forms of grief and loss he confronts in the world over time help him become reconciled to the loss of Arthur Hallam. Carefully traces through the individual lyrics the poet's gradual ability to come to accept the absence of his friend. Suggests the fate of the one left behind is paramount in the poet's mind as he explores his sense of loss.

Buckler, William E. "*In Memoriam* in Aesthetic Context." In *The Victorian Imagination: Essays in Aesthetic Exploration*. New York: New York University Press, 1980.

Claims earlier critics have failed to heed Tennyson's remarks that the poem is impersonal, not biographical. Presents a reading which subordinates the poet's personal relationship with Arthur Henry Hallam to a larger theme: the quest of the modern poet to explore the nature of reality and the concept of the self in a world where traditional systems of belief are no longer accepted. The poem develops a myth for Tennyson's time, and by extension for modern times, to replace inoperative Christian myths. Discusses the importance of *The Divine Comedy* and Tennyson's "Ulysses" in shaping the poet's perception of the central theme of *In Memoriam*: the self in need of renewal and reintegration. Examines other Tennyson poems in which the poet uses symbolic techniques similar to those employed in his great elegy.

Buckley, Jerome H. "*In Memoriam*: The Way of the Soul." In *Tennyson: The Growth of a Poet*. Cambridge, Mass.: Harvard University Press, 1961.
Briefly describes the process of composition and the initial publication of the work. Discusses the structure, noting how the form affords Tennyson opportunities to explore his personal feelings. Highlights recurring imagery. Explains the function of sections on Victorian science and explores Tennyson's concern with the development of the self and the necessity for understanding the place of the individual in the world. Believes the poem is religious without being specifically Christian.

Culler, A. Dwight. "*In Memoriam*." In *The Poetry of Tennyson*. New Haven, Conn.: Yale University Press, 1977.
Lengthy, detailed analysis, arguing Tennyson consciously rejected the traditional form of elegy because he wanted to show the gradual progress of the speaker toward some understanding of his friend's death; hence, the poet could not include a *peripeteia*, suddenly moving from grief to joy. Careful examination of each of the nine "natural divisions" Tennyson suggested for the work, especially thorough review of the concept of immortality as Tennyson and his contemporaries understood it, and a discussion of the poet's distinction between knowledge and wisdom. Believes the epilogue was added as a way for the poet to move from "personal sorrow to some larger, even cosmic dimension."

Dawson, Carl. "*In Memoriam*: The Uses of Dante and Wordsworth." In *Victorian Noon: English Literature in 1850*. Baltimore: Johns Hopkins University Press, 1979.

Discusses the reaction of Tennyson's contemporaries to the publication of *In Memoriam* in 1850 and explains how the attitude of Tennyson and of his reading public toward Dante helped shape both the composition of the poem and its reception. Traces the popularity of Dante in the nineteenth century to show how his work influenced poets, especially Tennyson. Explains how Tennyson's contemporaries would have also compared *In Memoriam* with the recently published 1850 version of Wordsworth's long personal epic, *The Prelude*.

Goslee, David. *"In Memoriam."* In *Tennyson's Characters: "Strange Faces, Other Minds."* Iowa City: University of Iowa Press, 1989.
Claims this is the first poem in which Tennyson confronts the loss of Hallam directly, trying to come to grips with his loss while simultaneously preserving Hallam's memory. Examines the composition process with great care, using previously published scholarship and an analytical framework highlighting the poet's continual pattern of arranging lyrics already composed, then supplying additional new sections which offer further explanation of his feelings for Hallam.

Hair, Donald S. "'Heart-affluence in discursive talks': *In Memoriam.*" In *Tennyson's Language.* Toronto: University of Toronto Press, 1991.
Traces the influence of language theories of such diverse figures as John Keble, Samuel Taylor Coleridge, John Locke, and Lucretius on Tennyson's development of the form for this work. Discusses the importance of analogy as a means of approaching genuine knowledge of his subject. Concentrates on the poet's apprehension of the terms "faith" and "doubt." Extensive analysis of Tennyson's understanding of the nature and function of language as the basis for his method of composition; pays special attention to the poet's selection of words and tropes.

_____. "Tennyson's Domestic Elegy." In *Domestic and Heroic in Tennyson's Poetry.* Toronto: University of Toronto Press, 1981.
Carefully examines the poet's use of domestic images and settings to transform the traditional elegy into a work particularly appropriate for Victorian readers. Looks at each of the four major divisions of the poem and the Christmas lyrics which divide them; points out the significance of Christmas as a Victorian family celebration and the mythic dimensions of the birth of the Christchild ushering in a new age. Sees Tennyson creating Hallam as a heroic figure within a domestic setting. Explains why Tennyson chooses to use marriage as a central metaphor for his relationship with Hallam.

Hellstrom, Ward. "*In Memoriam*: A Prelude"; "*In Memoriam*: The Poem." In *On the Poems of Tennyson*. Gainesville: University Presses of Florida, 1972.

Deals with the perennial critical problems of meaning and unity. Sees Hallam as a useful tool in Tennyson's plan to examine "the unity behind the diversity and change of the cosmic process." Discusses the Liberal Anglican theology from which Tennyson draws ideas; points out how Hallam is used as Dante used Beatrice in his work. Focuses on the poem as a work of art rather than simply autobiography. Explains ways Tennyson employs poetic devices to achieve formal and structural unity.

Hughes, Linda K. *The Manyfacéd Glass: Tennyson's Dramatic Monologues*. Athens: Ohio University Press, 1987, pp. 135-154.

Claims Tennyson's experiments with dramatic monologues prepared him to write this poem; believes the poet uses techniques of the monologue, especially the distancing of the speaker from the poet, to allow him to expose his private feelings about Hallam without undue personal risk. Shows how Tennyson relies on readers' active participation in creating meaning. Carefully examines the structure, showing how the psychological movement is a vacillation between separation from and union with Hallam. Briefly discusses the function of the epilogue.

Hunt, John Dixon, ed. *Tennyson: In Memoriam, a Casebook*. London: Macmillan, 1970.

Collection of essays by nineteenth and twentieth century readers of the poem, offering a variety of assessments about the work's artistic merits. Eight brief excerpts from reviews by Tennyson's contemporaries suggest the range of critical opinion in the poet's day. Eleven more extended commentaries by twentieth century critics, all previously published, give a good sense of the poem's enduring qualities. Also includes two essays by Arthur Henry Hallam, the subject of Tennyson's elegy. Hunt's introduction surveys the history of criticism of the work.

Johnson, Wendell Stacy. *Sex and Marriage in Victorian Poetry*. Ithaca, N.Y.: Cornell University Press, 1975, pp. 135-144.

Discusses Tennyson's use of marriage in the poem; throughout, marriage is used as a metaphor for the union the speaker wishes to achieve with his dead friend, and his grief at the loss of Hallam is often described as being like that of a widow. Notes the poet's careful use of a real marriage and the birth of a child at the end of the elegy; this image is symbolic of hope, which Tennyson feels after passing through the various stages of despair and grief which initially swept over him when his friend was lost.

Jump, J. D. "Tennyson's Religious Faith and Doubt." In J. D. Palmer, ed. *Tennyson*. Writers and Their Background. Athens: Ohio University Press, 1973.
Considers the work Tennyson's most important religious poem, in which he gives expression to his desolation at the loss of Arthur Hallam and the hope he "wrung from a state bordering on despair." Carefully examines the nine-part structure Tennyson provided for the work. Describes how the poem is simultaneously personal and philosophical. Concludes with an explanation of the work's religious dimension.

Kincaid, James R. "*In Memoriam*." In *Tennyson's Major Poems: The Comic and Ironic Patterns*. New Haven, Conn.: Yale University Press, 1975.
Argues Tennyson attempts in this poem to re-create the spirit of medieval comedy to counterbalance the despair and irony which characterize the circumstances of the speaker's loss of his friend. The loss of Hallam suggests that all continuity of relationships may be impossible. Throughout the work the speaker seeks some assurance of the ability to establish such continuity. Claims the structure of the work cannot be easily defined because Tennyson is exploring the consequences of living in a world where structure seems missing. Looks carefully at individual lyrics to trace the tension between irony and comedy and the movement from an ironic to a comic perspective.

Kissane, James D. *Alfred Tennyson*. Boston: Twayne, 1970, pp. 66-78.
Extended analysis of the poem acknowledged by Kissane as the one on which Tennyson's reputation finally rests. Briefly reviews the work's biographical genesis; discusses the poet's use of his unusual stanza form and method of composition. Focuses on Tennyson's handling of grief and on the importance of memory as a unifying principle which gives shape to the disparate lyrics which make up the poem.

McSweeney, Kerry. "The Natural Magic of *In Memoriam*." In *Tennyson and Swinburne as Romantic Naturalists*. Toronto: University of Toronto Press, 1981.
Argues one of the major informing principles of the poem is the recompense for loss provided by memory and by "the ministration of the natural world." This recompense is insufficient for the poet, however, who strives to impose a supernatural dimension on the work.

Looks carefully at numerous lyrics to show how both memory and natural phenomena offer the speaker consolation for his lost friend. Pays considerable attention to Lyric XCV, which McSweeney considers "the positive climax" of the poem.

Pattison, Robert. *Tennyson and Tradition.* Cambridge, Mass.: Harvard University Press, 1979, pp. 103-130.
Points out the poem's tight structure and the public character of the work. Traces the classical sources of elegiac writing on which Tennyson depended. Discusses the "evolutionary question" at the center of the poem; also describes the poem's affinities with Dante's work. Explains how the structure mirrors Tennyson's need to discard traditional forms of elegy, and adopt more lyric modes, to truly celebrate Hallam, who comes to represent "humanity evolved to perfection through an organic though painful process."

Peltason, Timothy. *Reading "In Memoriam."* Princeton, N.J.: Princeton University Press, 1985.
Systematic, detailed, personal reading of the poem, focusing on the individual beauties and the larger themes readers discover in the act of reading. Attempts to read the poem "consecutively and cumulatively," offering multiple possibilities for interpretation. An introductory chapter describes the poem's composition and discusses the unusual effect produced by the accumulation of short poems into the larger whole. Central chapters provide detailed analyses of individual lyrics; final chapter offers an assessment of the poem's epilogue.

Pinion, F. B. "*In Memoriam A.H.H.*" In *A Tennyson Companion: Life and Works.* New York: St. Martin's Press Press, 1984.
Briefly acknowledges early lyrics from which the elegy grew; sees the general movement from grief to assurance of immortality and reunion. Carefully summarizes the various sections of the work, concentrating on Tennyson's use of poetic devices to vivify the feelings engendered by the loss of Hallam. Includes commentary on the poet's ability to create scenes of beauty and significance.

Ricks, Christopher. "*In Memoriam 1850.*" In *Tennyson.* New York: Macmillan, 1972.
Reviews the composition history of the work; argues against claims for strong unity in the poem. Points out influences of Shakespeare's sonnet sequence on the poet's conception of his completed work. Discusses in some detail charges that Tennyson expresses a homosex-

ual love for Hallam. Pays some attention to the poet's use of the *abba* rhyme scheme.

Shaw, W. David. "The Autobiography of a Mourner: *In Memoriam*." In *Tennyson's Style*. Ithaca, N.Y.: Cornell University Press, 1976.
Claims the poem is an intentional mixing of genres, meant to provoke readers into seeing the multifaceted nature of the mourner's grief. Places the poem within the tradition of confessional literature. Believes the work looks simultaneously inward and outward, as the mourner's doubts are mirrored in those of the age. Shows how the mourner's catharsis is presented in five ways: through the formal features of verse, through biblical and natural imagery, through use of puns and epigrams, through "generic indirection," and through the use of visionary experiences.

Sinfield, Alan. *The Language of Tennyson's "In Memoriam."* New York: Barnes & Noble, 1971.
Detailed analysis of the language and poetic devices used by the poet to create his elegiac masterpiece. Devotes two chapters each to discussion of diction, syntax, and imagery, and single chapters to considerations of sound and rhythm. Explores ways the poet uses rhetorical and tropological devices to highlight themes. Concludes with a chapter on Tennyson's impact on modern poetry, especially the symbolist movement.

_____. "Matter-Moulded Forms of Speech: Tennyson's Use of Language in *In Memoriam*." In Isobel Armstrong, ed. *The Major Victorian Poets: Reconsiderations*. Lincoln: University of Nebraska Press, 1969.
Disputes earlier claims that Tennyson could not write highly structured poetry; contends *In Memoriam* provides evidence to the contrary. Focuses on Section XCV of the work, a passage central to understanding the nature of Tennyson's mystical experience in his attempts to bridge the gap between himself and his deceased friend. Uses exceptionally close textual analysis of individual words, lines, and stanzas to illustrate subtle shifts of mood and carefully selected images which allow the poet to represent to his readers a realm beyond reality.

Turner, Paul. "*In Memoriam*." In *Tennyson*. London: Routledge & Kegan Paul, 1976.
Detailed analysis of the many literary and nonliterary sources on which Tennyson drew for the poem. Discusses the poet's reliance on Arthur

Henry Hallam's writings about rational theology; his use of literary precedents, especially classical writers including Horace, from whom he borrowed the association of "human feelings with seasonal change" and the use of anniversaries; his affinities with Petrarch, Shakespeare, and Milton; his debt to Plato and Lucretius for the poem's philosophical underpinnings; and his adoption of ideas about evolution from Charles Lyell and Robert Chambers.

The Lady of Shalott

Albright, Daniel. *Tennyson: The Muses' Tug of War*. Charlottesville: University Press of Virginia, 1986, pp. 31-37.
Reads the poem as an example of Tennyson's criticism of "high imagination," the kind which cuts one off from the world. Makes extensive comparisons between "The Lady of Shalott" and "Elaine," one of the twelve *Idylls of the King*, to show how damaging this form of imagination can be. Discusses the use of the mirror and the river as symbols of the imagination. Believes "The Lady of Shalott" can be interpreted allegorically as the story of the soul of the artist being destroyed by its transformation into the real world.

Culler, A. Dwight. *The Poetry of Tennyson*. New Haven, Conn.: Yale University Press, 1977, pp. 44-49.
Careful examination of both plot and theme. Suggests Tennyson is working with a folk tradition in which a faery falls in love with a mortal. Points out the many contrasts between the Lady and Lancelot. Argues the Lady is emblematic of the artist who participates indirectly in life through the power of her art; once the artist enters the world, imagination is stifled. Notes how Tennyson's changes in the 1842 volume significantly altered readers' perception of Lancelot from that of the originally published version.

Hellstrom, Ward. *On the Poems of Tennyson*. Gainesville: University Presses of Florida, 1972, pp. 10-15.
Challenges traditional readings of the poem as a statement of the destructive effects of society on the artist; argues instead that Tennyson consciously revised the poem to highlight the lifelessness of the Lady's tower and the vibrancy of the world outside. Therefore, her decision to leave the tower is a positive affirmation of life. The paradox of this choice is that it leads to her death; but such is to be expected, since all life eventually ends in death.

Johnson, Wendell Stacy. *Sex and Marriage in Victorian Poetry*. Ithaca, N.Y.: Cornell University Press, 1975, pp. 114-116.
Compares the poem to "Mariana" and "Œnone"; all three deal with "loneliness," a "longing for death," and "the failure of love and marriage." The Lady lives isolated from the world; when she finally sees the man with whom she wishes to be united, she ventures after him, only to find death in society outside her tower. Notes how the poem may be read as emblematic of the poet's own fear of losing his poetic powers if he immerses himself in social concerns.

Joseph, Gerhard. *Tennyson and the Text: The Weaver's Shuttle*. Cambridge, England: Cambridge University Press, 1992, pp. 102-110.
Traces the history of criticism of the poem, showing how its meaning has shifted as critics have read the work in light of the prevailing critical paradigms of their generations. Explains how Tennyson's nineteenth century contemporaries reacted to the poem; how it fared with the New Critics; and how proponents of literary theory have read it. Focuses on the function of the image of the mirror, explaining what that image has meant to different critics.

Kincaid, James R. *Tennyson's Major Poems: The Comic and Ironic Patterns*. New Haven, Conn.: Yale University Press, 1975, pp. 31-35.
Claims the poem, expanded in the 1842 version, is clearly ironic. The Lady has no real choice between alternate lifestyles, but rather is condemned either to isolation from the world (remaining in her tower) or to death (the price she pays for leaving it). Argues the Lady represents an incomplete self who seeks fulfillment by leaving her place of isolation only to find "not freedom and expression" but "obliteration." The imagery of the poem shows life and death are represented equally and indifferently in this world. The irony is carried through to the end of the work, where no one, not even Lancelot, is able to explain the significance of the Lady's decision to seek self-ful-fillment in the world.

McSweeney, Kerry. *Tennyson and Swinburne as Romantic Naturalists*. Toronto: University of Toronto Press, 1981, pp. 42-45.
Brief but insightful analysis of a poem McSweeney considers one of the poet's finest. Sees it as one of several Tennyson writes to explore the conditions under which art is created and the Romantic notion of the necessity for the artist to remain isolated from society. Examines each part of the poem carefully, demonstrating the impact Lancelot has on the Lady; the knight, who represents an idealized version of human

love, causes the Lady to enter the world below, where natural elements which seemed benevolent when viewed from above are now seen as more threatening.

Pattison, Robert. *Tennyson and Tradition*. Cambridge, Mass.: Harvard University Press, 1979, pp. 47-50, 55-59.
Discusses the formal qualities of the work which attracted Tennyson. Believes the poem shares aspects of both idyll and epyllion. Describes Tennyson's borrowings and omissions from his Italian source; notes the poet's primary interest is in the character of his heroine, who seems to suffer from some unnamed melancholy. Compares the poem briefly to similar works in the Tennyson canon.

Shaw, W. David. *Tennyson's Style*. Ithaca, N.Y.: Cornell University Press, 1976, pp. 62-65.
Brief analysis of the poem, concentrating on the poet's craftsmanship. Points out the extensive revisions Tennyson made over the years during which he tinkered with the text. Reads the poem as a search for identity and attributes the tenuous nature of the lady's behavior, mirrored in the imagery, to the poet's desire to represent that search dramatically.

Locksley Hall

Albright, Daniel. *Tennyson: The Muses' Tug of War*. Charlottesville: University Press of Virginia, 1986, pp. 122-127.
Believes the poem displays an "exercise of supreme rhetorical power" which overwhelms any sense of coherence in the speaker's personality. The speaker simply rants against the injustices of the world, without any "steady sense of fact." Notes the highly sexual tone of the entire work. Compares the speaker to his re-created self in "Locksley Hall Sixty Years After" to show how much his imagination and his belief in the power of external forces has shrunk.

Buckler, William E. "In Defense of *Locksley Hall*." In *The Victorian Imagination: Essays in Aesthetic Exploration*. New York: New York University Press, 1980.
Insists the poem should not be read autobiographically. Cites Tennyson's own comments to show the real subject is the confrontation of youth with the disappointments of his society and his eventual resolution of his sorrow through acceptance of the social and scientific progress which signal a better life. Extended subtle analysis of the

speaker; notes how the form of the poem, the monodrama, is particularly appropriate for dealing with the subject Tennyson has chosen.

Goslee, David. *Tennyson's Characters: "Strange Faces, Other Minds."* Iowa City: University of Iowa Press, 1989, pp. 198-202.
Links the poem with "Enoch Arden" and "Aylmer's Field" as poems which use "a visionary figure" to explore the dangers of religious systems. Considers the work Tennyson's frankest assessment of sexuality and his most extensive attempt to deal directly with the source of sexual desire. Explores ways the poet tries to circumscribe the temptress Venus, whom he sees as a particularly threatening figure psychologically. Looks at unused fragments from manuscripts to support his reading.

Hughes, Linda K. *The Manyfacéd Glass: Tennyson's Dramatic Monologues.* Athens: Ohio University Press, 1987, pp. 119-122.
Brief discussion of the character of the speaker in the poem; notes how successfully Tennyson keeps readers focused on the consciousness of the young man. Also points out the emphasis placed on time: the speaker is entranced by both past and future, and the poem shows how he comes to reject possibilities for happiness in either. Also shows how deftly Tennyson integrates social commentary into an intensely personal poem.

Kincaid, James R. *Tennyson's Major Poems: The Comic and Ironic Patterns.* New Haven, Conn.: Yale University Press, 1975, pp. 54-57.
Sees the speaker in the poem as trivializing the dilemmas he faces, acting spitefully in blaming external sources for the problems he encounters. Claims there are no real crises in the work, only invented ills which allow the speaker to vent his spleen. Believes the speaker is really isolated from the world, unable to benefit from the progress he celebrates; he is characterized throughout by an "egoistic shallowness."

Kozicki, Henry. *Tennyson and Clio: History in the Major Poems.* Baltimore: Johns Hopkins University Press, 1979, pp. 71-75.
Explores the numerous and often conflicting views of history which inform the poem. Claims the hero vacillates between affinity for the process of evolution he sees taking place in society and a wish to destroy that society through violent revolution. Cites the importance of Carlyle's ideas about history to Tennyson's development of the poem's theme; believes the work suggests a change in the poet's position about the idea of history as a gradual process of change.

Pattison, Robert. *Tennyson and Tradition.* Cambridge, Mass.: Harvard University Press, 1979, pp. 87-90.

Discusses the poem as a culmination of a series of twelve brief idylls which explore "the warring forces of love and duty." Points out parallels to numerous other works by Tennyson and to Dante's *Divine Comedy, The.* Considers the work the finest of the early idylls in presenting "the fullest description of the emotional filaments that compound the vexed question of human happiness."

Rader, Ralph W. *Tennyson's Maud: The Biographical Genesis.* Berkeley: University of California Press, 1963, pp. 37-47.

Careful examination of the background and details of the poem to show how it has strong biographical influences. Notes the poet provides no hints that his speaker is fictional, and comments on the multiple appearances of similar stories in Tennyson's canon. Looks at both internal and external evidence to establish the date of composition at 1837-1838, a time when the poet had been recently jilted by Rosa Baring. Points out parallels between Rosa and Duncombe Shafto, her husband, and the fictional couple in "Locksley Hall."

The Lotos-Eaters

Buckler, William E. "Tennyson's *The Lotos-Eaters*: Emblem of a New Poetry." In *The Victorian Imagination: Essays in Aesthetic Exploration.* New York: New York University Press, 1980.

Argues that, within this poem, Tennyson introduces an entirely new kind of poetry into the literary tradition: a fusion of classicism (the Homeric story from which he draws his subject), Elizabethanism (in his use and modification of the Spenserian stanza form), and Romanticism (in his treatment of his subject). Maintains Tennyson is able to balance these traditions and let the action of the story have primacy while highlighting the self-discovery made by the mariners in their lotus-induced musings. Carefully explicates the poem, paying special attention to prosody and imagery.

Hellstrom, Ward. *On the Poems of Tennyson.* Gainesville: University Presses of Florida, 1972, pp. 15-17.

Brief commentary addressing the alluring message of the mariners. Claims that, because readers will recall the original scene from Homer's *Odyssey*, they will know the call to indolence must be rejected. Points out ways the structure of the work draws readers toward acceptance of the mariners' call, then forces them back to thoughts of the real world. Also shows how Tennyson's revisions for the 1842 version of the work strengthen the idea that the mariners' decision to remain in the land of the Lotos-eaters should be rejected.

Hughes, Linda K. *The Manyfacéd Glass: Tennyson's Dramatic Monologues*. Athens: Ohio University Press, 1987, pp. 87-93.
Briefly compares the work to others Tennyson wrote on classical subjects. Argues the success of the work depends heavily on readers' willingness to engage their imagination in the reading experience, filling in the gaps in the text which Tennyson intentionally created. Points out ways the poet generates sympathy for the mariners and ways he establishes distance between readers and these same mariners; shows how the 1842 revision of the work more clearly maintains this tension.

Kincaid, James R. *Tennyson's Major Poems: The Comic and Ironic Patterns*. New Haven, Conn.: Yale University Press, 1975, pp. 38-41.
Discusses the tension created within the poem: readers tend to find themselves "unable to resist the appeal of the mariners and equally unable to yield to it." The work achieves an unusual balance between sympathy and judgment: the appeal to peace and order is counterbalanced by readers' awareness that the mariners are abandoning their quest to return home and hence their responsibility. Argues the central appeal is really to self-indulgence.

McSweeney, Kerry. *Tennyson and Swinburne as Romantic Naturalists*. Toronto: University of Toronto Press, 1981, pp. 65-68.
Compares the poem with several others by Tennyson, especially "The Hesperides" and "Tithonus," as well as "The Palace of Art" and "The Vision of Sin"; in each the Romantic version of the artistic mode of existence is contrasted with the requirements for people to interact with others in society. Notes how the contrast is dramatized in alternative stanzas. Discusses the impact of changes Tennyson made to the 1832 ending for republication ten years later; these highlight the psychological tensions the mariners feel.

Shaw, W. David. *Tennyson's Style*. Ithaca, N.Y.: Cornell University Press, 1976, pp. 66-70.
Brief stylistic analysis of a poem Shaw believes is the best example of the young Tennyson's "ability to refine sensation, refracting it through thought." Looks at the irony and paradox present throughout the work. Examines Tennyson's use of specific verbs and verbals, and his sen-

tence structure. Pays special attention to the choric song which the
Lotos-eaters sing.

Lucretius

Albright, Daniel. *Tennyson: The Muses' Tug of War*. Charlottesville:
University Press of Virginia, 1986, pp. 141-147.
Argues the poem is Tennyson's most ambitious attempt to imagine
what the deity is like. Claims it is an indictment of the poet's age, which
had transformed its deities into simple figments of the imagination; the
work shows the effects of "the decay of mythology." Lucretius is an
example of skeptical modern man; like several other Tennyson characters, he wishes to become disembodied and freed of his identity, but
finds this impossible.

Brashear, William R. "Lucretius and Despair." In *The Living Will: A Study
of Tennyson and Nineteenth Century Subjectivism*. The Hague: Mouton, 1969.
Points out parallels between Tennyson and the historical Lucretius.
Claims the poem shows the impossibility of living in complete harmony with nature. Discusses the prominence of sexual references and
the significance of the three dreams which appear early in the work;
shows how the hero, a victim of his own overdeveloped intellect, is
unable to achieve a true integration of self, leading to his death.

Hughes, Linda K. *The Manyfacéd Glass: Tennyson's Dramatic Monologues*. Athens: Ohio University Press, 1987, pp. 226-233.
Considers the work one of Tennyson's finest dramatic monologues.
Demonstrates ways the poet is able to fuse readers' sympathy for and
judgment of Lucretius: his understanding that his mind is failing
engenders great pathos. Also shows how completely Tennyson assimi-
lated the historical Lucretius' philosophy and scientific knowledge,
and how he re-creates and vivifies these ideas in the poem. Notes how
much the poet sees himself in Lucretius; this monologue allows him
to explore these similarities while maintaining appropriate psychological distance from his subject.

Kincaid, James R. *Tennyson's Major Poems: The Comic and Ironic Patterns*. New Haven, Conn.: Yale University Press, 1975, pp. 141-143.
Considers the poem one of the best examples of Tennyson's late ironic
works. Argues Lucretius is not a satiric figure but rather is a man

intensely committed to finding meaning in a universe which is inherently meaningless. He is defeated by inconsequential forces, including a wife who betrays him; his failure represents the tragedy of all men's great hopes to find significance in nature and in their lives.

Kozicki, Henry. *Tennyson and Clio: History in the Major Poems.* Baltimore: Johns Hopkins University Press, 1979, pp. 155-163.
Argues Tennyson's conception for the poem is heavily indebted to the historical parallels he saw between Rome in the time of Lucretius and nineteenth century Britain. Believes the poet saw both ages as having overtones of apocalypse about them. Reviews the sources of Tennyson's knowledge of Lucretius' life story. Discusses the significance of dreams in the poem; points out parallels to other works by Tennyson, especially *Idylls of the King.*

Shaw, W. David. *Tennyson's Style.* Ithaca, N.Y.: Cornell University Press, 1976, pp. 108-114, 246-250.
Deals with the poem first as an example of the poet's ability to balance the elements of psychology and rhetoric in a single work, then as an investigation of the philosophical positions of idealism and materialism. Describes how Tennyson is able to portray the gradual divergence of thought and feeling in the speaker without losing control of the structure of the work. Believes the poem shows the limits of positivism and realism.

Maud

Albright, Daniel. "The Speaker of *Maud* as Adonis." In *Tennyson: The Muses' Tug of War.* Charlottesville: University Press of Virginia, 1986.
Focuses on the mythological qualities of the poem. Traces Tennyson's enduring fascination with myth, showing how many of his characters seek meaning by appealing to myths. Explains ways the speaker of *Maud* parallels several mythical figures, especially Adonis; he seeks to discover an archetype which will give significance to what seem only "random fits of mania and depression." Discusses the importance of the madhouse scenes.

Ball, Patricia M. "If I Be Dear to Someone Else." In *The Heart's Events: The Victorian Poetry of Relationships.* London: Athlone Press, 1976.
Claims *Maud* deals with the vulnerability of individuals who give themselves completely to love. Tennyson's hero is a hysterical person-

ality, obsessed with his beloved; he is doomed to become temporarily deranged when she rejects him because he has invested too much emotionally in the relationship. Ball provides a detailed reading of the poem to illustrate how Tennyson dramatizes "the power of love proving as shattering as it was ecstatic."

Buckler, William E. "Tennyson's *Maud*: New Critical Perspectives." In *The Victorian Imagination: Essays in Aesthetic Exploration.* New York: New York University Press, 1980.

Considers this a thoroughly modern poem in which Tennyson explores the possibilities of creating a character and re-creating various phases of passion wholly through modulation of language. Discusses the significance of the poem's form, the monodrama, as a particularly apt vehicle for Tennyson's purpose; readers know the speaker only through the language he uses to describe himself and his predicament. Believes Tennyson is less concerned with suggesting a definite theme or moral than with exploring the many possibilities of meaning which can be expressed through poetry that is primarily symbolist.

Buckley, Jerome H. *Tennyson: The Growth of a Poet.* Cambridge, Mass.: Harvard University Press, 1961, pp. 140-147.

Defends the poem as Tennyson's most tightly constructed long work. Explains its difficult nature by noting that Tennyson's hero undergoes radical shifts in sensibility; his changing moods provide a central interest in the work. Sees the poet using war as a framework for this monodrama; warfare in various forms serves as "the expression of unreason" in both self and society. Also discusses the poet's use of madness. Believes Tennyson has written a successful symbolist poem. Briefly comments on hostile reviews by Tennyson's contemporaries.

Byatt, A. S. "The Lyric Structure of Tennyson's *Maud*." In Isobel Armstrong, ed. *The Major Victorian Poets: Reconsiderations.* Lincoln: University of Nebraska Press, 1969.

Argues the central concern of the poem is "the human being's capacity to discover his own identity, through the use of his senses." Discusses the aesthetic, sensual qualities of the work to show how Tennyson moved his readers to understand his hero's plight. Examines the dramatic and lyric qualities of the poem, devoting special attention to one of the lyrics as an example of Tennyson's method of combining the particular and the universal. Believes Victorian readers better appreciated the formal complexity of the work than do those of the twentieth century.

Colley, Ann C. *Tennyson and Madness*. Athens: University of Georgia Press, 1983, pp. 74-84.

Demonstrates Tennyson's reliance on both scientific and literary traditions for materials used to create his portrait of the poem's mad hero; cites several nineteenth century medical treatises and Robert Burton's seventeenth century *Anatomy of Melancholy* as examples of works from which Tennyson drew his information. Discusses the progress of the hero throughout the poem as a case study of someone dominated by an *idée fixe*; claims the hero does not regain his sanity at the conclusion of the poem, though he does speak truly about the evils of the age, which is itself diseased in its obsession with material wealth.

Culler, A. Dwight. "Maud, or the Madness." In *The Poetry of Tennyson*. New Haven, Conn.: Yale University Press, 1977.

Argues the poem deals with humanity's "primitive impulses and feelings." Explains in detail how it fulfills the generic requirements of the monodrama; describes Tennyson's relationship with Dr. R. J. Mann, the poem's first critic and the first to use the term to describe it. Traces the poet's awareness of the clinical conditions and symptoms of madness. Describes the ways Tennyson develops his portrait of madness: not only is the speaker mad, but the age possesses certain characteristics of madness as well.

Drew, Philip. "Tennyson and the Dramatic Monologue: A Study of 'Maud.'" In J. D. Palmer, ed. *Tennyson*. Writers and Their Background. Athens: Ohio University Press, 1973.

Provides an explanation for Tennyson's methodology in the poem, justifying its origin and the poet's rhetorical and structural ploys. Sees the speaker in the work moving from hysteria through rapture and mania to sanity. Carefully examines the text to illustrate the poet's manipulation of the speaker's state of mind. Explains how Tennyson's apparent glorification of war makes sense in the context of the poem. Compares the work to numerous others in the Tennyson canon which deal with similar themes.

Fletcher, Pauline. *Gardens and Grim Ravines: The Language of Landscape in Victorian Poetry*. Princeton, N.J.: Princeton University Press, 1983, pp. 53-58.

Argues Tennyson uses the garden as a metaphor for describing problems of social status in contemporary England. Compares his use with that of earlier writers such as Alexander Pope. Though the garden in *Maud* seems Edenic, it actually loses its innocent qualities as the poet describes its "sinister overtones." Provides brief explication of selected passages to show how Tennyson uses garden imagery to vivify social themes.

Harrison, Antony. "Irony and Ideology in Tennyson's 'Little *Hamlet.*" In *Victorian Poets and Romantic Poems: Intertextuality and Ideology.* Charlottesville: University Press of Virginia, 1990.
Examines the many works which influenced Tennyson's development of this poem. Focuses on the poet's borrowings from Shakespeare's *Hamlet,* a source for both situation and techniques of presentation; special attention is given to psychological parallels between the heroes of both works. Claims in *Maud* Tennyson is intentionally ambivalent in his attitudes toward society's problems and potential solutions. Also discusses the influence of the Spasmodics on the work.

Hellstrom, Ward. "*Maud.*" In *On the Poems of Tennyson.* Gainesville: University Presses of Florida, 1972.
Offers a symbolic reading of the poem, focusing on ways Maud becomes a symbol of the hero's redemption; she is much like Beatrice in Dante's work. Points out parallels between the beginning of the poem and Carlyle's work, especially *Past and Present.* Shows how the hero moves from the hell in which he finds himself to a state of regeneration through the influence of Maud. Argues Tennyson's collection of images used to describe Maud present her as a symbol of both natural and spiritual love. Defends the poet's use of the Crimean War as an appropriate symbol of the hero's commitment to larger social goals.

Hughes, Linda K. *The Manyfacéd Glass: Tennyson's Dramatic Monologues.* Athens: Ohio University Press, 1987, pp. 158-174.
Shows how the poem is an outgrowth of *In Memoriam*; points out parallels in structure. In *Maud,* Tennyson is able to render multiple levels of consciousness simultaneously; his hero vacillates constantly between sanity and madness. Traces that vacillation in the structure and rhythm of the work. Examines rhyme and alliteration to show how the poet creates a carefully crafted subtext which highlights his hero's instability.

Jump, John D., ed. *Tennyson: The Critical Heritage.* London: Routledge & Kegan Paul, 1967.
Four selections by Tennyson's contemporaries giving a balanced view of the reaction to the poem by its first readers. Includes Goldwyn Smith's criticism of the war passages; a long, sympathetic analysis by a Cambridge critic; a selection from R. J. Mann's *Tennyson's Maud*

Vindicated (1856), the first extended commentary on the work; and
Emily Ritchie's reminiscence of the poet's public reading of the work.

Kincaid, James R. *"Maud."* In *Tennyson's Major Poems: The Comic and
Ironic Patterns.* New Haven, Conn.: Yale University Press, 1975.
Calls the poem a dark comedy, in which love is seen as a problem, not
a solution. Finds a pattern of death and resurrection in the work: the
individual ego first dies and then is reborn. The narrator must learn to
deal with the personality-shattering experience of loving Maud; his
commitment to war is an ironic rebirth. Brief explanation of reasons
for the poor critical reception by both nineteenth and twentieth century
critics. Careful analysis of Parts I and II to demonstrate the hero's
gradual disintegration as he is betrayed by love.

Kissane, James D. *Alfred Tennyson.* Boston: Twayne, 1970, pp. 140-145.
Modest assessment of the poem's lyric qualities and its social message.
Briefly reviews the plot of the drama, focusing on Part I, in which the
speaker falls under Maud's spell and is eventually driven to the brink
of madness. Considers the poem anticipatory of twentieth century
writers' fascination with insanity. Deals frankly with the poem's jingo-
istic ending, noting it is impossible to explain away the speaker's
glorification of war.

Kozicki, Henry. "The Political Poems and *Maud.*" In *Tennyson and Clio:
History in the Major Poems.* Baltimore: Johns Hopkins University
Press, 1979.
Believes the poem is similar to *Idylls of the King* in several ways. Sees
the hero as a "symbolic scapegoat" representing the commercial age in
which he lives. Through the action of the poem, he undergoes a process
of purgation, exorcising personal grief and affirming his belief that
involvement in the historical process can lead to society's improvement.
Traces the function of Maud throughout the work. Notes the prevalence
of imagery suggesting a Hobbesian world in which nature is ruthless.

Mermin, Dorothy. *The Audience in the Poem: Five Victorian Poets.* New
Brunswick, N.J.: Rutgers University Press, 1983, pp. 34-42.
Traces the development of the poem from its genesis in an early lyric
to the fully developed dramatic piece in which the speaker's views are
challenged and altered by his interaction with "representatives of the
ordinary world." Discusses the poet's use of lyric verse to heighten the
emotional impact of the contemporary world on the sensitive hero,
who, like other Tennyson heroes (Ulysses, Tiresias), is withdrawn from

society and disdainful of it. Describes the plot and the narrator's growing madness; explains the appropriateness of the ending, which seems to glorify violence.

Pattison, Robert. *Tennyson and Tradition*. Cambridge, Mass.: Harvard University Press, 1979, pp. 128-134.
Brief but insightful analysis of Tennyson's use of the traditions of both lyric and idyll in shaping this dramatic monologue. Shows how the poet introduces plot through skillful interplay of these traditions without resorting to traditional narrative techniques. Sees the work as a prelude to *Idylls of the King*, in which the poet will use the form of the idyll (traditionally employed to present a static view of character or idea) as a means of presenting a narrative.

Pinion, F. B. "The 'Locksley Hall' Poems and *Maud*." In *A Tennyson Companion: Life and Works*. New York: St. Martin's Press, 1984.
Warns against biographical interpretations; suggests readers consider the poem a combination of lyric and dramatic elements which allow Tennyson to explore the nature and dangers of madness in a character much like Shakespeare's Hamlet. Briefly summarizes the plot, focusing on Tennyson's revelation of his hero's interior conflict and psychotic tendencies. Defends the poet's apparent glorification of war in the closing section.

Rader, Ralph W. *Tennyson's Maud: The Biographical Genesis*. Berkeley: University of California Press, 1963.
Offers an explanation for Tennyson's intense involvement with and emotional attachment for this poem by reconstructing the biographical background on which Rader believes the poem is based. Suggests the work captures the series of important emotional relationships Tennyson established to fill the void left by Arthur Henry Hallam's death in 1833. Devotes chapters to study of the poet's involvement with Rosa Baring, Sophy Rawnsley, and Emily Sellwood, whom he married in 1850. Lengthy concluding chapter offers an autobiographical interpretation of the poem.

Reed, John R. *Perception and Design in Tennyson's Idylls of the King*. Athens: Ohio University Press, 1969, pp. 29-47.
Argues the poem should not be read as autobiography; rather, the poet has carefully crafted a moral design in which his narrator begins with a selfish interest in Maud but eventually divests himself of this feeling and accepts the idea that his salvation lies in acceptance of a "divine

plan" which requires him to subordinate personal desires to greater causes. Extensive examination of the development of the narrator, who moves from self-delusion to self-awareness as the poem progresses.

Ricks, Christopher. "*Maud* 1855." In *Tennyson*. New York: Macmillan, 1972.
Discusses the poet's personal involvement with the subjects this poem treats: unrequited love and madness. Examines the composition process and reflects on contemporary reactions to the work, especially negative responses to its martial ending. Sees the hero struggling to overcome feelings for a lover he never possessed; displays ways the dramatic monologue is the appropriate vehicle for dealing with the kind of hero Tennyson creates.

Shaw, W. David. "Lightning Under the Stars: *Maud*." In *Tennyson's Style*. Ithaca, N.Y.: Cornell University Press, 1976.
Considers the poem a great accomplishment, spurred by Tennyson's personal confrontation with madness and disappointment; the hero is able to rise above adversity and "remake and remold himself" as a result of his personal trial. Reads the work as a bitter satire on nineteenth century values, in which Tennyson reverses the value of many cherished ideals in society, mocking them because they appear to the speaker to mask hypocrisy. Demonstrates how the poet's manipulation of stylistic devices helps him achieve the sense of despair his speaker feels.

Slinn, E. Warwick. "Absence and Desire in *Maud*." In *The Discourse of Self in Victorian Poetry*. Charlottesville: University Press of Virginia, 1991.
Deconstructionist analysis of the poem, seeing it as an example of Tennyson's continuing presentation of the notion that "completion and fulfillment" are not possible in the present. As a result, individuals such as the hero of *Maud* strive in vain to achieve union with the absent object of their desire; any achievement of union will end in the death of the self, which defines itself by its "lack," its constant need for this union. Maud becomes a signifier of the "other" toward which the hero strives. Examines several key images in the poem to show how they function to illustrate Tennyson's central concern.

Turner, Paul. "*Maud*." In *Tennyson*. London: Routledge & Kegan Paul, 1976.
Careful examination of the many sources upon which Tennyson drew for his poem. Briefly reviews composition process. Looks at autobio-

graphical elements, citing Tennyson's use of settings drawn from the
surroundings at his new home on the Isle of Wight. Cites literary
sources, including Homer, Theocritus, Horace, and Shakespeare; also
notes other, more contemporary sources. Reviews contemporary issues
with which Tennyson dealt, especially the Crimean War. Shows how
the poet's treatment of madness is based heavily on ideas promulgated
by Dr. Matthew Allen, a prominent physician in the nineteenth century.

Œnone

Albright, Daniel. *Tennyson: The Muses' Tug of War*. Charlottesville:
University Press of Virginia, 1986, pp. 84-88.
Believes Tennyson is not successful in creating a fully realized character in the work; rather, Œnone remains an indistinct shape within the
landscape, which is presented in great detail. Through the persona of
the nymph Tennyson is able to present the excesses and abundances of
the natural landscape. Offers brief comparisons with the companion
poem written by Tennyson much later, "The Death of Œnone."

Buckler, William E. "Enlarging the 'Miniature Epic': The Panic Subtext
of *Œnone*." In *The Victorian Imagination: Essays in Aesthetic Exploration*. New York: New York University Press, 1980.
Offers a highly detailed, line-by-line explication of the poem to show
how Tennyson, working within the conventions of the epyllion established by classical writers such as Theocritus, examines the character
of Œnone as an emblem of an order which is passing away. Suggests
Tennyson intends readers to see multiple meanings within the poem,
but the poet wishes to fix none of them as the work's primary theme.
Notes the importance of Œnone as a daughter of the god Pan, whose
passing is often seen as symbolizing the fall of the Greek gods to the
onslaught of Christianity and a new world order.

Hair, Donald S. *Domestic and Heroic in Tennyson's Poetry*. Toronto:
University of Toronto Press, 1981, pp. 71-76.
Discusses this poem as a superb example of Tennyson's use of the
epyllion, a mixed form incorporating elements of the lyric, narrative,
and dramatic. Provides background on the epyllion's classical origins
and a twentieth century definition against which this poem can be
effectively measured. Explains how Tennyson's use of imagery and
allusion allows him to vivify the contrast of foreground and background in the work.

Hughes, Linda K. *The Manyfacéd Glass: Tennyson's Dramatic Monologues.* Athens: Ohio University Press, 1987, pp. 79-83.
Considers the poem a useful experiment in dramatic monologue,
though Tennyson is not fully successful in using the form to achieve
his thematic purposes. Notes how the work presents a fictive subject
very well but also maintains a subjective, personal tone. Explains how
both the narrative and dramatic elements work together in the poem.

Ricks, Christopher. *Tennyson.* New York: Macmillan, 1972, pp. 85-88.
Brief remarks about a poem Ricks considers only a limited success.
Believes the critical section, in which the goddesses debate, is a failure.
Faults the poet for excesses of style; finds his language too self-
conscious and polished. Cites commentary from several of Tennyson's
contemporaries who also disapproved of the poem. Praises the poet for
his ability to use landscape description to create an erotic mood.

Schur, Owen. *Victorian Pastoral: Tennyson, Hardy, and the Subversion
of Forms.* Columbus: Ohio State University Press, 1989, pp. 38-47.
Looks at ways Tennyson modifies the pastoral tradition to achieve his
desired effect. Carefully reviews the poet's borrowings from classical
sources, especially Ovid, who also examines from Œnone's perspective the story of Paris' choice among the three Greek goddesses.
Believes the exceptional consciousness Tennyson shows in his borrowings is a strength. Claims he creates "a new language of pastoral idyll"
through his manipulation of classical sources.

Shaw, W. David. *Tennyson's Style.* Ithaca, N.Y.: Cornell University Press,
1976, pp. 81-84.
Describes the poem as "a cross between a Theocritan idyll and a
dramatic monologue." Believes the poet's introduction of Athene's
moralizing speech is a weakness, as she is simply used as a mouthpiece
for Victorian attitudes. Claims the portrait of Œnone is much more
successful; analyzes the syntax of her argument and apology. Briefly
reviews Tennyson's skilful use of the frame which introduces and
concludes the tale.

The Palace of Art

Culler, A. Dwight. *The Poetry of Tennyson.* New Haven, Conn.: Yale
University Press, 1977, pp. 70-76.

Analysis of background and intellectual sources for the poem. Notes Tennyson's reliance on Shelley for the pantheon of literary heroes depicted in the work. Reviews the role of Tennyson's Cambridge friends in shaping the poem; also points out its reliance on English tradition of housing great art collections in country houses and palaces. Claims Tennyson is pleading for England not to be too democratized by reform, but for the aristocracy to share the treasures that rightfully belong to all.

Kincaid, James R. *Tennyson's Major Poems: The Comic and Ironic Patterns.* New Haven, Conn.: Yale University Press, 1975, pp. 50-53.
Discusses the poem as an example of Tennyson's continuing attempt to deal with the conflict between comic and ironic visions of the world. Argues the speaker in the work struggles to reconcile the urge for self-indulgence with competing demands for social significance in his endeavors. Examines the setting described in the poem to show how its very completeness suggests its self-sufficiency, making it an attractive safe haven from the outside world; hence it presents a great temptation for the speaker to abandon social responsibilities.

McSweeney, Kerry. *Tennyson and Swinburne as Romantic Naturalists.* Toronto: University of Toronto Press, 1981, pp. 47-50.
Argues in this poem Tennyson is too heavy-handed in his attempt to impose a moral on the story. Believes it is inferior to "Mariana," "Mariana of the South," "The Hesperides," and "The Lady of Shalott." Suggests that, if considered as a psychological study of the artist, the work offers an insightful commentary "about the expansion of consciousness through the stimulus of art" and its demise when the absorption in self leads to isolation from life. Claims Tennyson fails to convince readers of the soul's conversion, however; he simply imposes a moral solution on a complex psychological problem.

Pattison, Robert. *Tennyson and Tradition.* Cambridge, Mass.: Harvard University Press, 1979, pp. 59-63.
Acknowledges the conscious allegory of the work; sees the soul's search for beauty through all forms of art as a penetrating study of the attractiveness of the doctrine of Pantheism. Argues Tennyson was himself attracted to that doctrine but ultimately rejected it because it does not allow for the presence of God distinct from His creation. Discusses ways the form of the poem, the idyll, is an apt vehicle for presenting its theme.

Ricks, Christopher. *Tennyson*. New York: Macmillan, 1972, pp. 92-95.
Brief commentary pointing out the many flaws in a work Ricks believes is "vitiated by flummery." Argues the moral of the poem is stressed in a heavy-handed manner which makes any sense of genuine debate about the virtues of art impossible. Finds some merit in the psychological complexity of the second half of the work.

Shaw, W. David. *Tennyson's Style*. Ithaca, N.Y.: Cornell University Press, 1976, pp. 56-59.
Generally negative assessment of the work, claiming it shows all the defects of "a poetry of pure sensation." Believes Tennyson is indiscriminate in accumulating sensuous details, so much so that no part of the work seems to become distinguishable. Shows how the poem fits within the genre of the progress poem, a form popular in the Renaissance and eighteenth century.

The Princess

Albright, Daniel. "Disenchantment in *The Princess*." In *Tennyson: The Muses' Tug of War*. Charlottesville: University Press of Virginia, 1986.
Calls the work "one of the most original long poems in English." Discusses the care Tennyson took to develop the idea of multiple authorship for his story. Believes the poet wishes to show there is a unity beneath the disparate elements of human nature; men and women must grow to realize this fact. Includes a discussion of the lyric "Tears, Idle Tears," which appears near the midpoint of the narrative. Also discusses recurrent imagery in the work, especially the images of statues.

Bergonzi, Bernard. "Feminism and Femininity in *The Princess*." In Isobel Armstrong, ed. *The Major Victorian Poets: Reconsiderations*. Lincoln: University of Nebraska Press, 1969.
Examines the poem as an ideological treatise on the issue of woman's essential nature and women's rights. Posits Tennyson's oblique presentation stems from his desire to explore ideas with which he is not completely comfortable. Notes the strong interest in feminism throughout; concludes the poet is more concerned with examining all sides of the issue than in taking a stand on the question of women's rights. Believes the character of the Princess is insufficiently delineated.

Buckler, William E. "Tennyson's Function of Poetry at the Present Time: A Parabolic Reading of *The Princess*." In *The Victorian Imagination:*

Essays in Aesthetic Exploration. New York: New York University Press, 1980.

Relates this poem to Tennyson's other three major long works by showing how all of them are experiments in form. Argues the poet is not primarily concerned with his ostensible story, the battle of the sexes, but rather with ways in which literature can be used to explore any subject of contemporary interest to help readers see the seriousness of the issue under investigation. Tennyson uses literary form not only to shape his argument but also to give his subject proper perspective. Discusses the way the poet fuses oral and written traditions to develop his multipart narrative. Extensive discussion of the techniques used in the six intercalary songs.

Buckley, Jerome H. *Tennyson: The Growth of a Poet.* Cambridge, Mass.: Harvard University Press, 1961, pp. 94-106.

Claims the poem is not simply a burlesque targeting feminist causes; believes Tennyson was supportive of the women's movement, as his generally sympathetic portrait of the Princess indicates. Explains the function of the Prince's "weird seizures," which Tennyson added to the work after its initial publication. Extensive analysis of the character of the Princess and the Prince; brief discussion of the songs used to link the various sections of the poem.

Culler, A. Dwight. *"The Princess."* In *The Poetry of Tennyson.* New Haven, Conn.: Yale University Press, 1977.

Discusses the background of the women's movement with which Tennyson had to deal in shaping his poem. Believes the poet selected his form so he could explore various positions on the issue without having to take sides. Discusses the function of the modern-day frame and the significance of the young men and women engaged in relationships similar to those in the tale they tell. Comments in some detail on the character of the Prince. Believes Tennyson seeks a reconciliation between the sexes, but he is not in favor of homogenization.

Fletcher, Pauline. *Gardens and Grim Ravines: The Language of Landscape in Victorian Poetry.* Princeton, N.J.: Princeton University Press, 1983, pp. 24-27, 66-70.

Argues Tennyson's use of the garden in this poem is particularly noteworthy because the imagery contrasts with earlier, Romantic notions of landscape. In *The Princess* "the garden attains its highest development as an embodiment of social and political values." Tennyson's portrait of a landscape dominated by gardens (both in the story of Princess Ida and in the frame wherein the young men and women create Ida's story) is a metaphor for England, which the poet sees as a perfect society, organized on authoritarian lines with strict class boundaries.

Hair, Donald S. "Romance: *The Princess*." In *Domestic and Heroic in Tennyson's Poetry*. Toronto: University of Toronto Press, 1981.
Examines the poem in relation to the tradition of the romance, which Tennyson found a congenial form. *The Princess* repeats a central action of all of Tennyson's best romances: "the hero's approach to the heroine, and the awakening of vitality in her." Discusses the poet's use of the modern frame for his medieval story and his handling of conventions of romance, especially the "patterns of opposites and threes." Sees the central conflict between men and women resolved in the figure of the child.

Johnson, Wendell Stacy. *Sex and Marriage in Victorian Poetry*. Ithaca, N.Y.: Cornell University Press, 1975, pp. 124-135.
Reads the poem as one concerned chiefly with relations between the sexes, especially with the proper roles men and women should play in marriage. Believes Tennyson seeks a middle ground between extreme positions regarding either sex: good marriages require compromise of both parties. Examines the various characters in the poem and briefly comments on the function of the lyrics. Concludes Tennyson believed the ideal union of the sexes in marriage was not yet possible but was a noble goal for society to pursue.

Kincaid, James R. "*The Princess*." In *Tennyson's Major Poems: The Comic and Ironic Patterns*. New Haven, Conn.: Yale University Press, 1975.
Sees Tennyson attempting to "forge a new genre" pitting heroic and domestic comedy against each other. Ida's heroic attempts to liberate women from the domestic conventions which have made them subservient to men finally fail, but the Princess is not seen as wrongheaded; hence the poem contains a tension which resists easy resolution by readers. Discusses the significance of the songs and of the image of the child, a symbol of domestic harmony the Princess' opponents try to foist upon her. Ida is defeated by the forces of convention, which are too strong to be overcome by assertion of individual will.

Kissane, James D. *Alfred Tennyson*. Boston: Twayne, 1970, pp. 93-99.
Considers the poem flawed but interesting. Compares the work to Alexander Pope's *The Rape of the Lock*, claiming Pope had firmer

ideas about women's rightful place in society; Tennyson is unsure of his attitudes toward women's roles and hence vacillates between satire and sympathy for Princess Ida. Sees the principal theme of the poem the progress toward self-understanding. Both the Princess and the Prince develop an appreciation of femininity and masculinity; lesser figures in the work complement, by parallel or contrast, the development of these two. Believes Tennyson intended readers to see acceptance of one's sexual identity as an integral part of self-knowledge.

Pattison, Robert. *Tennyson and Tradition*. Cambridge, Mass.: Harvard University Press, 1979, pp. 94-102.
Focuses on the formal qualities of the work; shows how Tennyson blends the idyll with the lyric, epic, and romance to create his medley. Points out parallels with other idylls in the poet's canon. Discusses the function of statuary, the principal metaphor in the work. Explains Tennyson's use of lyrics, which are effective only when they advance the plot or serve a larger theme. Concludes the work is not as successful as later long poems because Tennyson does not achieve a full synthesis of the various forms he uses.

Pinion, F. B. "*The Princess*." In *A Tennyson Companion: Life and Works*. New York: St. Martin's Press, 1984.
Discusses Tennyson's interest in the issue of the women's movement in his day, and especially in women's education. Claims the poet felt women should be given greater status in society than they were accorded in the nineteenth century. Faults the poet for the ridiculous story he used to convey his ideas, and for his use of a needlessly complex structure for presenting the tale. Examines the function of the lyrics and of the Prince's weird seizures.

Ricks, Christopher. "*The Princess* 1847." In *Tennyson*. New York: Macmillan, 1972.
Believes the poem is ultimately a failure; despite its verbal and stylistic achievements, Tennyson is guilty throughout of evading a series of issues important to him or to his contemporaries. Among these are the questions of women's education, the issue of social responsibility, the poet's relationship to Arthur Hallam and to his father, and the rising concern over the discoveries being made in geology. The strengths of the work lie in its presentation of landscapes and in the lyrics which link the sections. Devotes attention to several of these intercalary poems.

Shaw, W. David. *Tennyson's Style*. Ithaca, N.Y.: Cornell University Press, 1976, pp. 114-131.
Narrowly focused analysis of the phenomenon Shaw describes as "narrative indirection." Discusses the poet's effective mixture of genres. Comments on the psychological dimensions of the work, especially the indirect expression of repressed sexuality. Concentrates on the lyrics linking the various segments of the poem, highlighting stylistic devices which call attention to the poet's principal themes.

Turner, Paul. *"The Princess: A Medley."* In *Tennyson*. London: Routledge & Kegan Paul, 1976.
Provides an overview of the poem. Discusses Tennyson's ideas about feminism, suggesting he was a moderate. Cites numerous literary sources for the story, including F. D. Maurice's novel *Eustace Conway*, Froissart's *Chronicles*, and Shakespeare's plays. Examines the character of the Princess, for whom Tennyson has great sympathy. Shows how the poet's view of women's gradual emancipation has parallels in geological writings of his day.

Tithonus

Hughes, Linda K. *The Manyfacéd Glass: Tennyson's Dramatic Monologues*. Athens: Ohio University Press, 1987, pp. 223-226.
Brief commentary focusing on revisions Tennyson made to his earlier poem "Tithon"; shows how the changes transform the original work into a highly successful dramatic monologue. Also points out that, in the later version, responsibility for the ironic gift of immortality falls on Tithonus; he owes his plight and his lifetime of sad reflection to his own error in judgment, not to outside agencies. Claims in this poem and other late monologues Tennyson achieves full mastery of the form.

Kincaid, James R. *Tennyson's Major Poems: The Comic and Ironic Patterns*. New Haven, Conn.: Yale University Press, 1975, pp. 45-47.
Brief discussion of the ironic overtones of the poem. Claims it is a "bleak parody" of "Ulysses," which argues for an extended lifetime of experience; "Tithonus" shows the horrors of unending life. Notes how Tennyson uses the dramatic monologue to force readers to suspend judgment of Tithonus and even to build sympathy for him. Also notes some of the "incongruous echoes from the comedy of manners" which create further irony within the poem.

McSweeney, Kerry. *Tennyson and Swinburne as Romantic Naturalists.* Toronto: University of Toronto Press, 1981,. pp. 63-65.

Abbreviated review of the major themes of the poem, claiming it is Tennyson's most polished version of a wholly naturalistic world in which death is acceptable. Describes Eos as a symbol of erotic love but simultaneously as an emblem of the creative process and the "timelessness of natural process." Believes the poet is able to control the potentially explosive sexual elements of the work by balancing their appearance with a constant series of referents that create a sense of longing for the past.

Schur, Owen. *Victorian Pastoral: Tennyson, Hardy, and the Subversion of Forms.* Columbus: Ohio State University Press, 1989, pp. 78-90.

Notes the principal theme: an exploration of death and resignation in the face of suffering. Sketches biographical and literary sources, concentrating on Tennyson's borrowings from classical literature. Points out the poem's affinities with Keats's work. Explains how Tennyson uses the conventions of the pastoral to explore the nature of melancholy; highlights the ironic nature of the poet's treatment of his theme.

The Two Voices

Albright, Daniel. *Tennyson: The Muses' Tug of War.* Charlottesville: University Press of Virginia, 1986, pp. 94-103.

Discusses the complexity of Tennyson's persona, whose argument with the two voices urging radically different alternatives is a model for the struggles many of Tennyson's later characters undergo. Traces the urge toward suicide depicted in other nineteenth century works. Believes the presentation of the two sides of the argument is a bit forced, since all the voices exist within the speaker's mind. Notes how closely linked the speaker is to the voice promoting suicide.

Johnson, Wendell Stacy. *Sex and Marriage in Victorian Poetry.* Ithaca, N.Y.: Cornell University Press, 1975, pp. 119-124.

Notes the central interest in this poem is in the speaker's internal debate over the question of suicide. Suggest the scales are tipped in favor of life over death when the speaker sees a couple with their child, a scene described in terms many critics find overly sentimental. This image is central, however, to understanding both this poem and later works by Tennyson; it is the poet's vision of an ideal relationship, one in which love has produced new life.

Kincaid, James R. *Tennyson's Major Poems: The Comic and Ironic Patterns*. New Haven, Conn.: Yale University Press, 1975, pp. 53-54.
Reads the work as an attempt to provide some answer to a perennial dilemma: humankind's desire to find meaning in a word where cosmic forces are characterized by wastefulness and purposelessness. Notes the resolution in favor of an optimistic belief in humanity's ability to find or create meaning in life stems from a process of turning the ironic viewpoint against itself: the uncertainty represented by the dark voice, which argues people cannot be certain about the nature of the universe, is used by the principal character in the poem to prove one cannot therefore be certain there is no purpose to life. The speaker ends up rejecting the voice of despair and adopting a comic perspective on life.

McSweeney, Kerry. *Tennyson and Swinburne as Romantic Naturalists*. Toronto: University of Toronto Press, 1981, pp. 52-57.
Praises Tennyson's ability to manage his materials in the terse rhyming triplets which focus readers' attention and sharpen the debate between the competing voices. Finds the resolution disappointing, however, believing it too facile a way to dismiss the serious claims made by the voice which advocates suicide; claims the poem would have been a fine example of the Romantic agony of self-consciousness and isolation had it ended before the moralizing verses with which it concludes.

Reed, John R. *Perception and Design in Tennyson's Idylls of the King*. Athens: Ohio University Press, 1969.
Argues against autobiographical interpretations of the poem. Reads it instead as an example of a work in which the poet has imposed a moral design; the dramatic presentation focuses readers' attention on opposing ideas about the topic of faith. Believes the two voices are within the same speaker, who weighs the alternatives before rejecting the appeals of suicide. The speaker is redeemed by opting for love, even though there is little rational basis for making this choice.

Ricks, Christopher. *Tennyson*. New York: Macmillan, 1972, pp. 103-107.
Claims Tennyson wrote the poem to explore a feeling quite personal to him: questions about the value of existence. Dispels the notion that the poem was inspired by Arthur Hallam's death; notes its partial composition before that event. Shows how the voices all exist within the speaker's mind. Posits there are actually three voices, two distinct from the speaker's consciousness. Believes the voice promoting suicide makes the stronger argument.

Tucker, Herbert F. "Vocation and Equivocation: The Dialogue of Genres in Tennyson's 'The Two Voices.'" In Jerome J. McGann, ed. *Victorian Connections*. Charlottesville: University Press of Virginia, 1989.

Careful, detailed, and sensitive examination of the poem, showing how Tennyson handled the dialogue to his best advantage. Argues that, in the context of the work, the poet is pitting two forms of poetry against each other: the meditative lyric and the descriptive idyll. Analyzes the central passage in which the speaker witnesses a family and community going to church and a Victorian family to demonstrate that, far from being simply cliché, the scene serves as a powerful antidote to the speaker's solipsism. Presents cogent evidence of Tennyson's link to his Romantic predecessors and his reliance on them for imagery and theme in this work.

Ulysses

Culler, A. Dwight. *The Poetry of Tennyson*. New Haven, Conn.: Yale University Press, 1977, pp. 92-98.

Believes Tennyson chooses this scene, only suggested by Homer, partly because it had been the subject of a long tradition; traces that tradition through Greek writers to Dante and Bacon, showing how Ulysses had become transformed into a Romantic hero by Tennyson's day. Argues the poet intends readers to see Telemachus sympathetically; he and Ulysses represent two different but equally viable lifestyles. Claims the ending, though clearly symbolic of a voyage toward death, does not represent an irresponsible act on Ulysses' part, because he sets out to do noble work, a virtue admired by the Victorians.

Hellstrom, Ward. *On the Poems of Tennyson*. Gainesville: University Presses of Florida, 1972, pp. 17-20.

Acknowledges the critical controversy over Ulysses' actions in the poem: some see him as heroic, others as escapist or suicidal. Believes the hero's choice to leave Ithaca in search of new adventures is the right one, because his life in Ithaca is "not life but a kind of death." What Ulysses rejects in leaving his homeland is a kind of passivity which should be avoided; even actions leading to death are preferable to doing nothing.

Hughes, Linda K. *The Manyfacéd Glass: Tennyson's Dramatic Monologues*. Athens: Ohio University Press, 1987, pp. 94-99.

Describes the highly personal nature of the poem; cites evidence from

Tennyson's friends to show how Hallam's death affected all of them. Also explains ways the poem is simultaneously objective, as Ulysses' story is subject to critical analysis independent of the details which link the poem to Tennyson's life. Looks carefully at both the language and poetic devices Tennyson employs, and his skillful use of gaps between the verse paragraphs which invite readers to fill in their own explanation for Ulysses' behavior.

Kincaid, James R. *Tennyson's Major Poems: The Comic and Ironic Patterns.* New Haven, Conn.: Yale University Press, 1975, pp. 41-45. Reads the poem as a statement about the power and the danger of the heroic will. Ulysses is essentially an egoist, bent on abandoning community duties and values in pursuit of self-fulfillment. Though the hero comes to a personally satisfying resolution, readers find themselves disturbed by the implications of his attitude and his treatment of his son Telemachus. Claims the final argument of the poem is high-blown rhetoric intended to win over both the mariners and readers to Ulysses' point of view.

Kissane, James D. *Alfred Tennyson.* Boston: Twayne, 1970, pp. 132-135. Highlights the many contradictions in the poem, noting how appropriate Tennyson's Ulysses is as a symbol of the Victorian hero. Cites the Greek warrior's desire to confront life by escaping it, his urge to seek new experiences though his life is nearly over, his abandonment of social responsibility to seek heroic adventures, and his fear that the age may not sustain or appreciate heroic acts.

Mermin, Dorothy. *The Audience in the Poem: Five Victorian Poets.* New Brunswick, N.J.: Rutgers University Press, 1983, pp. 26-34. Notes similarities between this poem and two others by Tennyson: "St. Simeon Stylites" and "Tiresias." All three contain auditors whom the speaker wishes to convince about the rightness of his behavior. Believes Ulysses is more concerned, however, with convincing himself about his intended course of action. Thinks Tennyson may have seen Dante's Ulysses as "a warning against the misuse of imaginative powers." Nevertheless, Tennyson seems to sympathize with his hero, even though Ulysses is abdicating his social responsibilities. Discusses the poet's addition of the Telemachus passage in which Ulysses appears to mock his son's virtues; also comments on the hero's appeal to his countrymen, a scene inferior to those in which Ulysses muses to himself about his present fate.

Pattison, Robert. *Tennyson and Tradition*. Cambridge, Mass.: Harvard University Press, 1979, pp. 83-86.

Brief but insightful analysis of the character of Ulysses. Compares him to other Tennyson figures concerned with the proper use of time and with self-fulfillment. Believes the hero's "total commitment to the principle of action" forces him to abandon many traditional values— home, family, society—in his desire to find fulfillment in never-ending adventure. As a consequence, "all human rapport is sacrificed to self and will."

Schur, Owen. *Victorian Pastoral: Tennyson, Hardy, and the Subversion of Forms*. Columbus: Ohio State University Press, 1989, pp. 66-78.

Detailed, coherent explication of the poem as an analysis of the "quest to recover the power of myth itself." Briefly summarizes the critical heritage of the work. Extensive examination of Ulysses as a mythic hero, displaced into the ordinary world of Ithaca. Makes clear Tennyson's use of Ulysses as a symbol of the human need to go beyond limits. Discusses the enigmatic ending, which confounds readers' attempts to establish a clear judgment of the hero.

Shaw, W. David. *Tennyson's Style*. Ithaca, N.Y.: Cornell University Press, 1976, pp. 85-89, 93-95.

Highly laudatory assessment of Tennyson's ability to create a character who can balance elegiac and heroic attributes. Believes Ulysses considers himself superior to his son. Through his rhetoric, the Greek hero is able to master death; notes the frequency of elegiac undertones in the hero's strident rhetoric. Also provides a brief analysis of the closing lines to show how Tennyson keeps the elegiac and heroic modes balanced.

Turner, Paul. *Tennyson*. London: Routledge & Kegan Paul, 1976, pp. 87-89.

Brief review of the plot. Cites Tennyson's reliance on both Homer and Dante for his portrait of the Greek hero; suggests the poet is more inclined to view his hero sympathetically, drawing on Homer for many of his good qualities. Believes the portrait of Ulysses is straightforward and optimistic; the poem emphasizes the necessity for those who have little future to make the most of life.

Chapter 13
JAMES THOMSON

General Studies

Shaw, W. David. "Feuerbach and Thomson: The Rending of the Veil." In *The Lucid Veil: Poetic Truth in the Victorian Age*. Madison: University of Wisconsin Press, 1987.
Brief exploration of the theological basis of Thomson's work and commentary on his use of discursive techniques in *The City of Dreadful Night*. Thomson is seen as a disciple of Ludwig Feuerbach, who held that the proper focus of religious studies was on human beings, who act in godlike ways. Discusses the poet's figure of Melancholia as an example of Feuerbach's ideology brought to life in poetry. Also remarks on Thomson's use of deliberate fragmentation as a means of representing "the schizoid inner life of his speaker."

Thesing, William B. "James Thomson: The City as Wasteland." In *The London Muse: Victorian Poetic Responses to the City*. Athens: University of Georgia Press, 1982.
Believes Thomson's vision of the city is farthest removed of all Victorian poets from Blake's optimistic hope that London will be transformed into a new Jerusalem. Claims Thomson used his personal nightmare vision of city life as a springboard to examining more universal characteristics of the enervating nature of city life on humankind. Traces the poet's progress from qualified optimism to bitter realism through a half-dozen representative works. More detailed analysis of *The City of Dreadful Night*, in which the city becomes an emblem of unrelenting hopelessness and despair for individuals who inhabit it.

The City of Dreadful Night

Williams, Raymond O. *The Country and the City*. New York: Oxford University Press, 1973, pp. 235-239.
Discusses ways Thomson's poem exploits the symbolic dimension of the city. Williams argues that the poet represents the city symbolically as "the condition of human life." Quotes liberally from the

poet's work to illustrate ways in which Thomson uses the cityscape to portray the loss of belief and purpose in human life. The poet envisions the city as "the physical embodiment of a decisive modern consciousness."

Chapter 14
OSCAR WILDE

General Studies

Beckson, Karl, ed. *Oscar Wilde: The Critical Heritage*. New York: Barnes & Noble, 1970.
Collection of excerpts from 127 reviews, essays, and letters, most written contemporaneously with the publication of Wilde's major works. Provides a sense of how Wilde's work was received by the reading public in late Victorian England and abroad, especially in America, where Wilde's speaking tours had made him quite popular. Approximately two dozen selections focus on Wilde's posthumously published *Collected Works* and on his reputation in the first quarter of the twentieth century.

Bloom, Harold, ed. *Oscar Wilde*. Modern Critical Views. New York: Chelsea House, 1985.
Collection of essays by leading artists and critics of the twentieth century, including William Butler Yeats, G. Wilson Knight, and Richard Ellmann. Provides overview of Wilde's literary output; helpful for understanding the development of his aesthetic outlook and his attitude toward society. Passing references illuminate the background of *The Ballad of Reading Gaol*. Includes brief selected bibliography.

Ellmann, Richard. *Oscar Wilde*. London: Hamish Hamilton, 1987.
Definitive biography, exhaustively investigating numerous published and unpublished sources to set out the events of Wilde's life and explain the geographical as well as the artistic genesis of his works. Presents Wilde as a modern hero whose aesthetic sentiments were ahead of his time. Illustrated throughout with photographs of Wilde and his circle. Deals extensively with the artist's many literary and personal relationships. Notes and index provide information for further study.

_____, ed. *Oscar Wilde: A Collection of Critical Essays*. Englewood Cliffs, N.J.: Prentice-Hall, 1969.
Collection of critical essays, reminiscences, poems, and retrospective evaluations written during the last decade of the nineteenth and the first half of the twentieth centuries. Includes analyses by George Bernard Shaw, William Butler Yeats, W. H. Auden, Thomas Mann, Jorge Luis

Borges, André Gide, John Betjeman, and James Joyce. Commentary on Wilde's life and its importance in shaping the literature he produced.

Ericksen, Donald H. *Oscar Wilde*. Boston: Twayne, 1977.
Claims criticism often ignores the literary merits of Wilde's individual works in an attempt to use them merely as examples of the Decadent movement at the end of the nineteenth century. Places primary emphasis on analysis of individual writings. Devotes chapters to examinations of the poetry, short stories, criticism, Wilde's novel (*The Picture of Dorian Gray*), and his drama to show the "essential artistic unity of Wilde's creative output."

Fraser, Hilary. "Aestheticism: Walter Pater and Oscar Wilde." In *Beauty and Belief: Aesthetics and Religion in Victorian Literature*. Cambridge, England: Cambridge University Press, 1986.
Examines Wilde's critical attitudes, especially his version of aestheticism, which stands in sharp contrast to the moral earnestness of critics of the preceding generation. Shows how the strong influence of religious thinking prevalent in the period affected Wilde's beliefs about the role of the artist and of the critic. Demonstrates how Wilde's ideas emerged not only in his critical writings but in his poetry as well.

Gagnier, Regenia. *Idylls of the Marketplace: Oscar Wilde and the Victorian Public*. Stanford, Calif.: Stanford University Press, 1986.
Study of the way Wilde reached out to the public to promote his special brand of aestheticism. Believes a proper understanding of Wilde's relationship with the public can help answer a much larger question: "the place of art in a consumerist society." Individual chapters explain how Wilde created an audience for his works, appealed to the consumer society in later nineteenth century Britain, and turned his back on that society in his greatest work, *De Profundis*. Includes a useful bibliography.

Hyde, H. Montgomery. *Oscar Wilde*. London: Eyre Methuen, 1976.
Detailed biography written for the scholar and general reader. Focuses on the events of Wilde's life, examining the biographical significance of his works. Stresses the heights to which Wilde rose in the eyes of his public and the depths to which he sank as a result of public trials for homosexuality. Includes numerous photographs and a useful bibliography of secondary sources.

Mikhail, E. H. *Oscar Wilde: An Annotated Bibliography of Criticism*. Totowa, N.J.: Rowman & Littlefield, 1978.

Listing of bibliographies, published reviews of Wilde's works, books devoted wholly or partially to criticism of the writer, and periodical articles about his life and writings. Also includes a listing of reviews of productions of Wilde's plays, dissertations on Wilde, sound recordings of his works, and satires which appeared in *Punch*.

Miller, Robert Klein. *Oscar Wilde*. New York: Frederick Ungar, 1982.
Comprehensive study of Wilde's life and writings. Excellent, brief biographical chapter provides insight into Wilde's unusual, peripatetic life; deals frankly but tactfully with his homosexuality and its influence on his writings. Individual chapters discuss the author's major works of prose fiction, criticism, and drama; a chapter is devoted to analysis of writings inspired by Wilde's two-year incarceration. Concluding chapter offers an analysis of Wilde's aesthetic theory.

Raby, Peter. *Oscar Wilde*. Cambridge, England: Cambridge University Press, 1988.
Attempts to define Wilde's distinctive "voice" as an artist, separating it from the amalgam of critical and literary forebears the writer imitated in his work. Sees Wilde as being continually conscious of the public role of the artist to affect the taste and sensibility of his reading public. Argues Wilde is essentially a dramatist, both in his life and in his art; even his later nondramatic works share affinities with his best dramas. Surveys the writer's career to show how his development as a writer is consistent despite the many forms he chose for expressing his aesthetic doctrine.

Shewan, Rodney. *Oscar Wilde: Art and Egotism*. Totowa, N.J.: Barnes & Noble, 1977.
Systematic study of Wilde's writings, aimed at exploring "Wilde's relationship with literature." Argues Wilde devoted his entire career to "investigating that most elusive subject," the "self." His art is a consistent attempt to express his changing ideas about the nature of the self. Demonstrates how firmly grounded Wilde was in the classical, humanist tradition. Contains a detailed chronology and a useful bibliography of secondary sources.

The Ballad of Reading Gaol

Beckson, Karl, ed. *Oscar Wilde: The Critical Heritage*. New York: Barnes & Noble, 1970.

Excerpts from five reviews which appeared immediately after Wilde published the *Ballad*; at least three reviewers did not know the author's identity, so their comments are not tainted by familiarity with or contempt for Wilde's lifestyle. Scathing comments by W. E. Henley are balanced by Arthur Symons' sympathetic reading. In addition to these selections, comments about the *Ballad* are scattered throughout other excerpts in the collection.

Ericksen, Donald H. *Oscar Wilde*. Boston: Twayne, 1977.

Traces the history of the poem's composition as it sprang from Wilde's personal experiences in Reading Gaol. Discusses the difficulties Wilde had in finding a publisher. Offers close textual examination of the poem's various cantos, explicating individual stanzas which reveal the propagandistic note Wilde openly wished his readers to recognize. Argues the primary aim of the poem is to "communicate experience and its effects in terms of those who suffer man's institutionalized cruelties." Believes this poem is closer to the work of Hardy and Housman than to its Victorian predecessors.

Gagnier, Regenia. "Art for Love's Sake: 'Salome' and 'Reading Gaol.'" In *Idylls of the Marketplace: Oscar Wilde and the Victorian Public*. Stanford, Calif.: Stanford University Press, 1986.

Brief analysis at the end of a chapter which discusses Wilde's attitude about physical love and its destructive as well as salvific powers. Claims the poem is not simply or even primarily about the torments of prison life, but rather deals with the passions and the consequences of those passions, especially love. Sees Wilde torn between his allegiance to the community of prisoners and his abhorrence at being cast out of society.

Miller, Robert Klein. *Oscar Wilde*. New York: Frederick Ungar, 1982.

Considers the *Ballad* as a product of Wilde's experiences in prison; compares it favorably to *De Profundis*, noting how Wilde is able to avoid "mawkishness" by focusing on the sorrows of another prisoner rather than dwelling on his own ill fortune. Offers a careful explication of the poem, pointing out how, through the story of the condemned murderer whom Wilde chooses as his hero, the poet is able to construct a bitter indictment of social institutions which have perverted the notion of Christianity in modern times. Notes the realism with which Wilde depicts characters and situations; combined with the poet's plain diction and stark imagery, the realistic portrait highlights the degradation of prison life.

Shewan, Rodney. *Oscar Wilde: Art and Egotism*. Totowa, N.J.: Barnes & Noble, 1977.
Brief analysis of the poem, showing how it illustrates one of Wilde's many attempts to understand the concept of self and to find fit expressions for that concept in his art. Argues the hero, presented on the surface as an outcast, is in reality representative of the type who wishes to ostracize him: the majority, who are guilty of murdering that which they love in one way or another.

Woodcock, George. "The Social Rebel." In Richard Ellmann, ed. *Oscar Wilde: A Collection of Critical Essays*. Englewood Cliffs, N.J.: Prentice-Hall, 1969.
Considers the poem primarily about the horrors of hanging, which Wilde saw as a form of enormous cruelty sanctioned by the state. Judges the work one of the most successful examples of propaganda written in English, noting the irony of Wilde's producing this kind of socially conscious literature while professing that art should be pure and distinct from the sphere of everyday life. Argues the poem demonstrates how Wilde is really a great humanist, much more concerned with social ills than his critics have acknowledged.

AUTHOR INDEX

SUBJECT INDEX

ABOUT THE AUTHOR

Laurence W. Mazzeno is Vice President for Academic Affairs and Academic Dean at Ursuline College, Pepper Pike, Ohio. A native of New Orleans, Louisiana, he received his B.A. from Loyola University and his Ph.D. from Tulane University. He served on the faculty at the U.S. Military Academy and the U.S. Naval Academy, where he was Chair of the English Department from 1986 to 1989. From 1989 to 1992 he was a Dean at Mesa State College, Grand Junction, Colorado. He has published widely on British and American authors and compiled *The Victorian Novel* (1989) for the Magill Bibliography Series. He is also the author of *Herman Wouk* in the Twayne U.S. Authors Series (1994). For eight years he was an editor for *The Arnoldian: A Review of Mid-Victorian Culture*; from 1988 to 1992 he edited *Nineteenth-Century Prose*, a journal featuring scholarship on nonfiction prose of the nineteenth century.